HAWAI'I

Favorites, Tips, and Secrets of the Diving Pros

BELOW

by Rod Canham

Hawai'i Below

Favorites, Tips, and Secrets
of the Diving Pros

by Rod Canham

Watersport Publishing, Inc.
Post Office Box 83727
San Diego, CA 92138

First Printing 1991
Watersport Publishing, Inc., P.O. Box 83727, San Diego, CA 92138

Printed in Malaysia

International Standard Book Number
ISBN 0-922769-21-4

Library of Congress Catalog Card Number: 90-071402
Canham, Rod
      Hawai'i Below

Dedication

This book is lovingly dedicated –

To my father Leslie Canham... a friend who has always
been there, regardless of the road

To Paul Grulich... a friend who has encouraged me
every step of the way

To my wife Kathy... my best friend

Acknowledgements

The completion of this project was possible only with the cooperation of so many people who contributed their expertise, advise, enthusiasm, and support.

Its inception started with Paul Tzimoulis, who challenged me with, "If you want to make money writing, . . .". It continued with Ken Loyst, who said the three words writers love to hear from their publisher, "Let's do it!", and then got behind this project with unbridled support.

My wife Kathy, contributed her time and patience editing, her industry, objectivity, wisdom, support, strength, the ability to keep focused, and her love at every point when I needed it the most. She graced most of the photographs as the model unless otherwise noted.

My dear friend Paul Grulich gave of his enthusiasm, support, and expertise with editing a very raw product - all in the midst of his own flight training and otherwise busy schedule.

Tim Kern provided his wizardry on a Macintosh computer coupled with friendship, trust, and artistry to culminate in the professional quality graphics within these pages.

Ultimately the informational base came from the experts in the business - the professional dive charter operators, instructors, and guides, that gave of themselves completely and freely.

On Kaua'i: Ken and Linda Bail of Bubbles Below set the tone for the interviews, and gave me their blessing in naming the book. Mauro Civica of Fathom Five Divers, Terry Donnelly of The Poipū Dive Company, Peter Ricciardi of Aquatics Kaua'i, and Scot and Mary Rysdale of Sea Sage Diving Center, also contributed from the "Garden Isle".

On O'ahu: Site data was provided by Marc Pearlman of South Seas Aquatics with a gift for detail, Scott Turner of Elite Dives Hawai'i who gave freely of his boat and his expertise, only to have his life turned upside down for two days looking for my computer that I left onboard. Steve Holmes, Rick Richey and Alan McAdams from Steve's Diving Adventures fleshed out many of the sites around the south eastern corner, then got me on the Corsair. Paul Robinette and Tomo Kimura of Dan's Dive Shop contributed the informative site info and basic drawings of the YO-257, and provided unlimited tanks on O'ahu. Zane Bilgrav, Marvin E. Dean, Mark Gillbreath of Pacific Quest Divers gave me the Windward sites. Nicholas G. Bierchen of Divestar Hawai'i, Ray Ehrgott of Aaron's Dive Shops, and Jackie James of Aloha Dive Shop also contributed to the project.

Several people helped put together the data base for the graphics on the *Mahi* starting with the staff of The University of Hawai'i Sea Grant Program headed by Ray Tabata. Donna Stewart-Erhard of South Seas Aquatics, Brad Revis of Ocean Adventures, and Kim Anderson, contributed a detailed data base from which to build the model. Michael Wilson and Jeff Pugh of Atlantis Submarines Hawai'i, LP provided support for the YO-257 data collection.

On Maui: I wish to give my love and appreciation to Pete and Jane Cambouris and the entire staff of Central Pacific Divers with whom I had a long and rewarding relationship, including Bill Cauldwell, Byron Dunn, Dave Fleetham, Neil Graber, Jeff Hughart, Bill Moore, and Greg Wood. Pauline Fiene-Severns and Mike Severns of Mike Severns Diving, Bill Clifton of Bill's Scuba Shack, and Peter Hilley formerly of Lahaina Divers, shared their knowledge and their adventures.

A very special note of thanks goes to Mark Ferrari and Deborah Glockner-Ferrari who helped me realize the dream of Chapter 2.

On Kona: Lisa Cocguette and Tom Shockley of Dive Makai, introduced me to Miss Piggy and proved that turtles really can be like people. Jim Light, Dan Ruth, and Clay Wiseman of the *Kona Aggressor*, Turner Lett of Kohala Divers and Bob Weisman of Red Sail Sports filled out the data for the balance of the sites.

A number of very talented individuals contributed their photographic accomplishments to enhance the project. Their work is credited by their photographs. They include Kathy Canham, Deborah Glockner-Ferrari, Mark Ferrari, Dave Fleetham, Paul Grulich, Mike Severns, and David Watersun.

I would also like to thank the following for their respective input and assistance: Brett and Beth Whittington on Oʻahu, Grant Asti on the "Big Island", Len Todisco from the International Diving College, Steve Anderson of South Seas Aquatics, Joanne Hay and Kirsten Anderson of Dolphin Quest, Blanca Stransky, Kendell Thompson, and Lori Lirette of the USS Arizona Memorial National Parks Service, T.J. LaPuzza, Public Affairs Office of the Naval Oceans Systems Center in San Diego, Herb Schreiner of Paradise Cruise, Ltd., Jon Bryan of the Hawaiʻi Maritime Center, Betsy Otsu of the Film Department of the State of Hawaiʻi Tourism Board, David R. Cannalte of the Pacific Fleet Submarine Memorial Association, Duke Gonzales and Marj Awai of the Waikīkī Aquarium, Luly Nakanishi of Martin & Associates Advertising Inc. for Sea Life Park, Ann Fielding, Dan Moriarty of the Kīlauea Point National Wildlife Refuge, Karen, Jonathan and Emily McCarthy from Atlantis Submarine Hawaiʻi, LP and Eugene T. Nitta of the National Marine Fisheries Service.

My heartfelt thanks and lifelong appreciation go out to Jim Light, Dan Ruth, and Wayne Hasson of the *Kona Aggressor*, the Coast Guard flight crew out of Barbers Point, and the Doctors and Staff at the Hyperbaric Treatment Center, University of Hawaiʻi School of Medicine in Honolulu, whose fast action and clear thinking prevented any permanent damage when I got "hit".

Last, but definitely not the least, to Pastors Steve Kaneshiro, Mark Hoshizaki, Don Bennington, the late Don Kaufman, Ken Rogers and to the Word, for showing me what is really important in life - and finally, to my church family at Kahalui Baptist, who prayed me through some really difficult times.

To all of you that I mentioned, and those that I may have neglected to, I send you my love, appreciation and gratitude for all you have done. God Bless -

Rod Canham
Maui, Hawaiʻi
August 1990

Table of Contents

Table of Contents

Table of Contents

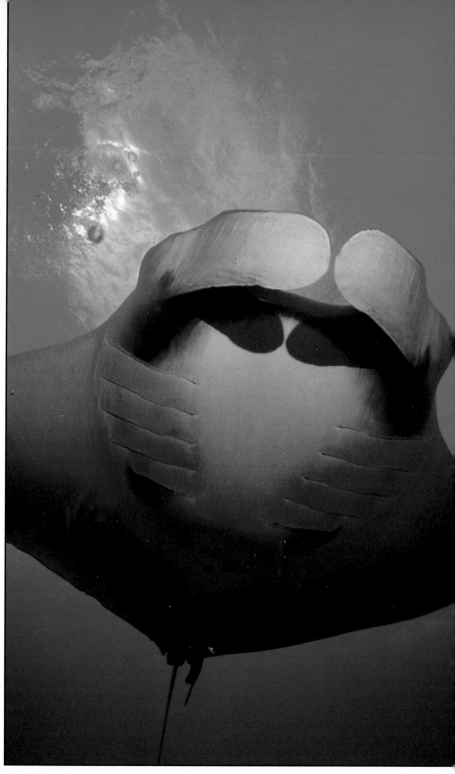

Giant Manta Ray

Getting Acquainted

On a windless day in October, boat captain Peter Hilley was hitching a ride from Maui to Lāna'i for a day of diving. During the one hour transit a disturbance was noticed ahead on the water's flat surface. As the boat slowed down, he observed two giant manta rays swimming in lazy circles and touching each other with their wings. As soon as the engines were shut down, the mantas came to the boat and continued circling. The charter customers grabbed their snorkeling equipment and slipped into the clear, blue water with the rays. The gentle pelagics would swim away, and then return in single-file to the boat, imitating each other's moves in slow, graceful motions. After fifteen minutes, the snorkelers returned to the boat.

Noticing the rays' reluctance to leave the area, Peter re-entered the water. The larger of the two (12 feet) dived deep, but the latter, and smaller one (10 feet), swam just beneath the surface, right under Peter. He grabbed hold of the ray on the flat part of its forehead between the two cephalic lobes that project forward from each side of its head, and rested his forearms on its sandpaper-like skin. Two remoras, also hitching a ride, accommodated Peter by moving to the underside of the manta. For the next five minutes he was given the experience of a lifetime. The ray cruised just beneath the surface at snorkeling depth, following the larger manta to a point about 100 yards from the boat, then returning. Next to the boat the larger ray did a slow barrel roll before diving deep. The smaller one followed, taking Peter with him to a depth of 30 feet, where he released his grip and slowly surfaced.

One minute later the ray returned and again Peter climbed on for a ride. Before the 30 minute encounter was over, two other snorkelers got a chance for an exhilarating experience. Leaving the area of the boat, the two rays regrouped and slowly swam off together.

The fourth leading dive destination in the world, Hawai'i offers an abundance of marine delights. The islands are surrounded by an underwater shelf less than 600 feet deep extending two to three miles from shore. From there, the bottom plummets to the abyssal depths at 6,000+ feet. Cooler water temperatures and rough seas inhibit the profuse coral and sponge formations normally found in the Caribbean. Nevertheless, a veritable palette of tropical fish color the otherwise monochromatic backdrop of alluring lava formations. Daily encounters with octopus, green sea turtles, moray eels and whitetip reef sharks, both charm and excite, while "blue water" sightings of manta rays, whale sharks and other pelagics offer what are usually once-in-a-lifetime memories on a regular basis.

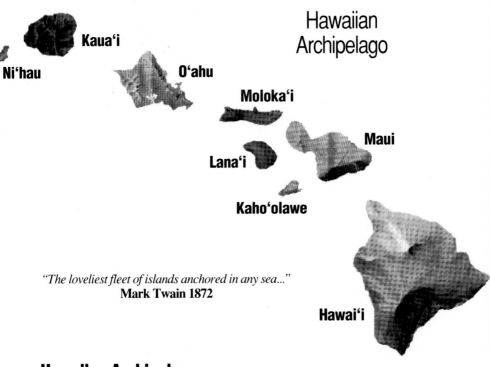

Kaua'i

Ni'hau

O'ahu

Moloka'i

Maui

Lana'i

Kaho'olawe

Hawaiian
Archipelago

"The loveliest fleet of islands anchored in any sea..."
Mark Twain 1872

Hawai'i

Hawaiian Archipelago

The Hawaiian Archipelago consists of 132 islands spread across a span of 1523 miles. All of the islands are the very tops of immense shield volcanoes that have built up from the ocean floor over the eons. They rest upon a section of the earth's crust called the Pacific Plate, four miles beneath the water's surface. Magma pours through a fissure in this plate - building up over the millennia, eventually breaking above the surface of the sea, to create an island. As the land mass increases, the foundational plate begins to sag beneath its own weight, and the island starts to recede back into the sea. All the while this is happening, the Pacific Plate is inching its way to the northwest at the rate of two to four inches annually. Eventually the pipeline of magma is cut off, turning the active volcanoes into dormant ones, and the dormant ones eventually become extinct. Immediately upon breaking the surface, other forces begin to take effect, with wind, rain, and the ocean sculpting the face of the islands we see today. The further northwest in the chain, the more ancient, weathered and receded the islands become leaving low lying atolls which will eventually fade beneath the waters. But to the south, the eight main islands have a personality unique and totally distinct from one another. In the millennia to follow, other new islands will eventually break the surface, adding to, and perpetuating the Hawaiian Island chain.

Overview: The Hawaiian Islands

Area ....6,450.4 miles
Coastline .... 750 miles
Population   1,104,600 (12/31/88 estimate)
        (15% of the state's population is military and their
        dependants, with over 99% of those on O'ahu)
State capital .... Honolulu
Distances from Honolulu (in miles):
        San Francisco 2,397
        Los Angeles 2,557
        Seattle 2,679
        Anchorage 2,781
        Chicago 4,179
        New York 4,959
Time lag from the mainland
    Standard Time:
        .... behind San Francisco by 2 hours
        .... behind New York by 5 hours
    Daylight Savings Time:
        .... behind San Francisco by 3 hours
        .... behind New York by 6 hours

Climate

Hawai'i's central Pacific location places the state completely in the tropics, making the resultant climate one of the islands' biggest draws. The surrounding waters serve as a gigantic thermostat controlling the weather, with year-round temperatures moderated by gentle trade winds and comfortable humidity, but the conditions can vary radically though from one side of an island to the other. Rainfall ranges from an annual average of a desert-dry seven inches at Puakō on the "Big Island", to the world's wettest 486 inches at Mount Wai'ale'ale, on Kaua'i.

Hawai'i essentially has two seasons: summer (from May through October), and winter (November through April). Northeast trade winds buffer the high temperatures with cooling breezes ranging from almost 10 to over 13 miles an hour. The islands are relatively (though not completely) segregated from the paths of tropical storms. In the past 40 years only five hurricanes have struck the islands, the last one being Hurricane Iwa in November of 1982.

A Quick Look at Hawai'i's Climate

Month	Temperatures (°F)	Precipitation (inches)	Humidity (%)
January	72.6	3.79	72
February	72.8	2.72	68.5
March	74.3	3.48	65.5
April	75.7	1.49	63
May	77.5	1.21	60.5
June	79.1	0.49	60
July	80.1	0.54	60
August	81.0	0.60	61
September	80.6	0.62	60
October	79.5	1.88	62
November	76.6	3.22	67
December	74.0	3.43	70

Dealing With The Sun

Much has been written about the ill effects of sun worship. Whether actively seeking a tan, or passively sightseeing, shopping or watching, the sun is a force to be reckoned with. There is no longer such a thing as a "healthy tan". Along with all of the warnings, experts say not to panic. Just use some simple precautions:

· stay out of the sun when it is at its strongest (from 10:00 a.m. to 2:00 p.m.)
· wear a hat, visor or some protective head covering
· wear a pair of good-quality, polarized sun glasses, especially if you plan to spend any amount of time out on the water
· use a sun block or screen (preferably waterproof), with an SPF of at least 15 or greater (the numbers mean that if you could normally withstand exposure to the sun for one hour, a lotion with an SPF of 15 would allow you to stay out for 15 hours for a comparable exposure).
· drink plenty of fluids to stave off dehydration

Dressing The Part

Aloha shirts and mu'umu'u's aside, the only recognized dress code for Hawai'i is casual. Shorts, comfortable tops and optional footwear is the norm, and a hat or visor is recommended. Rare is the restaurant that requires a dress or jacket as part of the accepted dining apparel, and at those that do, you can expect to pay for that privilege. When the thermometer plummets to the low 70's, most visitors are rejoicing in the balmy conditions, while we locals are breaking out the denims, sweaters, jackets and throwing extra blankets on the bed at night. Even as a transplanted East Coaster, I have discovered my blood has "thinned out", and I have nowhere near the tolerance for the cold that I used to. In the winter months, the windward and elevated parts of the islands are notoriously cooler and excursions to Mauna Kea, Mauna Loa or Haleakalā (all 10,000 foot plus) send the heartiest souls clamoring for protection.

Culture

Approximately 1,200 years ago, native South Pacific seamen, probably from the Marquesas, traversed 2,400 miles of open ocean and settled in the Hawaiian Islands. It was a disease-free and uncrowded life, for the warlike, pagan people. Within the next 200 years, settlers from Tahiti, and other islands in the South Pacific, immigrated to the islands and eventually took them over.

On January 18, 1778, the British explorer Captain James Cook, sailing aboard the *Resolution*, first landed on Kaua'i. He named his discovery after his most ardent benefactor, John Montagu, the fourth Earl of Sandwich. The Sandwich Islands were never again to be remote. The reputation spread of how free the islanders were with their food, drink, and sexual favors. From a population estimated at 400,000 to 800,000 people, venereal disease, brought in by the sailors, reduced those numbers to less than 26,000 in a little over a century.

At the time of Captain Cook's arrival, each of the islands were autonomous. The "Big Island" was ruled by Kalaniopu'u, who had

designated his son Kiwalaō to inherit the throne, and his nephew, Kamehameha, to be the keeper of the family god, Kūkā'ilimoku. However the restless nephew had his own ideas; Kiwalaō was killed in battle and nine years later Kamehameha finally gained control. Not happy with just the one island, he set out to conquer all of the individual realms, and unite them under one monarchy - his. Within four years, all of the islands were in line with the young warrior king, and the monarchy was to reign for the next 77 years.

King Kamehameha I is annually honored on June 11th with a parade and festivities. Floral leis, up to 30 feet long, adorn his statue, in front of the Ali'iolani Hale, in Honolulu, for days following the celebration known as "King Kam Day".

King Kamehameha I held onto the old ways of paganism that served as guidelines for business, religious and ecological practices, and he encouraged trading with outsiders. A few tangible traces of the ancient civilization remain in fishing villages, ponds, petroglyphs and *heiaus*.

Heiaus

The term *heiau* means "temple", where the ancient Hawaiians worshipped their gods. *Heiaus* held a prominent role, not only in their religious culture, but politically as well. They were completely exposed to the heavens, not under a protective cover, and are believed to have served a dominant position within view of the entire following. The temples had three class distinctions: *luakinis* were built for kings, where in honor to their idols, sacrifices (including human) were made, the *waihau* were for the kings and chiefs, and the last were for the common people. In 1819, King Kamehameha's son, Liholiho, overthrew the idolatrous practices affiliated with the *heiaus*. Though several hundred of the ancient temples have been located to date, countless others have been lost to the antiquities.

The Haleki'i and Pihana Heiaus are located atop a bluff overlooking the Kahalui Harbor in Maui.

King Kamehameha died May 8th, at the age of 70. The following September, the first whale was killed in Hawaiian waters, and on October 23rd, the first missionaries set sail for the islands. Through these three unrelated events, 1819 marked the year the religious, cultural, and economic destiny of the Hawaiian Islands were to be altered forever.

Whalers, Missionaries and Traders

In September of 1819, the whaling vessels *Balena* and *Equator* recorded the first sperm whale killed in Hawai'i's waters at Kealakekua Bay. This event was to set the destiny of the islands. Drawing whalers from around the world, the fertile grounds surrounding the Hawaiian Islands were quickly and systematically decimated. The whales moved to new grounds off Japan, Russia and the Aleutians requiring longer voyages (from three to four years) for the whalers which necessitated reprovisioning, repairs and a restful break from the tedium and rigors of exploiting the valuable behemoths. With Japan's ports closed to outside visitors, the central Pacific location of Hawai'i was ideal to suit those needs.

The islands became so popular to whalers that the numbers of the vessels rivaled even the largest New England ports at New Bedford, Provincetown and Nantucket. In 1846, for example, 429 vessels were registered making stops in Lahaina, and 167 in Honolulu.

What made the islands so appealing to the whalers, besides the climate, provisions, and a break in the routine, was the liberty. A popular saying among the sailors was "there is no God west of Cape Horn". James Michener wrote in his book, *Hawai'i*, of a song mournfully sung in the seaports of New England,

"I want to go back to Owyhee,
Where the sea sings a soulful song,
Where the gals are kind and gentle
And they don't know right from wrong!"

Both beliefs proved short lived. In October of 1819, the first Congregationalist missionaries, aboard the brig *Thaddeus*, out of Boston, landed on the "Big Island" of Hawai'i. In the wake of King Kamehameha's death that same year, they converted the queen mother Keōpuōlani and the chiefess Kapi'olani. Within two years they had put together a written form of Hawaiian and published the first Hawaiian bible. From that point on they were to intercede against the amoral whalers, leading to several conflicts, and at one incident, the shelling of a missionary's house from one of the ships.

Three events brought the whaling era to a close. In 1859, petroleum was discovered via a crude oil drill in Pennsylvania. Then, during the Civil War, 46 whaling ships were sunk by the Confederacy and 40 more were used by the Union forces as a blockade on Charleston, South Carolina. Finally in the autumn of 1871, 33 ships were trapped north

Erected in 1837, by the first missionaries to the islands, the Moku'aikaua Church, on the "Big Island" of Hawai'i, is the oldest and a still active church in the state.

of the Bering Straits. The growing pack ice literally crushed all but the last vestiges of the pioneer whaling era.

With the decline of whaling and the income it brought to the islands, the agriculture industry was developed to maintain economic prosperity. But the islanders' numbers were declining from disease, and their aversion to field labor necessitated importing manpower first from China, then Japan, Portugal and the Philippines to work the sugar fields and eventually the pineapple plantations. It laid the groundwork through intermarriage to what we now know as Hawai'i being the "Melting Pot of the Pacific."

Language

The Hawaiian language is a beautiful flow of Polynesian communication that actively thrives on Ni'ihau and a few isolated villages throughout the islands, but has been squeezed out of the mainstream by the influx of Western Civilization. Its visual remnants grace the names of villages, streets and sites throughout the islands, and salts the everyday conversations of local residents. At first glance it looks like an unpronounceable mish mash, but actually is easy to learn and fun to try. There are only 12 letters in the Hawaiian alphabet, seven consonants (h, k, l, m, n, p, w) and the five vowels (a, e, i, o, u). An apostrophe is a glottal stop between two syllables. A rule of thumb is to try to pronounce each letter individually. The following are lists of commonly used Hawaiian terms, you are most likely to hear in conversation:

DAY TO DAY CONVERSATION:

How It Looks	How It Sounds	What It Says
'a'a	ah-ah	rough lava flow
ali'i	ah-lee-ee	Hawaiian royalty
aloha	ah-loh-hah	hello, welcome
haole	how-lee	white man
kama'āina	kah-ma-eye-nah	local resident
kapu	kah-poo	stay out, taboo
keiki	kay-kee	children
lānai	lah-nigh	balcony, porch, veranda
lei	lay	garland of flowers, shells or leaves
lū'au	loo-ow	Hawaiian feast
mahalo	mah-hah-low	thank you
mauna	mow-nah	mountain
Menehune	may-nay-hoo-nay	legendary little people
nēnē	nay-nay	Hawaiian goose
pāhoehoe	pah-hoy-hoy	smooth billowy lava
pali	pah-lee	cliffs
pau	pow	finished
poi	poy	repugnant lū'au dish
pūpū	poo-poo	appetizer
wahine	wah-hee-nay	women

ON THE MENU:

How It Looks	How It Sounds	What It Says
'ahi	ah-hee	yellowfin tuna
aku	ah-koo	skipjack tuna
mahi-mahi	mah-hee mah-hee	dolphin fish, dorado
ono	oh-noh	wahoo fish
uku	oo-koo	grey snapper fish
ulua	oo-loo-ah	crevalle jack fish

ON THE DIVE BOAT:

How It Looks	How It Sounds	What It Says
makai	mach-eye	towards the sea
mauka	mow-kah	towards the mountains
moku	moh-koo	island
puka	poo-kah	hole, cave, crevice, tube

Another form of communication that commonly surfaces in everyday talk is **pidgin** - a simplistic derivation of…

LOCAL SLANG:

How It Looks	How It Sounds	What It Says
brah	bra	brother, pal
da kine	dah-kine	a substitute for anything
shaka	shah-kah	hand gesture meaning it's cool, take it easy
t'anks	tanks	thank you

Family Activities

On top of being a Polynesian paradise to traveling singles, Hawai'i is the quintessential family vacation destination. There are places to go, people to see, and things to do for everyone, young and old. The islands as a whole could be planned in a combination package, to get just a flavor of each island, or as a single destination, each could be visited repeatedly without seeing all their offerings. Deciding upon a vacation to Hawai'i is the easy part - planning on where and how to go about it can be a little more difficult.

"Shaka brah" – everything's cool.

Topping seven million visitors annually, tourism is the leading income source for the islands, and with it comes all of the attractions and trappings. Shopping abounds with major commercial malls and centers in or near all of the metropolitan areas, while shops, boutiques and galleries line the streets and fill the lobbies of all the resort centers. Restaurants run the gamut from a plethora of fast foods to exquisite continental cuisine. The confluence of European, Oriental, South Pacific and native Hawaiian cultures contributes to the culinary delights. Seafood is caught fresh daily and offered in a variety of fresh dishes appealing to the most discriminating palates. Of course no Hawaiian vacation would be truly complete without - at least once - experiencing a real Hawaiian *lū'au*. On the other hand, many hotel rooms and condominiums have self-contained kitchen facilities, for visitors that do not wish to be 100% restaurant dependent.

Room accommodations vary as much as the dining options. Bed-only hotel rooms, guest houses, bed and breakfast inns, and fully furnished condominiums are available. Some are equipped with full kitchens, washers/dryers, swimming pools, hot tubs and balconies (*lānais*) that overlook the ocean.

Yet, Hawai'i is much more than just catering to the tourist traffic. The natural beauty that first drew the outside world to the islands, continues to invite, astonish, and inspire. There are mountainous vistas that overlook the splendor of volcanic creation, weathered by time, and bordered by the azure waters of the Pacific. Beaches of various tones and textures ring every island in the state attracting sun worshippers, socializers, and the watchers.

Windsurfing enthusiasts ply the ideal waters off Maui's Ho'okipa Beach.

Surfing is an integrated part of life in Hawai'i for the young and the young at heart. The surf is caused by wind driven waves and storms thousands of miles away. The huge breakers that thrill the adventurous and observer alike, are generated from winter storms transiting north of the islands. When these breakers "spill", they create "tubes" - pathways for spectacular rides for the successful, or thunderous jaws that seem to swallow up the not-so-skilled.

A common site around the islands is the finned tails (skegs) of surfboards atop a beat up "cruiser", or a bicyclist negotiating traffic while balancing a board under the arm. The sport dates back as far as a thousand years, and has gone through an evolutionary development of its own, from the unwieldy solid *koa* wood board, to the computer designed, lightweight materials that ride the waves today. The North Shore Pipeline is world renown for its spectacular wave sets, and is the site of international competitions every November and December, including the Triple Crown Hawaiian Pro Surfing Championships.

For those without the skills or equipment for board surfing, boogie boarding is a popular alternative.

Riding the wind and waves on a board with a sail has been refined, since its inception in 1970, to an Olympic event. Every November, Hoʻokipa Beach on Maui is the site of the world windsurfing championships.

Each island has a subculture of speciality shops that cater to instruction, rental, sales and repair of all these water sports activities. It is best to check with the shops' experts at your respective destination for recommendations about sites, conditions, and limitations that best suit your particular skill level.

Hawaiʻi's waters are home to some of the most exciting blue water game fishing in the world including: marlin, sailfish, *mahimahi* (a type of dorado) and tuna. Record catches have been taken off the "Big Island" of Hawaiʻi, while tournaments for trophies and some large cash prizes are offered for the serious competitor. For a good many, the experience turns out to be an enjoyable afternoon of relaxing, and "talking story" at sea, but for others, it can be a dream come true.

The One That Didn't Get Away

In a sport where exaggeration abounds about the one that got away Byron Dunn brought home the proof. In May of 1989, Byron, a dive boat captain and friend, was fishing aboard the *Wizard of Id* with two friends. Trolling the backside of Lānaʻi, they hooked on, and the fight began. For an hour and forty five minutes it was a struggle of will and determination over survival. Until the catch was alongside the boat, they didn't know what it was on the other end of the line, except that it was big and powerful. When it finally came into view, it was the dream of all sport fishermen - a blue marlin, 750 pounds and 13 1/2 feet long.

They towed the fish for over an hour before finally boarding it. Needless to say, the 21 foot boat sat a bit lower in the water after boarding the prize catch. The fish was believed to be one of the top ten ever caught out of Lahaina, and expected to be the biggest take of the year. Three months later, the fishing vessel *Manō Kēlā*, working off Olowalu boarded an 890 pounder, the second largest ever caught out of Lahaina. But for that day, Byron had his moment in the sun, and the restaurants were offering marlin as their "fresh catch of the day".

Sport fisherman Byron Dunn, and his "dream" catch.

23

Charter operators on all of the islands offer full and half day trips in pursuit of the big one, but boats do not come cheap and the catch is customarily kept by the crew. Know exactly what you want, and what you can expect to get for your dollar before you book.

Parasail, jet ski, and water skiing operations collectively fall into the category of "thrill craft", and though exciting, are the center of controversy with the residents, ecologists, and government in the state. The point of contention centers around the noise generated by the craft, and the intrusion of the near-shore shallow waters favored by the humpback whales for calving during the winter months.

Snorkeling is an experience that can be shared by the entire family. Most dive and snorkel operators offer free maps of recommended sites to explore the marvels of our underwater world. When the conditions are inclement, or the predominate currents prove threatening, it is best to explore the lee waters and protected coves where boating traffic is light. There are several operations that offer snorkeling charters aboard boats that vary from "six pack" inflatables, to large catamarans, carrying scores of passengers to some of the more inaccessible and pristine areas. Some destinations have a resident populace of fish acclimated to the snorkelers and their food offerings.

With 120,000 scuba divers traveling to Hawai'i annually, it is rated the fourth leading diving destination in the world. There are upwards of 80 retail and charter operations to choose from. Most are run by serious-minded, service-oriented professionals - instructors or divemasters that are involved for their shared passion of the sport, the sea, and its inhabitants. They do this because they choose to, so avail yourselves of their expertise, and get to develop a more intimate relationship with Hawai'i below.

This book is not designed to be a scientific tome, but rather a handbook and a quick reference, written for divers, from a diver's viewpoint, to help you realize the most out of your underwater experience in Hawai'i. It is hoped that it will find a place in your dive bag, to give you a quick introduction to the sites you may be diving and a reference for after-the-dive about the critters you encountered below.

Section I deals with the marine life that you are most likely to encounter while diving, some you probably will not meet, and an introduction to our underwater world for the entire family. **Section II** is a compilation of several favorite dive sites from island to island. Most of this information was drawn from surveys and interviews of the operators that dive these sites daily. **Section III** is an introduction to destinations, sights and activities that may occupy your time between and after your diving. The **Appendices** are a quick reference of pertinent phone numbers, inter-island flights, diver's first aid for marine encounters, and marine life listings. I hope that you find this guide useful in planning your dive vacation to the Hawaiian Islands - *Mahalo.*

Section I

Exploration into Discovery

"Strange fishes, strange in shape and color – crimson, blue, orange, rose, gold - such fishes as flash like living light through the coral groves of these enchanted seas..."
Isabella Bird 1881

The cataclysmic activity that created the Hawaiian Islands above the ocean's surface left a volcanic legacy of cavernous formations beneath. In waters too cool for extensive coral building, the lava structures serve as the centerpoint for marine habitation, protection and propagation. What the monochromatic formations lack in color is augmented in a spectrum of tropical fish.

To date, over 450 species have been identified in Hawai'i with 90 to 135 believed to be endemic - found nowhere else in the world. Critters considered rare treats to encounter in other parts of the diving world are experienced here on a daily basis. Humpback whales make Hawai'i their home during the winter months, and the rarest classification of all the underwater world, the ocean swimming pelagics, provide the electricity to energize any diver's enthusiasm, no matter how seasoned and well-traveled.

The marine life and their habitats are what make diving in Hawai'i so wonderful. The potential for sighting new or unusual animals and their behavior is what keeps me "juiced" after 17 years in the business. Learning with other professionals, who daily "live" the shared experience, always leads to new discoveries. With a good eye, some patience, and a share of grace, Hawai'i below can fulfill your greatest diving fantasies.

Chapter 1

Blackside hawkfish patiently wait for unsuspecting prey.

Habitats and Residents

The volcanic origins that formed the Hawaiian islands above the water, continue now, as they have since the beginning of their creation, to play a role in the architecture of the underwater world. Much of Hawai'i's underwater topography was first formed above the water. It eventually settled beneath the surface to be assembled into ridges, pinnacles, archways, and overhangs. Interlaced with caves, lava tubes and caverns, it provides a photogenic backdrop for shutterbugs craving to capture the moment. The lava foundations serve as a substrata for coral growth, a habitat for a rainbow of tropical fish and unusual invertebrates, and a limitless source of exploration. Pockmarked with *pukas* (holes), they can yield a treasure trove of discoveries.

The best way to experience any dive area, and especially here, is to take your time and keep your eyes open, for the big as well as the small. Hawai'i has a large number of marine personalities, that when encountered, leave an indelible impression with the participants. Many divers spend their time swimming as hard and fast as possible hoping to run into the "big guys", missing almost all of the secrets the ocean has to offer, and end up with a disappointing experience. To enhance your opportunities for discoveries and encounters, this chapter has been divided into the various types of underwater topography in Hawai'i, and what is most likely to be found in and about them.

In mentioning the marine life the first time in each chapter, I have written the formal common name followed in parentheses by the name most commonly used to identify the critter in the islands, either the nickname or in Hawaiian: white-tipped reef shark (whitetip), or blue-lined snapper fish (*ta'ape*). Every subsequent mention within that chapter will only be written as its most commonly recognized name. Appendix D has a complete listing of the marine life mentioned in the text listed in alphabetical order by their formal common name, followed by the Latin designation, completed with the Hawaiian name when known.

The Reef

Hawai'i is too far north to support the substantial coral fields common to the South Pacific and the Caribbean. Nevertheless, cauliflower coral is the most common type found in Hawai'i's waters. The first to colonize on new lava flows, it is prevalent on much of the shallow substrata, and in isolated instances, precariously growing in rubble fields. It is quite common to see either an arc-eye or blackside (Forster's) hawkfish resting between the branches, laying in wait for unsuspecting prey. I once found one with a "popsicle stick" protruding from its mouth. At close inspection it turned out to be a juvenile trumpetfish, swallowed whole, tail first, and not quite fitting.

Hard-to-find harlequin shrimp feed upon textile sea stars eating all but one of its arms.

These fish make great photographic subjects when approached slowly. The coral heads also often contain small crustaceans living in the protection of their branches.

Cauliflower coral with a bleached white appearance has been victimized by either a pincushion starfish (shark's pillow) or the poisonous crown-of-thorns sea star. These echinoderms encompass the coral, extrude their stomachs over the branches, and digest the polyps before moving on. One of the few natural predators of the starfish is the Triton's trumpet, the largest snail in Hawai'i waters and an active nocturnal feeder. Feeding on the pincushion starfish, the snail extends its proboscis to either drill a hole in the leathery body or completely encompass it. With the crown-of-thorns, the proboscis enters directly through the stomach, literally sucking the life from the animal. Unfortunately, the cornucopia shaped shell of the snail is highly prized by collectors, and its harvesting has decimated its numbers. On either of the starfish, tiny shrimp called emperors can often be found, but hands-off is the rule with the crown-of-thorns, as its venom can leave a painful wound when punctured by one of its thorny spines.

Antler corals are in the same family as the cauliflower corals, but grow to a much greater size. These four to six foot ecosystems are inhabited by juvenile yellow tangs, moorish idols, and communities of Hawaiian

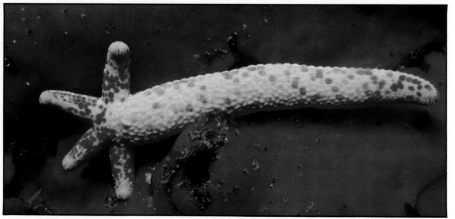

The common starfish will regenerate its missing arms, thus renewing the food source for the delicate harlequin shrimp.

dascyllus (shadow or moon) damsels. When threatened, the fish will signal with a "chirping purr", swim closer to the coral head, and eventually take refuge in the protection of its largest branches until the threat passes.

Swimming crabs, juvenile lionfish, and sometimes harlequin shrimp can be found inside the coral. The small, and delicate harlequins are ornately configured and very colorful. These qualities are very appealing to underwater photographers, but mishandling these fragile creatures can lead to damaging or destroying them. Harlequins feed upon textile starfish with reckless abandon, but are aware of preserving their food source. The starfish have the ability to regenerate lost limbs, so the shrimp will eat all but one of its arms. Soon new buds will form on the starfish and the process is renewed.

Densely packed formations of finger corals provide an endless source of food, habitation and protection for fish as well as invertebrates. It is often seen decorated with purple collector urchins, but the best time to appreciate a reef of finger coral is at night, when all of the critters hidden during the daylight hours emerge to feed. Several species of shrimp and mollusks can be found, including the tiger cowry that grows up to seven inches.

Reef Fish

The ubiquitous tropicals are at every site. Some school in abundance; others are solitary, alert, and curious. Seen on practically every dive are parrot fish, snapper, surgeon fish, wrasse, innumerable butterfly fish, and trailing a long, streaming dorsal fin, the yellow, black and white striped moorish idol.

Fish feeding allows close interaction at dive sites where tropicals have been conditioned to accept the hand-outs.

Photo Tip: Feeding and Photographing Fish

One of the methods of providing an opportunity to photograph marine life close-up and interacting with a diver is by feeding. Animals that might normally shy away from a diver sometimes drop inherent inhibitions for a free hand-out, but using food can be a double edged sword.

While food may serve to attract fish, it may also bring in too many to photograph with any kind of order to the set-up. Once fed, they may not know enough to leave, providing you with undesired escorts throughout the duration of the dive.

The type of food being offered makes a big difference to the quality of the image and the reaction of marine life:
- **Bread** – a favorite for feeding fish, clouds water a milky white.
- **Fish Food Sticks** – are packed in a biodegradable bag. The granulated food floats.
- **Peas** – another favorite, cannot be concentrated in a single area and will show up in any part of a shot.
- **Canned mackerel** – is oily and if used by the photographer, can find its way to the camera and optics.
- **Squid** – seems to be the overall best, but is often hard to find and expensive at that.

Continued . . .

Feeding and Photographing Fish *Continued...*

Food Containers

Different types of containers to carry the food have various advantages and disadvantages:

Tin cans with plastic, easy-to-remove lids are ideal. The food's aroma can be sealed inside until opened, and the can may be covered with colored decorator's tape as a prop.

Mesh bags allow the aroma of the food to drift out. The resultant attraction gives the mixed blessing of curious animals, but a bit out of control.

Plastic bags hide the smell of food but allow its full visibility. If lost, they are a danger to the marine life. Fish caught inside will suffocate, and turtles, mistaking them for jellyfish, can choke while feeding on them.

A last word about food – remember that fish at one dive site may not be as responsive to food as the same kind of fish at a different site. Conditioning by divers has a lot to do with it. If an area is not known for being a fish feeding spot, the results may prove disappointing.

Do Not Handle Scaled Fish. Fish secrete a mucus that protects them from bacteria in the ocean. Handling fish with scales removes that shield which eventually will kill them.

Ridges

Volcanic ridges form the basic building blocks of several dive sites in the Hawaiian Islands. They vary in size from small projections growing out of a sandy bottom, up to the height of buildings several stories tall and a city block long, fringed by a skirt of coral rubble. The ridges often house lava tubes and caves, as well as support a trellis work of archways and overhangs. Combine these with the *pukas* (holes) that pockmark their surface, and the corals that anchor on the substrata, to get an aquatic maze of habitation and secrets waiting to be unveiled by curious divers.

Black, long-spined sea urchins look menacing to touch, and for the most part are. Their long sharp spines snap off easily, and can leave a painful reminder of the encounter. Look closely, however, and you will often find a long, thin commensal shrimp perfectly camouflaged by precisely aligning itself within the spines.

Several species of nudibranchs can be found in and on the ridges. A few of the most common include the scrambled egg nudibranch, a jumble of colors in black, white and yellow, with a putrid smell out of the water, and an acrid taste to predators. The appropriately named gold laced nudibranch has a translucent white body with threads of gold weaved throughout. Its frilly black and white rhinofores and gills make it a macro delight. Aeolids look like a long string of purple pasta with curly cue cerata that ruffle when touched from front to back. They feed on coelenterates, incorporating their stinging cells into their own defensive mechanism, and can leave an itchy rash if handled with bare hands.

The Picasso's triggerfish is more affectionately known as the humuhumu nukunuku ā pua'a.

The Official State Fish

It only seems natural that with Hawai'i's inextricable ties to the ocean, the state would have an official fish. That distinction goes to the Picasso's trigger fish *Rhinecanthus aculeatus*. It is also known as the painted trigger and reef trigger fish, but it is most well known in Hawai'i as the *humuhumu nukunuku ā pua'a*. Its name translates "snout like a pig" or "fish that makes a noise like a pig", depending upon who is asked. The six and a half inch, shallow water fish is solitary, very skittish, and next to impossible to photograph, ducking for cover whenever approached.

Flatworms, often mistaken for nudibranchs, can be found hugging the lava as they glide along the surface looking for food. Easiest to find under rocks, they come in either an array of brilliant colors or unappealing hues that blend in with their environment.

Pinnacles

Pinnacles or sea mounts are peaks that rise from the ocean floor. They provide a concentrated variety of diving at various depths on a relatively small topographical formation.

Black coral trees can be found established on pinnacles, as well as walls, from 35 feet to depths exceeding safe diving limits. Most of the black coral in shallow waters has been harvested for jewelry, leaving the largest, and most spectacular specimens too deep to enjoy for the average diver. Fortunately, some areas are protected from this pillage giving divers an opportunity to observe this self-contained microcosm. The rare and skittish long nose hawkfish can often be found resting within its willowy branches, only to dart to a more protected branch when threatened.

31

Careful searching and a good eye can lead to the well-camouflaged angler fish.

Another species of black coral is the long, green, spiralled wire coral that extends from the wall facing into the current to catch microscopic plankton as it passes by. Commensal shrimp can be found on some of the stalks as well as tiny gobies. Both are well adapted to their host, with elongated green bodies that blend in too well to see without a meticulous search.

On one pinnacle I have found a number of angler fish - a lure feeder that uses a threadlike projection from its rostrum to attract unsuspecting prey. Perfectly still, and camouflaged, it waits until the moment of truth, then inhales its victim with a lightning fast gulp. Known as frog fish, their camouflage makes them difficult to find, and they are always considered a special treat. Many professional divers can count on one hand the number of times in their careers they have ever seen one. Colors range from bright yellow or burnt orange to the less ostentatious grays and mottled combinations. Slow swimmers, and thus easy to catch, they will inflate their stomachs when distressed, to distort their size.

"*Pukas*", Lava Tubes, Caves and Caverns

As lava flows from a volcano, the surface, cooled by its contact with the air, hardens. The lava underneath continues to flow in a molten state through a channel known as a lava tube. As the lava flow subsides, and eventually ceases, the hollowed out tube remains. Divers experience these remnants underwater in the forms of tubes, caves, and caverns.

"*Puka*" is the Hawaiian term for hole. Any kind of cut, crevice, hollow or cave falls into this broad category. *Pukas* can be formed by a gas bubble, the process of erosion, or occasionally by marine life. The allure of exploring these dynamic formations to seek out their wonders and mysteries has drawn over a hundred thousand divers here annually.

The walls and ceilings of the caves are often colorfully encrusted with red, yellow and orange sponge as well as orange tube (cup) corals. Although we have no fire coral in Hawai'i, there is a related species called a hydroid. They resemble miniature ferns, either white or black. Avoid contact and you will avoid the uncomfortable itchy rash which they cause. Any kind of protective clothing, thermal or not, will shield against accidental contact.

Diving Hawai'i's Caves Safely

For the most part, cave diving in the islands is accessible by boat only. The guides know the sites intimately, what their strong points of interest are, as well as the potential hazards each particular cave may pose. But, some of the tubes, caves and caverns are easily accessible from shore. Regardless of what your diving background is, I strongly recommend that you hire a professional guide who knows the waters and the formations. The temptation to explore these *pukas*, without the services of a knowledgeable guide can sometimes lead to tragic consequences.

On July 7th, 1987, three marines from the Kāne'ohe Marine Corps Air Station on O'ahu dived a spot called Shark's Cove at Pūpūkea Beach Park. One of the entries to the site is by wading out to a shaft called the "elevator". Once at the opening, divers drop into the cavern through the shaft, then exit to open water. It is a maze of caves accessible during the summer months only. On that day, an ocean surge had stirred up the visibility in the shoreline formation. The reduced visibility caused them to get disoriented, and when they could not find the opening, they took one of the exits going off to the side, got lost, ran out of air, and drowned.

Take a dive light when exploring both the inside, as well as the outside of the formations. Rock boring urchins patiently carve a network of channels, providing endless homes for juvenile fish, eels, mollusks, and invertebrates.

Some of the first critters usually seen when entering a cave is a school of shoulderbar soldier fish (menpachi or *'ū'ū'*). Their large eyes are common to nocturnal feeders, while they cluster in the dark recesses of the caves for protection during the daylight hours.

Crustaceans thrive in this type of environment. The slightest crack may be the home to red and white banded coral shrimp. Ghost shrimp, a relatively large species with a white body, a distinctive lateral red stripe, and very long antenna, are often found in large fissures inside caves. Several species of colorful lobster use the natural formations to congregate, as well as protection from several predators - most notably man. The small Hawaiian lobster is bright orange in color, clawed, hairy in appearance, and grows to eight inches. Slipper lobster can grow to 18 inches and resemble a lobster tail with eyes. Spiny lobster do not have large claws, but grow to 16 inches and are delectable. A rare crustacean is the long-handed spiny lobster, found in some of the more pristine, less dived recesses. Other species include the mole and the target lobster. Every once in a while, a prime choice of lobster lovers, the spiny lobster, will be seen within reach. Then, with a quick grab, the successful hunter will inspect the new catch, only to find the shell without the prize. This abandoned skeleton is a "molt", deposited by a bug that has outgrown its case. Left with only a soft outer

Photo Tip: Capturing Turtles On Film

If you are really insistent on a souvenir of your encounter, green sea turtles are some of the most photogenic "big" critters in the islands. A wide angle shot of a turtle with a diver in the background is a great addition to any photographer's portfolio. Shy by nature, swimming directly towards a turtle is intimidating, and the response is usually a hasty exit. If one is swimming in the open water, swim at a slight angle closing the distance slowly. If they are resting, again approach slowly without being aggressive. The rule of thumb is - the less threatening, the more of a chance you have of being accepted.

Paul Grulich shares a moment with "Scratch", a friendly, but threatened green sea turtle.

If you are using a diver in the shot, try to position yourself and the model on either side of the turtle. Though feeding them squid has been well publicized, it does alter their behavior. They can become very aggressive looking for handouts. More importantly DO NOT feed the turtles because they can get too acclimatized to the diver's handouts, and become much more vulnerable to poaching. Keep in mind - DO NOT touch, caress, handle or ride the turtles. They are a threatened species, and it is against the law to do so.

shell, the lobster will grow one to two millimeters before starting the cycle anew. Season for lobster ranges from September to May, but most conscientious dive operations will not allow collecting at all.

Two of the more unusual and very large crabs found tucked into *pukas* are the 7-11 and the sponge. The 7-11 crab is named for the pattern of spots on its shell. It has two formidable pincers that will make anything in its grasp wish it wasn't. The sponge crab is often difficult to locate when looking right at it. It has a unique method of camouflage. It tears a large piece of yellow sponge off the wall of a cave, holds it over the back of its green body with its rear two pincers, then walks headfirst into a *puka* leaving the

A Turtle Primer

There are three types of turtles found in Hawai'i's waters:
- **Green sea turtle** (honu) *Chelonia mydas*
- **Hawksbill** ('ea) *Eretmochelys imbricata*
- **Leatherback** *Dermochelys coriacea*

- The rare hawksbill is found around the "Big Island" of Hawai'i and off Moloka'i. They are small to medium sized by comparison. The leatherback is the only sea turtle without a hard shell and rarely comes near Hawai'i's shores. It is sighted regularly in the open ocean, where it feeds entirely upon jellyfish, and can grow to 1,500 pounds. The green sea turtle is named for the color of its body fat and grows to 400 pounds on a vegetarian diet. Since this species is the most common, and the one divers most often encounter, it is the one I will be referring to throughout the balance of this book as "turtle".

- Sexually mature and immature turtles feed and nest throughout the main islands. It is believed that it takes from 10 to 60 years for them to reach maturity, and only then do they become distinguishable from one another. The female's tail barely reaches the end of her shell, while the tail of the mature male is enlarged and elongated, extending beyond its hind flippers. It is estimated that about 750 resident adult females nest every one to three years. To do so, they have to migrate from their feeding grounds up to 800 miles away to a small area on the French Frigate Shoals.

- Hawai'i's green sea turtles are a threatened species. It is one step below endangered, which means the species is likely to become endangered in the near future. Regardless, they fall under the protection of the Federal Endangered Species Act of 1973 and Hawai'i state law:

  - It is illegal to "take" a protected species.
  - To "take" is defined as, to: harass, harm, pursue, hunt, shoot, wound, kill, capture, collect or to attempt any of the listed.

Several of the green sea turtles, both here and in Florida, are afflicted with virus related tumors. The immediate threat it poses is the resultant impaired vision that hinders their ability to forage. Long range threats stem from: shoreline development, pollution, increased recreational use of the ocean, driftnets, floating plastic debris (which they mistake for jellyfish and eat), and direct exploitation for their by-products.

inquisitive to see only the sponge displayed. The crab can grow from eight to ten inches across and is equipped with a good set of pincers.

A rare find in recessed pockets is the bluestripe pipe fish. The pipe fish grows to about six inches in length with a very thin, cylindrical, translucent, white body. A lateral red stripe runs along the side of this fish that is closely related to the sea horse.

Ash-colored (mustache) conger eels can often be found at the entrance to caves and in hidden recesses. The eels can get quite large and have two pectoral fins that cover their gill slits. Having no teeth to speak of, the eels have often been given names like "Gummy" and "Gramps". The long gray body has smooth and durable hide, which makes it very desirable for wardrobe accessories such as wallets and hand bags. Sources for that industry come from commercial farms and not from the wild.

Last but not least, one of the largest creatures to be found in caves is the green sea turtle. Holding their breath up to two and a half hours, they use the underside of ledges and caves to rest. Normally wary by nature, they usually leave when threatened by a diver's presence.

Diving off the north side of Maui, we came upon a turtle with a five-foot carapace. This was one big turtle that seemed relatively nonplussed by my looking into its bedroom chamber. When some of the other divers came over to the entrance to see what was inside, the startled turtle got up a head of steam and bowled over several of us, making a rather powerful exit.

In areas where divers frequent, several turtles have become acclimated to their presence, and go about their daily business unaffected. This is usually misinterpreted as a "come-on" to the over-exuberant enthusiasts, who try to caress, fondle and even ride the, by now, terrorized reptile. Despite some promotion for diving in Hawai'i undertaken years ago, we do not harass the turtles by riding them for three simple reasons: they cannot surface to breathe, they leave, and it is against the law.

Slabs and Ledges

Huge chunks of lava are scattered about several dive sites. Some are isolated and others are stacked in a haphazard array. Their undersides provide another source of habitation for several species of marine life. 'Ū'ū's, mentioned earlier, as well as yellowfin goatfish, cluster in safe numbers within the confines. The very rare Tinker's butterflyfish is found around lava slabs and boulders in depths starting at 130 feet, at a very few sites. They have a white body with a black triangle and gold stripes. These beautiful specimens are prized by aquarium collectors and as such, this is the only mention of them, so as not to give away their whereabouts.

Hawaiian sergeant (major) fish are members of the damsel fish family. Normally yellow and white with black stripes, after the eggs are laid the males change color to a gray with black stripes, and avidly defend the purple patch of eggs encrusted on the lava. When divers approach, they flee for cover, opening the door for opportunistic predators to move in and feed on their charges. When the diver leaves, the sergeant major rushes back to the area and quickly disperses the marauders.

Hawai'i has several species of puffer fish as well. They are often sighted, and sometimes cornered, in caves, *pukas* and beneath ledges. Spotted puffer (white spotted balloon fish) are also known as velcro fish from the feel of their body when inflated. They have a formidable beak to munch coral, and caution is advised when handling them.

The very rare Tinker's butterflyfish is highly prized by fish collectors, and is normally found at depths exceeding 130 feet.

An unusual encounter, that I experienced, was near the end of a dive at Molokini Crater. I saw white "smoke" emanating from a small puka. When I went over to investigate, I saw the tail ends of three white spotted balloon fish actively wagging. Taking the tails of the outer two, I gently pulled the three of them out. They were all partially inflated, but the one on the far left was clamping onto a fourth scarred up balloon fish that made me believe the other three were feeding on him. However, as I continued to pull them out of the puka, the fourth had bit into the same spot on a fifth, just in front of the caudal fin, and to the right of the spine. The fifth was clamped onto a sixth at the identical spot, and the chain continued for nine puffer fish all connected at the same spot. I have spoken to several experts that have never heard of this phenomena. I regret that it was probably a mating cycle interrupted.

Other pufferfish include the porcupinefish. They are difficult to catch and harder still to hold onto. Their primary defense mechanism is to swim, and once under steam can easily outdistance a diver. When cornered and caught, they inflate with once matted down spines that now protrude in sharp points. Using their tails in a back and forth motion, the resultant thrashing tears on the hands with the spines. They are more approachable and easier to catch at night, but they too have very sharp beaks. A distressing sight is to see them with damaged top and bottom spines caused by divers crushing down on them with rocks, knives, lights and strobes to catch them, rather than try bare handed. This hinders the fish's chance to defend itself.

The undersides of ledges are also great places to find several varieties of sea shells that live in Hawai'i. The majority of the shells found are cowries, but tuns, bonnets and augers are common. Some charter operators forbid collecting, with the philosophy that anything taken from the sea reduces the community. Though seemingly insignificant for one, multiply that by 120,000 tourists each year and the impact becomes devastating. Other operators turn a blind eye to it, and still others avidly seek them out. If you are **collecting sea shells**, follow a couple of guidelines:

1) **Know the rules** of the area to see if it is legal - some spots are designated as State Marine Life Conservation Districts and nothing is allowed to be taken.
2) If the **original animal** is still inhabiting the shell - **leave it.**
3) If the **shell has been reoccupied** by a hermit crab - **leave it.**
4) If there is **any doubt** - either **ask** your guide, or **leave it.**

Photo Tip: Feeding and Photographing Eels

Food that is brought out to attract an eel will also attract other critters by the droves. Moray eels become very aggressive when fed, and do not always nab only the food being offered. I have found that having my dive partner stay out of the frame, with the food, will attract the fish away from the camera, while the activity excites an eel's curiosity resulting in a successful shoot.

Strategically hiding food out of sight will attract the attention of the eels, while keeping bothersome fish out of the viewfinder.

When reaching into recesses for shells, or any other thing for that matter, be forewarned, Hawai'i has several species of resident moray eels. From the friendly whitemouth, to the very large yellowmargin, moray eels are found daily at most of the sites. Many have gotten used to the divers, and can be found at exactly the same spot day in and day out. The yellowmargins and the whitemouths can grow to intimidating sizes, yet despite their girth,

A rare blue spotted urchin, Astropyga radiata

some individuals are very approachable, providing modeling services for the photographers. They have acquired pet names that often match their temperament, and though most morays are used to the guides handling them, others have a somewhat less amenable temperament. I strongly recommend (out of personal experience) that you do not handle the eels unless the guide gives you the lead to do so. Otherwise, nips, bites and stitches can result. Another species of eel, not seen as often, is the canine-toothed (viper) moray. This species can aerate its gills by contracting its neck muscles rather than pumping water with its mouth. This allows a full wide open display of its overly toothed mouth when threatened, and a firm warning to keep hands off.

The underside of some of the lava slabs and ledges provide a rest stop for whitetip reef sharks, that prefer having nothing to do with divers. The timid sharks do not have to keep moving in order to aerate their gills. When disturbed by gawking divers they usually circle around in a tight pattern under the ledge until they find an opening to escape, then just swim away to look for another haven. I have observed them as small as a foot long to a full adult size of around seven feet. They are also sighted resting in the sand and sometimes cruising the sites for octopus.

Rubble

Some of the terrains that visiting divers ignore are the fields of rubble that skirt almost every large lava formation, and lie in the path between anchored boats and the main arena of the dives. Most people swim over these visually unappealing areas, missing out on some great discoveries and encounters.

The most apparent finds are the urchins that abound here feeding on the algae. Red slate pencil sea urchins have thick spines about as sharp as a finger, and with a vivid red color that provides a pleasing garnish to any photograph. Rough spined sea urchins are not as photogenic, but easy to find and safe to handle. A concentrated mound of stones, bits of shells, and whatever, might signal the presence of a pebble collector urchin. This curiosity uses anything it can get its tentacles on to cover and protect its white spined body. One very rare species is the blue spotted urchin. It has a white body (test) with five gold lobes arrayed in a starlike pattern. The lobes are lined with rows of blue spots. Its tentacles are gold at the base, ending in red at the tips. The unusual critter is every bit as colorful as it sounds. I have only found two of them, both in 35 feet of water. Checking with the Waikīkī Aquarium, they have only had two brought to them from deep water trawls off Kauaʻi. One was damaged and died, the other is still healthy and on display.

Countless species of fish can be seen grazing on the unlimited food source provided in the rubble fields. Moorish idols are attracted by overturning a rock. Oblivious to photographers, they compete with wrasse to feed on the newly exposed sponge. Rockmovers (clown wrasse) and yellowtail coris flip rocks to feed on the brittle starfish and juvenile urchins hidden beneath. A dragon wrasse (an ornate juvenile rockmover) flits about the top of rubble like a solitary leaf in a light breeze, until threatened, then dives out of sight for protection. A white cloud of sand is usually sign of a goatfish actively hunting with sensory barbels for morsels beneath the surface.

Cone shells can be found living in rubble. They have a unique offensive system used to prey on other shells. Extending a proboscis, they sting their victims with a venomous radular tooth. Cautious handling is advised as some of the species are dangerous to man.

Spaghetti worms have long, white, stringy tentacles that radiate from the central tube of the animal. Sensitive to touch, they uniformly retract when handled.

Devil scorpionfish are quite at home among the rubble. Totally camouflaged in their surroundings, they lay undisturbed, waiting in ambush for lunch to swim by, then gulp it up. Their spines have venomous sacks at their base, and if punctured, can cause a painful wound. Leaf scorpionfish are tiny members of the same family. They do have a leafy appearance, and are often brightly colored. The orange mouth lizard fish, named for its reptilian appearance, is another resident that will lay motionless on the bottom. Reaching lengths of 14", this voracious feeder snatches any unsuspecting prey in a lighting fast lunge.

Two elusive and very colorful eels that live in rubble are the leopard (dragon) and snowflake moray eels. Neither species attains a very large size or are threatening to divers. The dragon eel has a blend of white and orange markings with rostrum appendages. Snowflake eels are white with gold spots ringed in black. Both species are timid, rare and visually appealing to photographers.

The shy day octopus is one of two species found in the Hawaiian Islands.

Three unusual species of crabs live in and under rubble as well. The hairy hermit crab has a brilliant orange striped body and is covered with a thick coat of hair follicles. They are often found in the shells of Triton's trumpets, a victim of the crab's predation. A species of hermit crab can attach anemones from rocks to its shell in a symbiotic relationship. The crab provides a food source for the anemone, which in turn protects the crab with its stinging cells. Smaller xanthid crabs wear a set of anemones on the foreclaws like pom poms, and readily use them for defense like a pair of boxing gloves.

To me, the star of the rubble finds is the ubiquitous octopus, an elusive, shy, and gentle member of the mollusk family. Octopus find, steal, or make their own *puka* to live in, then line the porch with a concentric pattern of coral rubble or rocks (a dead give away in finding one of the critters). There is nothing this species of octopus can do to hurt divers, but a lot that can be done to harm them, usually through mishandling. It is best to signal a dive guide after discovering one, and have experienced hands coax the octopus out of its home, and calm it down for introductions and photos. The octopus will be very excited when it's first brought out, and will ink up a storm in an attempt to get away. But they tire easily, and will soon settle down on the diver's arm for security.

Ta'ape (bluestripe snapper) were introduced to O'ahu from the Marquesas Islands as a food fish. They have taken well to these waters, spreading throughout the islands, and are often sighted schooling in the hundreds. When they are in the area, conscientious guides will leave the octopus alone, as the *ta'ape* fend off the efforts of divers, and strip off the ends of the octopus' tentacles.

41

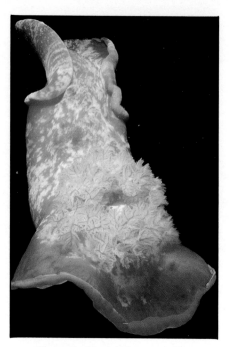

Spanish dancers, the worlds largest nudibranch, can reach 10" in diameter, but most often are found in smaller sizes. Clusters of eggs, resembling a rose in full bloom, give evidence to the presence of the nudibranch named for its undulating swim pattern in open water. Overturning several rocks may eventually yield a find, but the easiest time to find them is at night.

Sand Channels

Another area that can yield a treasure trove of marine life that divers often overlook is the sand channel. The top of the sand is seemingly littered with sea cucumbers. Some of the species, eviscerate a sticky white cluster called cuverian organs as a natural defense when handled. The large spotted (peacock) flounder do not give away their whereabouts until divers swim almost directly on top of them. Occasionally an eastern flying gurnard is sighted, its pectoral fins swept back into a delta wing configuration while at rest, then opening to a completely circular foil, rimmed in purple, that allows the fish to swiftly glide away from predators with a kick of its caudal fin. Peacock (razorhead) wrasse have a unique method of escape. When threatened, they dive headfirst into the sand, leaving no trace of their entry. Waiting a few inches beneath the surface, they re-emerge when the coast is clear.

The exotic Spanish dancer nudibranch can grow to 10 inches, and is most frequently found at night.

Helmet shells (conch) are a large species that are almost always found buried halfway beneath the sand. They favor deeper waters, but move up to shallow waters during certain times of the year.

The surface of the sand gives telltale signs of critters living just beneath. Straight furrows point out the path of a mitre shell or a marlin spike auger, while a small hump may yield a box crab. Sink hole patterns mark the locations of sea mouse, six to eight inches below. A cylindrical hole about an inch in diameter with two lobed eyeballs in retreat points out the home of a mantis shrimp. Starshaped patterns a foot in diameter mark the spots where sunburst starfish have been feeding. They live beneath the surface, and finding them is difficult. Their large size and bright golden arms makes for a great photographic subject, but careful handling is urged as they are fragile.

Mitre and auger shells are most commonly found beneath the sand. However, collecting live specimens is discouraged by conservation-oriented dive charter operators.

The sunburst starfish is a hard-to-find echinoderm living beneath the surface of the sand.

Several species of eels make their home in the sand. The large Henshaw looks like a critter that has crawled in to die. Only the top of its head protrudes from the granular bottom, until its prey swims by. A cloud of sand marks the flurry of activity and the eel is gone. Snake eels leave a wavy pattern in the sand as they swim just beneath its surface. They can be found, their heads protruding above their gill slits, in wait for food, but will recede into the protection of its tube when threatened by approaching divers and large fish. Small, thin garden eels stretch out of their holes without leaving them, and face into the current, undulating with the moving waters to nab any food that might pass by.

Out in the Blue

Pelagics are defined as ocean swimming creatures traveling freely to their own schedule and destination. Encounters with large schools of yellowfin tuna, families of gray sharks, and any meetings with hammerheads or oceanic whitetip sharks provide a lifetime's memory to those fortunate enough to encounter them. But the true stars of this show are giant manta rays that reach wing spans up to 14 feet, and the whale shark that can grow to 45 feet. Both are extremely gentle plankton feeders that are curious towards divers. Whale sharks tend to cruise an area, and swim on, nonplussed when a diver hitches a ride. On the other hand, manta rays,

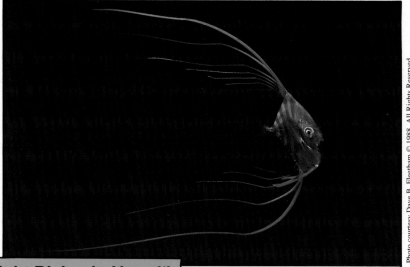

Night Diving in Hawaiʻi

Threadfin ulua *is one of the rare treasures of Hawaiʻi.*

The first time I ever read about diving at night was out of a dive shop brochure from the Florida Keys. It sent a chill up and down my spine. All that I could imagine was everything (with lots of teeth) that would be lurking just beyond the range of my light, or directly in back of me. My experience with this facet of diving has been a joy of discovery. There is a real sense of serenity and total solitude. The opportunity to maximize the use of macro and close-up photographic equipment on critters, otherwise intimidated during the daytime, was an added bonus. Most diurnal marine life hides, or is very approachable, at nighttime (usually stunned by the intrusion of the diver's light shined directly into their eyes). Several species of tropicals put on a "night cloak" - a change in the pattern and color from that during the daytime. Many creatures hidden during the daylight come out to forage after the sun goes down.

In Hawaiʻi, most operators do more of an "early evening" dive, just after sundown. I personally prefer going between 1:00 and 3:00 a.m. when everything has "transitioned over". Several species of crustaceans and mollusks give up their protective confines at night. Conger eels free swim in search of a meal. The crimson Spanish dancer nudibranch will mesmerize a diver with its mid-water undulating swim. Periodically check that midwater area - discoveries of squid, and the very rare thread-fin jack fish (thread-fin *ulua*), might be the reward. A different species of octopus, appropriately called a night octopus, can be seen in the sand channel. It has a linear spotted pattern beginning at the tip of its head radiating to the ends of its tentacles. If you lay your hand in front of the octopus, it will aggressively "pounce" on top of it, immediately back off 18 inches or so, then slowly extend one tentacle to scout out this thing it had hoped was a potential meal.

If you have never dived at night before:
- Try to dive the site during the daylight hours first, to get a mental imprint of its layout.
- Take a night diving seminar to learn equipment needs (lights, back-ups, Cyalume™ sticks), signaling procedures and safety orientation.
- Take a charter boat - even if it is a local night dive that could be done from shore.
- Relax - what lurks beyond the range of your light is the same thing that is just out of sight during the daytime.

when not intimidated by aggressive, overeager divers, will stay around, displaying a shear joy of underwater flight.

Do not charge after the critters. Every animal I have ever encountered underwater, when approached aggressively, has turned to swim away. It has led to many missed opportunities and several unappealing tail shots. The best way to increase the chances of a real close encounter, is to **stop and let them approach you.** They often have a curious nature and will swim as close as a couple of feet away. If pelagics do not feel threatened, they may stay around for the duration of the dive, or swim off, and then return. It is an exciting experience, and one that you will never forget.

Photo Tip: Shots of Opportunity

Imagine lying on the bottom of a sand channel 65 feet deep. Your model is feeding squid to a moray eel that lives in a fringing coral head, and you are using a wide angle format to record the feeding. While you are waiting for the eel to respond, you glimpse up, into the blue, and see a large figure slowly approaching your area. The bulk of the body and squared off silhouette of its head immediately identifies it as a whale shark!! It is the first time you have ever seen this rare creature, and it now becomes the only thing that occupies your senses.

An encounter with a pelagic whale shark is a rare thrill for any diver, and a once-in-a-lifetime "shot of opportunity" for an underwater photographer.

This is called a **shot of opportunity** - an unusual encounter that takes immediate priority over your planned set-up. It might be an encounter with a manta ray or other pelagic, an unusual invertebrate, or an interaction sequence between different marine life. Whatever the situation is, it is unusual, tells a story, and would make a great shot.

This is also where the adrenaline starts to take over, and where a photographer can most likely make a big mistake and come back with nothing usable on film.

To take the best advantage of this very rare situation, the photographer must have a **discipline of shooting**.

- **Check the focus, aperture and shutter speed settings.** Set the focus to five feet or greater (the critter probably will not come closer than that anyway).
- **Check the strobe settings.** Set a multipowered strobe to "Full" power. Pelagics are not highly reflective and you will need all the light that you can get.
- **Be patient** and wait for the critter to come to you. If you swim after it, it will swim away.
- **Do not start shooting until the critter comes to within range** and the shot will be dynamic.
- Once you start shooting, **make sure the strobe has time to recycle** before firing again.

Going through this checklist will only take a couple of seconds, and increase your odds of bringing back that once-in-a-lifetime encounter on film.

Chapter 2

The Mysterious Humpbacks and Other Marine Mammals

Hawai'i's winter season is a special time of the year. Rumors of whale sightings start circulating in the late fall, and within weeks, they become a daily occurrence. Fantastic stories are passed around about these leviathans swimming right up to transiting boats to take a closer look, and sometimes interacting with them. Endearing tales of mothers with newborn calves are long remembered. Even more thrilling is the awesome spectacle of a 40-ton behemoth launching straight out of the water, turning slightly, and then cascading back with a thunderous spray of sea water.

This is the season of humpback whales migrating to the Hawaiian Islands from the North Pacific Rim area of Alaska and British Columbia. It is believed they come to give birth to their calves, and it is known they nurse them during those first critical months in Hawai'i's ideal shallow waters. They are here as well, to propagate their endangered species, and fight for survival against overwhelming odds. The whales offer visitors and residents alike a chance to see, at close range, some of the last of the sea's magnificent cetaceans. More importantly, their short visit provides scientists an opportunity to identify and record them for census and distribution studies, observe their curious behavior, and sort out the puzzle that is the humpback whale.

The winter sojourn of the Pacific humpback whale, in the Hawaiian Islands, provides scientists an opportunity to study this mysterious mammal, and the public a chance to witness one of earth's most magnificent creations.

Description

From the front of its 45 foot long body to its flukes, the humpback whale is distinctive in appearance from all others. The top of the head is rimmed with knobs resembling "stove bolts", so named by whalers of old. Their underside is pleated with long ventral grooves that expand to cavernous proportions when feeding during the summer months in the north Pacific. Fifteen foot long pectoral fins, that extend a full third of the whale's length, may initially seem oversized. However, watching their slow, graceful movements in this liquid environment for which they were so adeptly created, puts any notion of clumsiness quickly to rest. Their scientific name, *Megaptera novaeangliae* (big winged New Englander), is inspired in part by their long pectoral fins. The common name is derived from a distinguishing hump in front of the dorsal fin made evident before each dive. The serrated tail fluke, measuring 20 feet across, is used to propel the beast gracefully through the water, and when called upon, to generate the power necessary to break the water's surface, launching the giant into a display called a breach.

Season and Distribution

Beginning as early as October, but most often in late November, reports of sightings by mid-channel fishermen and inter-island pilots start circulating throughout the islands. The level of excitement and anticipation builds for the impending season. In December, sightings become more frequent and widespread, reaching their peak during February and March, then gradually tapering off. By the end of May the whales are gone again, leaving Hawai'i's waters void of their presence, and empty of their song for another summer and fall.

Humpback whales are considered the "Nomads of the Sea". The sojourn between their northern home and southern breeding grounds is monumental in its scope, as they actually divide themselves among three locales; Hawai'i, Mexico and Japan. One individual has been positively identified in Hawai'i and Mexico during the same season. No one knows exactly what route is taken, or the varied attraction between the grounds. Nevertheless, their moniker is well earned.

It is not uncommon during Hawai'i's whale season, to see humpback mothers with their calves, and a male escort, in nearshore waters. It is an event that is evident by the number of cars pulled off to the side of the road - occupants armed with video cameras, telephoto lenses and binoculars all aimed seaward.

It is known that not all of the North Pacific Humpback whale population (estimated at 1,500) migrates to the Hawaiian Islands at one time. That figure, as well as the duration of their stay is at this point still guess work.

The waters of the North Pacific Rim are rich with krill, mackerel and plankton, the natural food sources of the humpbacks, but Hawai'i's waters are barren of this aquatic porridge. So, either they are opportunistic feeders, or they apparently fast during their stay, drawing sustenance from their own blubber reserves.

While all of the islands in Hawai'i share in the whales' presence, the shallow basin waters of Maui County between, Maui, Moloka'i, Lāna'i and Kaho'olawe, have the heaviest concentration. The next largest number comes from the "Big Island" of Hawai'i, primarily because the flat, calm waters off the Kona Coast are conducive to more sightings.

Calving

Whether the calves are actually born enroute to Hawai'i, or after their arrival, is unknown. No one has witnessed first-hand, or recorded on film, an actual birth. After an 11 to 12 month gestation period, the mother gives birth to a 14 foot, 1,500 pound light-colored calf.

With one violent thrust, one of a pair of competing humpback whales exposes its fluke in a powerful display.

The shallow waters surrounding the islands are ideal for newborn humpbacks' first few months of life. Their growth rate is phenomenal. Nourished from mothers' rich milk, the calves double their size within a year's time.

School is in session for the baby as well. Tail lobs, pec slaps and breaches are observed and mimicked by the youngster displaying as much energy and enthusiasm as any rambunctious toddler.

Mating

Mating is also believed to occur in Hawai'i during the whales' sojourn. Again, no proof of sightings or film can verify this claim, but the behavior of the animals seems to confirm this.

Within the pod, confrontations among males to claim pecking rights to the female is usually physical and violent...

In transit to Molokini, uninhibited whale activity was observed a couple of hundred yards off our port beam. We shifted to neutral and watched the waters thrash about with an occasional glimpse of the whales breaking through the surface. All the time this was happening, they were moving along in a straight course. As these pugilists drew closer to the stern of our boat, we observed them swimming side by side, constantly bumping into each other. They used their pectoral fins to beat on the back's of one another - both seemingly oblivious to our presence. Passing about 20 yards off our stern, we noticed that the backs of both whales were cut and bleeding, yet they continued unabated. A few minutes later, one of the two powerfully thrust its fluke high out of the water, trailing an arc of spray. Then they dove and were gone.

Mothers and calves are most often seen with a third whale acting as an escort. It was often believed to be another female, but later through behavioral studies and sexing, it proved to be a sexually active male. Studies have also proven that the whales conceive yearly rather than every other year as was originally thought.

Whale Watching

"What once used to be the whaling capital has now become the whale watching capital of the Pacific" – **the Hawai'i Maritime Center.**

Fishing, snorkeling, and dive charter boats double up duty, as transit times turn into whale watching ventures. With high expectations, all eyes become alert for the telltale plume of a whale's spout. Seldom are viewers disappointed.

Photo Tips for Whale Watching

From the curious displays of flukes raised toward the sky, to the resounding slap of a pectoral fin on the water's surface, or the aerial dynamics of a full bodied breach, humpbacks seem trained to be photogenic. Whale watching charters and inshore encounters afford more than ample opportunity to sate the hungriest photographer. Merely recording whales on film is easy, but doing it well – is not!!

Getting close enough for dynamic shots and exposing the film properly can be tricky. Here are a few hints on equipment, film and techniques to increase your odds of scoring that great one:

1. Secure Your Camera – Use a neck strap or wrist lanyard to keep from donating your camera to the drink when the boat rolls, or if you get bumped during all of the excitement.

2. Be Ready to Shoot – Most aerial displays happen fast, and only the more fortunate observers get to see a repeat performance. So keep alert and try to anticipate the action.

3. Be Patient – Don't waste too much film on whales several hundred yards away. Even with a telephoto lens and a very active whale, any encounter more than 80 yards away will result in a relatively small image that lacks the detail of a dynamic action photo. Close encounters usually happen when the boat's engines are shut down, and the whales take the initiative to approach the vessel.

4. Use a Telephoto Lens – If you own a disc camera or a point-and-shoot 35 mm camera, don't fret. View the long range action with binoculars, then photograph the whale when that close encounter does occur. Serious amateur and professional photographers are usually equipped with a zoom (70-210 mm) or fixed focal length (300 mm or above) telephoto lens. Any lens longer than 400 mm is too difficult to handle on a rocking boat. Keep in mind that the camera shutter speed should be greater than the length of the lens (for example – using a 300 mm lens, the shutter should be 1/500th or faster).

5. Use Higher Speed Films – The ASA rating of your film should be at least 100 or higher. A personal recommendation is Fujichrome 100 Professional or Kodachrome 200 Professional film when doing whale photography.

- **"High"** speed films need less available light which means:
  (1) a faster shutter speed – resulting in less camera movement with telephoto lenses
  (2) better depth of field so the whole whale can be in focus.

- **"Slow"** films have a couple of advantages as well:
  (1) Better color absorption – which is inconsequential as whale photography is relatively monochromatic
  (2) Better grain structure – which will start to show if prints are enlarged (for example 16" x 20").

Regardless of what film you choose, keep an extra roll or two handy. During an especially active or close encounter, a roll of film can be used up in short order.

6. Get the Best Exposure – Aim the camera at the water's surface when taking a light meter reading, and not the sky, for proper exposure. The brightness of the sky will fool the light meter and cause the whale to be underexposed or too dark. If you have a camera with an automatic or TTL metering system, use the "spot" metering control to properly expose the whale.

Protecting the Humpback - By Law

Designated the state marine mammal, Hawai'i's humpbacks fall under the protection of the Marine Mammal Protection Act of 1972 and the Endangered Species Act of 1973. The intent of the law is to deter the animals being hunted or harassed while they are in U.S. waters. Every effort is being made to keep the humpbacks coming back here, and from not moving to another destination for this most critical time in their life cycle. The laws are enforced by the National Marine Fisheries Service in waters within 200 nautical miles of the Hawaiian Islands.

The law forbids any aircraft to approach the whales within 1,000 feet, boats, or swimmers (yes, divers too) to approach within 100 yards of the whales, or within 300 yards of cow/calf waters. It is also illegal to disrupt the normal behavior or activity of the humpback whales. The whales don't know these rules, so nothing is wrong with them approaching you, just not vice versa. This means that no one can slip into the water with them while on scuba or snorkeling. The maximum penalty is vessel confiscation, a $25,000 fine and one year's imprisonment.

A humpback calf displays a head lunge in the Pailolo Channel between Moloka'i and Maui.

Behavior

A high percentage of whale sightings are at long range. As the boats approach the whales, their usual response is to dive and leave. Get your cameras ready, for often they will throw their flukes straight up (signaling a deep dive), then slip beneath the surface. It makes a quick but dramatic pose, and offers a glimpse of the pigmentation variation on the underside of the fluke. The pattern serves as a "fingerprint" in helping researchers identify individual whales. The circular still water where the whale was last sighted is called the "footprint", and caused by the turbulence of the dive.

Adult humpbacks can stay down an estimated 30 minutes and reach depths over 500 feet, but the average dives last from 10 to 15 minutes. Calves are limited to three to five minute dives before they have to surface. When an adult surfaces, it is unmistakable. A loud burst of air, will send a plume of misty salt water 20 feet into the air. It was a deadly giveaway for whalers who hunted them nearly to extinction in the mid-19th century.

The playful and friendly behavior of the humpbacks have endeared them to scientists, tourists and residents alike. It is easy to extend anthropomorphic (human-like) qualities to their behavior patterns, but it is at best, speculative. A whale slapping the surface of the water repeatedly with its fluke is demonstrating a **tail lob** or **fluke slap**. All surface behaviors are believed to be a form of acoustic communication with other whales.

Whales will often lay on their side and reach up with their pectoral fin. It can be an alluring greeting, witnessing a 15 foot long fin raised high and waving lazily. It seems to beckon observers…

The breach of a 40 ton adult humpback whale rivals any display in the animal kingdom.

Early one morning on the way out of Lahaina harbor, we noticed a mother and calf swimming along the roadstead, the mother on her side with her pec held high to the sky. The calf would intermittently mimic the mother as they visited each boat at their mooring, often elating live-aboard passengers to this unusual wake-up call. The whale was later identified as "Puamana" and known to be frequently seen in that area.

Humpbacks will also use their pectoral fins to slap the water's surface hard and repeatedly, generating a resounding crack. The display is known as **pec slaps**.

A whale's head rising out of the water not quite to eye level, then sinking back down repeatedly while swimming is demonstrating a **spy hop**. When a whale lifts its head above the water, then lunges back repeatedly, is a display called a **head lunge**.

Without a doubt, the greatest spectacle of individual animal behavior is the **breach**. Imagine a 45 foot long, 40 ton animal, leaping straight up out of the water, with anywhere up to two thirds of its entire body exposed, then doing a 180° turn before falling back with a thunderous cascade. This awesome display rivals anything in the animal kingdom. It is an action that is often seen once, but sometimes repeatedly by the same whale. One energetic calf was counted doing over 300 breaches over the span of a day's observations. We have seen two adults breaching simultaneously, and once saw three of them, breaching together and then alternating. I have personally noticed greater breaching activity when the seas are heavy. It seems the whales want to see where the source of the engine noise is, over the high, wind blown waves.

Singing

By now most of us have heard the recordings of humpback whales singing. Their mysterious orchestration of squeals, groans, bellows, and croons have entertained and fascinated scientists, as well as less educated ears, for decades. The purpose and reasoning behind their unique melodies are purely speculative, but some facts are known:

1 It is the **male of the species** that is the singer. Usually diving to a depth of about 100+ feet, the male will posture himself head down, extend his pectoral fins out to the side and begin. The songs can last a few minutes or several hours.

2 It is the **same song between breeding grounds** despite the distance that separates them. This gives rise to the speculation that at one time the whales could "communicate" with each other over a range of several thousand miles, before the noisy intrusion of man.

3 **The song varies from season to season.**

Whale watch boats are often equipped with hydrophones connected through a shipboard intercom system, that allows charter passengers a chance to hear the whale community "talk" to one another.

During the 1988 season we were crossing the 'Au'au channel between Lāna'i and Maui. The conditions were perfect; a bright, sunny day and glass flat water. At a distance we saw two whales swimming in a slow, lazy, circular pattern. We shut the boat down and watched as the mother and calf slowly circled closer and closer to our craft. With all of our attention focused on the two at the surface, it was startling when an escort whale (a large male) broke the surface, forcefully exhaled, threw up its flukes, and did a power dive directly beneath the boat. The conditions returned to dead silence until the crooning of the male filled the air around us. We had no hydrophone!! The amplification was so strong that it reverberated through the hull of our boat.

It is a rare day during whale season when divers can not hear whales singing during their dive. A divemaster placing a cupped hand behind his or her ear signals that a singing whale can be heard, so stop and listen. Sometimes a singer will be just out of visual range, but the amplification of its bellows literally vibrates through a diver's body, an experience that is never to be forgotten.

Interpretations

The interpretation of whale's singing and causal behavior is at best speculative and under investigation by a few individuals and organizations under federal permits.

When Jean-Michel Cousteau addressed a group of marine aficionados about the whales and what the scientific community knows about them, he stated that, "The only thing we can be absolutely sure of, is just how little we know of these gentle giants."

An Average Day at the Office

"We've got one, over there," yelled Mark Ferrari, as he started up the motor on the 15 foot Zodiac, and headed toward the whale activity. His wife, Deborah, grabbed the tape recorder and started making data entries. Mark said, "Get ready.", and I grabbed my mask, snorkel, fins and Nikonos (it is necessary to free dive with the whales, as exhaust bubbles are a normal sign given by whales to ward off intruders). We slipped into the water, careful not to make too much noise. For me, as we approached the whale, it was to be the fulfillment of one of my lifetime dreams. For the Ferraris, it was "another day at the office."

Deborah A. Glockner-Ferrari and Mark J. Ferrari

Deborah Glockner-Ferrari and her husband Mark, are Research Fellows for Wildlife Conservation International, a division of the New York Zoological Society. Licensed under federal and state research permits, they comprise the most compassionate whale research team in the Hawaiian Islands. In hopes of learning about the environment, behavior, and survival of Hawai'i's humpbacks, the Ferraris have spent their last 15 winters plying the lee waters of the 'Au'au channel off Maui, seeking encounters (above and below the surface), to record as much data and film as possible about the creatures that live so perilously close to extinction. In the past, studies were mostly conducted through postmortem examinations at whale processing plants. It is now done noninvasively through patient months of field study. During the remaining seven months of the year, while home-based on the mainland, their time is spent analyzing the data and slides they have collected. Working with the critters they passionately love, their steadfast diligence has resulted in substantial contributions to the total knowledge base we have on humpback whales.

Deborah discovered the hemispherical lobe at the base of the genital slit that identified the female species, to the subsequent realization that the escort whales, and singers, are sexually active males.

Whale #3208 is a "friendly" - one that is not intimidated by human presence. Over the years, they have developed a special relationship with that female they have come to know as "Daisy". She has allowed them close contact with her curious offspring, and for four consecutive years arrived with a newborn. Identifying individual whales over a several year span brought them to the conclusion that some whales calved annually, rather than every other year as was previously thought.

The 30 foot female yearling that we encountered the day I spent with them in their "office", was also a "friendly". We rotated filming and tending the boat, while the whale stayed with us for over two hours. We are alien visitors in the whales' element, so the duration and distance from the encounter are completely up to them. It was our good fortune that this one had no qualms about approaching within inches of us, swimming upside down, swooping by on her side, displaying the ventral slits along her underside, and just face to face encounters lying still in the water. There was no mistaking the intelligence when looking into her eyes. She was totally aware of our presence. Needless to say, she provided us with a wonderful photographic opportunity.

The most vivid image to come out of the encounter was one Mark recorded with a 16 mm movie camera. It is the opening sequence used in the Cousteau television program called *Land of the Living Totems*, part of their Rediscovery of the World series. Mark and Deborah were invited by Jean-Michel to join them in Alaska that following summer, to identify individuals known in Hawai'i's waters, to see if the calves are surviving the trek, and then be accepted by the North Pacific herds.

The Ferraris also contributed the live action footage of the humpbacks seen in the movie *Star Trek-IV: The Voyage Home*. Their still work has appeared in *Animal Kingdom, National Wildlife, Sports Illustrated*, and *Natural History* magazines, and recently illustrated a children's book titled *Humpback Whales* by Dorothy Hinshaw Patent published by Holiday House.

Mark and Debbie's passion is tempered by the reality that the whales' survival is still an uphill battle. Thrillcraft (jet skis, parasails, etc.) have chased the animals from the protection of the coastal shallows to deeper waters. Higher speed craft cannot react fast enough to a surfacing calf, and resultant collisions have led to serious and potentially fatal damage. Another concern is man's pollution of the seas could be the direct link to the increased sightings of sick yearlings.

The Ferraris established the non-profit Center for Whale Studies. Support for their important work is directly dependent upon individual, tax-deductible donations. For more information regarding the Center for Whale Studies, they can be contacted by writing them at P.O. Box 1539, Lahaina, Maui, HI 96767-1539.

Other Whales and Dolphins

Though five species of baleen whales and 19 species of toothed whales have been recorded either living or transiting through Hawaiian waters, very few species are seen on a regular basis. I am mentioning mammals that I have either personally encountered, or have most frequently heard about from other professional divers in the state. Though distributed throughout the Hawaiian islands, the greatest numbers of "blue water" sightings come off the Kona Coast of the "Big Island" of Hawai'i. This is due in large part to its southernmost location, next to the abyssal drop-off.

Appearing in the late spring through the fall, toothed Sperm Whales have, on rare occasion, been sighted offshore in the deep water areas surrounding the "Big Isle" of Hawai'i. Males can reach up to 55 feet in length, and were highly prized by whalers for their rich deposit of spermaceti oil in the box-shaped forehead of the leviathan. It was the sperm whale that inspired Herman Melville's *Moby Dick*.

False Killer whales have more often been mistaken for pilot whales than for true killer whales that they only superficially resemble. False killers can reach lengths up to 18 feet, weigh up to 3000 pounds, and are occasionally seen riding the bowplanes of boats. They have been spotted in groups of up to several hundred, but they are most often encountered in smaller pods.

Short-finned Pilot whales have been dramatically recorded off the Kona Coast in schools of hundreds. It is an oddity called "logging" where they will be resting on the surface, resembling floating logs. Most often they are seen in smaller numbers (20 to 40), and usually in the interisland channels. Though nomadic by nature, they have been sighted repeatedly in the same area, giving credence to the theory that they return to favorite areas. Sizes range a bit smaller than the false killers, with adults growing to 16 feet in length.

Pigmy killer whales reach a length of nine feet while averaging about seven and a half feet, and weigh in at approximately 370 pounds. When sighted, they are usually in the mid-channel area presenting tall, curved dorsal fins at the water's surface.

Dolphins

Dolphins have been the source of much sea lore over the centuries and with little wonder. Their fearless curiosity, playful behavior, and aquatic acrobatics can inspire even the gentlest spark of imagination. There is no season for dolphins, so Hawai'i's boaters are constantly treated to their accompaniment; riding the bowplanes of boats, body surfing in the boat's wake, and the circus-like antics of airborne spinner dolphins. Though the terms are often used interchangeably, technically speaking, Hawai'i does not have any species of porpoise, only dolphin.

Pacific bottlenose dolphins

Probably the most recognizable of the species, it is common to see Pacific Bottlenose dolphins riding the bowplane of transiting boats. Their command of their environment is simply breathtaking. Adults reaching eight to eleven feet long cluster in unison with their young, to hitchhike on the pressure wave being displaced by the bow of the boat. Sometimes one will roll on its side to look up at the passengers gawking over the bow; other times they will roll over on their backside, like stunt pilots at an airshow. Just how fast they can swim is demonstrated by their ability to swim away from a boat cruising at 20 knots, then glide back into the bowplane to continue their ride. I have observed them riding for five miles before they finally decided to disembark from our express run.

Divers will often hear the high pitched whistles and shrills of nearby dolphins, and will occasionally be cruised by the more curious ones, most aware of their aquatic superiority.

Along with the Pacific Bottlenose, and most commonly found in the open water, spinner dolphins display a true joy of life with their aerial demonstrations of spins, loops, and gainers. Delighting ocean travelers who happen upon these relatively small, three-toned dolphins, spinners are usually seen close to shore in large schools.

Pacific Spotted Dolphins closely resemble spinners. Reaching seven feet and up to 240 pounds, they are slightly larger than spinners, but are distinctive in appearance by their layer of spots, both on their top and undersides. They are usually encountered in mid-channel waters, and rarely observed accompanying humpbacks.

Monk Seals

One of the two species of true eared seals, Hawaiian monk seals can tip the scales at 600 pounds. However, the endangered pinnipeds (fin footed) are fighting for survival. At one time hunted for their fur, meat and oil, and now prey to sharks, and human intrusion, their numbers have fallen to between 500 – 1,400. They hover over the precipice of extinction.

Their greatest concentration can be found from Nihoa Island to Kure Atoll (ideally isolated for birthing). The monk seal, named for its preference to solitude, from humans as well as each other, rarely ventures south of these low lying northwest Hawaiian Islands. When they do, it is usually for a short period of time, and many critters familiar to divers at those particular sites coincidently start to disappear. It seems the seals have a voracious appetite eating up to 10% of their body weight daily. Eels, not endowed with good

The endangered monk seal, like this one photographed at Sea Life Park on Oʻahu, are often sighted basking along the shores of Lehua Rock.

sight or intelligence, are attracted to the approaching seal (closely resembling a diver), and gulp, they're history. The monk seals also like to feed on octopus, lobster, and small reef fish.

In 1988, a report was made of a seal giving birth and weaning her pup on the islet of Moku ʻAeʻae just off Kīlauea Point on Kauaʻi. Sightings off the nearby Niʻihau are becoming more prevalent as well, with interesting encounters as a result…

Nick Konstantinou was making a private dive at Lehua Rock, a remnant volcanic cone off the "Forbidden Isle" of Niʻihau. Because it is accessible only by a long boat trip, and protected by high winter seas, it is a pristine area rarely dived. That morning, as his boat stood at anchor in the shadow of the rock, he noticed between three and five monk seals. The unusual sighting was an exciting one, as the seals' continued existence is an "iffy" proposition at best.

Nick got into his snorkeling equipment, grabbed his camera, and slipped into the water. Two seals (100 and 200 pound youngsters) were waiting under the boat. The seals casually swam off, so Nick swam towards the cove where he had initially sighted them. At that point, the larger of the two swam to within 10 feet of Nick, stopped and stared. The other one stayed about 40 feet away to watch the activity. Nick shot about eight frames before the larger seal slowly swam off. He finished his dive around the cove and then returned to the boat. The gratification of the encounter came from the seal's initiating the approach. Though lasting only five minutes, it was precious time spent with one of the world's most endangered species.

As exciting as the encounters can be, experiencing the humpbacks at close range gives the viewer a deeper understanding of why researchers and conservation groups are fighting so hard to learn more about, and protect these endangered animals.

The decimation of the whale populace, as a result of unrestricted whaling, has left us with a few thousand creatures that struggle with the elements and man for survival. Harbor and resort development lead to more activity on the water and consequently more chances for harassment and displacement from preferred areas. Continued threats from pirate whalers, "legitimate" harvesting under the guise of research, thrill craft, pollution, oil spills, and drift nets spell impending doom not only to the whales, but dolphins, seals and other marine mammals as well.

One final point that Cousteau left us to ponder is the analogy of the aircraft in flight and our planet. If you picture each rivet that holds the aircraft together as a species, when a species becomes extinct, a rivet falls out of the aircraft. The aircraft can only tolerate a certain number of lost rivets. Beyond that critical point, the entire craft falls apart and crashes.

Chapter 3

A Glimpse of Hawai'i Underwater

Since the days of the ancient Hawaiians, the people of the islands have been acutely in tune with the importance of the sea to the welfare of Hawai'i. Today, as much as ever, awareness of the ocean, both above and below the surface, continues to be presented to the public. The education of the present generation assures its preservation for future generations to follow.

There are several different avenues that have been pursued in doing this chapter. I have selected those which best suit the nature of this book to inform individuals and families, both divers and nondivers alike, of why these waters are so precious to us, and their marine inhabitants. Though some of the organizations listed are commercial operations, they were strictly based on the spirit of public awareness by opening up the window to Hawai'i underwater through education, and the preservation of the ocean and its inhabitants.

Waikīkī Aquarium

The popularity of public aquariums in the United States has skyrocketed in the last decade. The heightened interest in the marine world has spawned a new era of high tech, interactive centers that allow visitors a close-up look at a world of which little was known thirty years ago. Built in 1904, the Waikīkī Aquarium is a small facility by mainland standards, but a progressive and internationally recognized research institution affiliated with the University of Hawai'i. It is located on the ocean side of Kapi'olani Park off Kalākauā Avenue, just past the crush of hotels and beaches of Waikīkī.

The aquarium displays 40 tanks with 250 species of fish from Hawai'i and the South Pacific in four thematic galleries. The most popular attractions are the 5000 gallon shark tank, an outdoor pool with two endangered Hawaiian monk seals, and the outdoor "Edge of the Reef". This is an interactive display allowing a "hands-on" viewing of inhabitants found along the rocky shoreline area, progressing to tide pools, then on to a quiet reef area. The entrance leading to the gallery area has the "Hawaiians and the Sea" section, depicting the ancient islander's vital link to their aquatic surroundings, through graphics and artifacts. New displays are on the docket including a living reef machine and a large outdoor tank for the larger ocean fish including the *mahimahi*, a type of dorado.

The common as well as the unusual are on display in the four galleries of the Waikīkī Aquarium, representing marine life throughout the Hawaiian Islands and the South Pacific.

Audio tours are available for a 50¢ rental at the front desk, in English and Japanese. In 1987, the aquarium published a very informative guidebook with full-color photographs and two-toned illustrations. Waikīkī Aquarium also offers education programs geared for adults which are open to members and nonmembers alike. Day and night reef walks are available, as well as a popular lecture series offered by the staff. A spring travel program with resident biologists is offered to areas throughout the South Pacific and the Galapagos Islands.

Though small, the Waikīkī Aquarium is by no means stagnant. The current displays are catching up to the lofty standards set by the country's leading public aquariums, and plans are on the drawing board for a natural history theater and an ocean science center by the turn of the century. The Waikīkī Aquarium is located at 2777 Kalākauā Avenue, and the phone number is (808) 923-9741. A donation is requested from adults, and children 15 and under are admitted free.

Sea Life Park

It is a scenic 15 mile drive from Waikīkī to Sea Life Park, nestled in an ocean side setting at Makapuʻu Point, against the backdrop of the Koʻolau Mountain Range. Opened in 1964, the park is modest by today's theme park standards, but fully cognizant of the public's love for the ocean, its inhabitants and their preservation. I first started coming to the park in the late 60's, and it still holds my fascination for the sea to which it first introduced me.

A white spotted balloon fish, in the 18 foot deep Hawaiian Reef Tank, is the source of curiosity and delight for Brett Whittington and his mother Beth, at Sea Life Park.

The initial and most impressive exhibit is the Hawaiian Reef Tank. Approximately 4,000 critters inhabit the 300,000 gallon aquarium, that can be viewed from the surface, 72 feet across, or via 17 large acrylic windows along a circular ramp that descends 18 feet to its base.

The Hawai'i Ocean Theater seats up to 400 for entertaining displays by dolphins, California sea lions and Humboldt penguins in a 175,000 gallon stage. The Whaler's Cove Show is set in a 2,000,000 gallon man-made lagoon. The most striking structure is the 5/8ths to scale replica of the whaling ship *Essex* - 70 feet long with a 66 foot high mast. The interior of the ship now has large acrylic ports to view the false killer whales, Atlantic bottlenose dolphins, and an unexpected hybrid of the two - a wholphin. Birthed on May 15th, 1985, *Kekaimalu*, meaning "the peaceful sea", has grown to eight feet and 600 pounds, and was recently unveiled to the public.

Interactive exhibits include the 1,500 gallon Touch Pool, where visitors can have a "hands-on" encounter with Hawai'i's marine world without actually diving, and the Sea Lion Feeding Pool. Less impressive, but equally important exhibits are the Rocky Shores intertidal zone exhibit, Kolohe Kai Sea Lion Show, and the Penguin Habitat. The park has a resident populace of the only endangered penguins in the world, the South American Humboldt Penguins. They now have a private beach, pool with a below-water viewing port, and several nesting sites.

Sea Life Park has established several preservation projects as well. The Hawaiian Monk Seal Care Center was recently built with the cooperation of the National Marine Fisheries Service. This 40,000 gallon habitat serves as a temporary home to stranded and injured monk seals. As soon a the endangered mammals have recovered, they are safely returned to the wild. Turtle Lagoon has three species of turtles and has hatched over 1,000 eggs for eventual release. The Leeward Isles Bird Sanctuary is visited by 20 species of marine fowl; red-footed boobies, albatross and the great frigate birds highlight the sightings.

The Shark Gallery is a static display of artifacts and photographs about the once feared predator. The privately owned Pacific Whaling Museum is a small collection of artifacts highlighted by a 36 foot long sperm whale skeleton, reconstructed from an adolescent that stranded and died off Barbers Point, O'ahu in May of 1980. The museum is free to the public and has a gift shop. The park also has the Sea Life General Store, the Sea Lion Cafe and the Rabbit Island Bar and Grill. There are mini lectures available, as well as behind the scenes tours. The park is open from 9:30 a.m. to 5:00 p.m. daily, and to 10:00 p.m. on Fridays. Further information may be obtained by writing Sea Life Park, Makapu'u Point, Waimanalo, HI 96795, or by calling toll free (800) 367-8047 ext. 348, or locally at either (808) 259-7933, or (808) 923-1531. Admission is charged.

Hawai'i Maritime Center

In 1984, a private, nonprofit organization was dedicated to establish a world class maritime exhibition on the Honolulu waterfront. The opening of the Kalākauā Boathouse in 1988, at Pier 7, was the fulfillment of that dream and the centerpoint of the Hawai'i Maritime Center. Located a short walk from the historic Aloha Tower, the center boasts a museum, a four masted ship, and a historic ocean going canoe. The museum is housed in

The Hawai'i Maritime Center houses a unique collection of artifacts and displays related to Hawai'i's inextricable ties to the sea. Part of the permanent display is the Falls of Clyde, *currently undergoing a complete restoration.*

the boathouse, which is named after King David Kalākauā, the last ruling monarch of Hawai'i, who was renown for his love of the ocean and the revival of Hawai'i's ancient culture. Dozens of exhibits present the various influences of the ocean on the islands: economic, historical, cultural, and recreational.

The imposing *Falls of Clyde* is berthed alongside the museum. This is the last surviving four masted square rigged ship in the world, and the last of the original Matson fleet. This turn of the century oil tanker plied the sea lanes between San Francisco and the Hawaiian islands, and is currently under restoration. On the other side of the boathouse is the historic *H ōkūle'a*, a replica of the Polynesian voyaging canoes believed to date back 1,500 years. Using ancient navigational methods, the *H ōkūle'a* has made two round trips to Tahiti and a two-year rediscovery voyage around Polynesia. Off-site field trips have been initiated when the center recently came to an agreement with the Coast Guard to run day trips to the Makapu'u Lighthouse, built in 1906.

Pier 7 Gifts is located in the lobby of the boathouse. An on grounds, open air restaurant, the Coasters, is open from 10:30 a.m. to 10:00 p.m. The museum hours are from 9:00 a.m. to 5:00 p.m. daily except Christmas. For information call (808) 536-6373. Admission is charged.

Whale Watch Cruises

The enchanting magnetism of the humpbacks, the pageantry of their display, and the mystique of their songs, excites even the most devoted land lubber. During the six month season, a sub-industry of whale watching springs to life, enabling visitors to get a close look at the curious mammals on full or half-day charters. Binoculars, telescopes, and cameras with telephoto lenses are ritually brought on all charters.

A humpback calf rolls gently off its mother's back as it ventured too close - to the delight of the transiting dive charter passengers.

Most frequent are long distance sightings of the whales swimming at a slow but steady pace, occasionally displaying their 20 foot tail flukes signaling a deep dive. But every so often . . .

During the 1987 season, we were transiting from Lahaina to Molokini Crater, off Maui, for a two-tank dive charter. At Olowalu we spotted some activity about 300 yards inshore and stopped the boat. For a period of 45 minutes the three whales, a mother, calf and escort, swam closer and closer to our boat. The captain shut down the engines, and with that the calf swam to within 20 yards of the port side of the boat.

Mother had decided that was close enough. She submerged, swam under the calf, and rising up, lifted her offspring completely out of the water. We watched in awe as the baby rolled harmlessly down its mother's back.

For those who do not function well on boats, there are over 30 different observation sites along the islands' coastline that are recommended as high potential sighting areas. During the height of the season (February and March), it is common to see dozens of cars pulled off the road. Observers applaud and cheer as the whales put on a show within a few hundred yards of the shoreline.

Dolphin Quest

On a trip to the "Big Island" of Hawai'i, I toured the Hyatt Regency Hotel at Waikoloa. Lunchtime was interrupted by a woman whose enthusiasm had broken through normal restraints and burst out, "I got to swim with them! I got to swim with the dolphins!" The announcement to her friend across the room (and subsequently everyone within earshot), was punctuated by flailing arms and a smile from ear-to-ear. She had realized her dream through Dolphin Quest's swim-with-the-dolphins program, which is open to the public, for anyone 13 or older.

A man-made lagoon on the hotel's grounds is now home to a number of Atlantic Bottlenosed dolphins (*Tursiops truncatus*) that adapt very well to their surroundings. Normally found along the east coast of the United States and the Gulf of Mexico, the dolphins, by nature, prefer the shallows of the coastal waters. Their Pacific cousins (*Tursiops gilli*) prefer the deeper waters of the open ocean, and would not do as well in captivity.

For a fee, individuals get a chance to learn much about dolphins, through lectures, demonstrations, and culminating in an interactive in-water encounter. The dolphins are not trained to do tricks, nor is this an amusement park ride. It is meant to "inspire appreciation of, and sensitivity towards all marine mammals, through personal, interactive, educational opportunities for adults and children to learn about our marine ecosystem."

This, as well as several other similar programs throughout the country, has generated much controversy. Complaints range from the depletion of wildlife stock, to the stress on the captive animals. Most come from individuals and organizations that have neither witnessed, nor pondered the benefits these programs offer. The few individual dolphins that have been

At the end of the Dolphin Discovery program while the other children were leaving the lagoon, I looked back to see Grant Asti getting in a last affectionate stroke.

captured for Dolphin Quest, spend only an hour a day in actual human contact. The balance of their time is spent in training, play, at rest, and feeding on the 18 pounds of restaurant quality fish they devour daily. The small numbers that have been taken are used to educate the public, and increase their awareness for proper conservation of the marine mammals. Balance this against the hundreds that died in the wild during 1989 from a poisonous plankton bloom, and the thousands that die annually in the fishing nets of the tuna industry. It seems to leave no question about the benefits of the programs. Yet the high profile of the controversial swim-with-the-dolphins program overshadows much of the other work that the multi-faceted Dolphin Quest is involved with.

Their research focuses on gaining a knowledge of the dolphins' vocalization, behavior and organization. They are also involved with a study of spinner dolphins in the wild, to help in developing a solution to their high mortality rate from the tuna industry. In the American tuna fleet, an average of 20,500 dolphins are caught in the industry's nets each year. The results are rarely good for the dolphins. That doesn't count the Pacific Fleet where the toll is much more dramatic and unaccounted for. The most tragic is the pelagic driftnetting that is estimated to drown between 100,000 to 250,000 dolphins annually. Working with the University of California Santa Cruz, caring researchers are developing a gate system that the dolphins can use to escape the deadly entrapment.

Dolphin Quest works closely with the Marine Mammal Fund, and is now endorsed by Greenpeace Foundation. Other objections arise about the money brought in from this successful venture, being done so at the "dolphins' expense". Besides their food costs, the income is used for security, staff salary, educational materials, and funding for several gratis programs, including two-day field trip programs for local schools, seminars, a summer youth program, and Make-A-Wish Foundation.

On my visit with Dolphin Quest, I witnessed their Dolphin Discovery program, catering to five to twelve year olds. The children do not swim with the animals, but are carefully introduced to them at the edge of the lagoon's shore. After a short lecture, and a couple of demonstrations on echo-location, speed, and their body design, the kids get to caress and feed them a snack.

The experience is carefully controlled by trainers who obviously love their work and the dolphins who appear none-the-worse for the experience. The children are left with an indelible impression of these lovable mammals, and hopefully a lifelong fervor to preserve the species for their generation, and those to follow.

Glass Bottom Boats

An insulated way to spend time on the ocean, and view the marine life below, without worrying what might try to nibble on your toes, is by taking a cruise on a glass bottom boat. Large passenger vessels make an enjoyable combination of cruising over nearshore reefs while a narrator describes the marine life and action passing beneath the hull. At some point, a diver is usually put overboard to bring interesting marine life within close range of the portals, or lure fish into view with hand held-food. It's much the same as an aquarium that rolls with the swell, and the action is a bit more spontaneous.

Submarine Tours

Instead of looking at marine life in the artificial settings of aquariums and underwater theme parks, divers and nondivers of all ages, can now enjoy Hawai'i's marine world in its natural element. The advent of **Atlantis Submarines** in Hawai'i enables passengers a chance to experience Hawai'i below in the confines of a fully enclosed, air conditioned vehicle. Established as the first public passenger submarine company, Atlantis has a long and successful track record in the Caribbean for safety, enjoyment and educating the public.

Atlantis opened their first Hawaiian operation in August of 1988 at Kailua-Kona on the "Big Island". Immediately setting out to develop an area teeming with marine life, they did it so successfully, that news spread quickly, and before long, a myriad of tropicals and eels moved to "Atlantis Reef". Now divers escort the subs and lure the fish to within a few feet of the wide angle viewing ports. The second operation opened in Waikīki in

One of Atlantis' divers lures a school of
ta'ape (bluestripe snapper) to within
inches of the submarine's viewing ports.
Jonathan McCarthy is able to point out
the fish with one of the identification
cards available at all of the stations.

September of 1989. Without having a good base reef to work with, the company procured a surplus U.S. Navy yard oiler, and sunk it on a sand bottom, to establish an artificial reef. I dived the "newest site off O'ahu" a few months after it was sunk, and was amazed at how quickly a marine community was established. Atlantis Submarines is committed to community education, and has established special tours for local school children.

The $3,000,000 submarines are certified by the U.S. Coast Guard and the American Bureau of Shipping to dive to depths up to 150 feet. Measuring 65 feet long by 13 feet wide, the 80 ton subs are battery powered, attain three knots at the surface, and a knot and a half submerged. Tours are run for 45 minutes, carrying up to 46 passengers and three crew. Thirteen 21 inch ports on each side of the submarine, and a 52 inch bow port allow more than ample viewing. Each viewing station has a fish identification card, and knowledgeable guides are narrating the tours to point out the highlights as they come into view. The pilots are skilled navigators keeping the submarines at least two to three feet off the bottom, and are ever so careful to not touch anything while submerged. Each submarine is equipped with 16 one thousand watt exterior flood lamps for night dives.

For more information concerning tours, booking information or the submarines, Atlantis can be contacted on the "Big Island" by writing, Atlantis Submarines Hawai'i, L.P., 74-5590 Ālapa Street, Suite A, Kailua-Kona, HI 96740, or by calling (808) 329-3175, FAX (808) 329-3177. On O'ahu the address is 560 North Nimitz Highway, Suite 201C, Honolulu, HI 96817, or by calling (808) 536-2694, FAX (808) 537-1193.

Intros, Refreshers and Orientation Dives

You have read about and seen photographs of marine life in books, magazines, and at static displays at museums. You have viewed critters through the glass at aquariums and marine theme parks. You may have even taken a submarine ride to view them in their natural environment through a porthole. All these methods have provided windows to take a glimpse into the underwater world. The bottom line is they all place a barrier to prevent you from reaching out to touch the sea. Nothing can replace the communion of actually being there.

"But, what can I do if I don't dive?" – "I don't know if I would like diving enough to commit the money and time for a course. Isn't there some way I can try it out?" "My spouse dives, but I'm not certified. How can I get to go along?" The answer to these questions is easy. Most dive charter operators offer **Introductory Dives**. They are usually open to anyone in good health, 15 years or older (some as young as 12), have rudimentary swim skills, and are comfortable in the water. The program starts out with a lecture from a scuba instructor about the equipment, dive procedures, safety precautions and the marine life. Some offer time in a swimming pool to practice skills - others go straight into the ocean, but do the same skills on a safety line, a few feet underwater. Then, one at a time, everyone descends to the bottom for a tightly controlled tour, and depending upon the size of the group, led by one or more instructors. So now you're doing it - the real thing, with real marine life, in their everyday, natural environment. The professionals will often find critters for you to hold - or touch (only if you wish). At the completion, you have had a wonderful experience, not a certification course, but hopefully a pleasant enough adventure to induce you to take sanctioned training.

"I've been out of diving for a long time. I know my certification card is good for life, but I don't feel comfortable about getting back into diving". Take a **Refresher Course**. It is run much the same as an Introductory Dive, in very controlled conditions. It helps shake off the rust and either gives you the self-confidence needed for you to get back into diving, or convince you to start from scratch and get recertified.

"I've dived a lot in lakes and quarries, but never before in the ocean." "I've never been diving in Hawai'i before. How can I get acclimated before taking a regular dive charter to waters I am not familiar with?" **Orientation Dives** offer the same experience as the Introductory or Refresher dives, but without the lecture and pool work. You should be well versed with your equipment and safety procedures already. You will benefit by setting your buoyancy correctly, and learning what thermal protection you will need without feeling the pressure of holding up regular charter divers.

Whatever reasons have kept you from trying this beloved sport in the past, there are avenues to introduce or re-acquaint you with our world underwater. Give it a chance and take the plunge.

Water Conditions

Water clarity depends upon a lot of different factors including plankton bloom, agricultural run-off, wind, surge and pollution to name a few. Hawai'i's waters are exceptionally clear when all the conditions are favorable, and better than average when all of the conditions are not. Visibility ranges from a low of 50 feet to well over 150+ with averages of 60 to 80 feet.

Hawai'i basically has two seasons - summer and "not quite summer". Water temperatures average 73 - 77°F in the winter to 77 - 81.5° in the summer, and are isothermal from the surface to the bottom. **Thermal protection** for visiting divers becomes a matter of personal consideration. Many "cold water" divers find a lycra suit, and/or an eighth inch shorty jacket sufficient. If you are planning to do a lot of diving you might consider a full suit or at least a farmer john. You will notice that all of the professional divers here wear full suits. Diving anywhere on a daily basis acclimatizes the body to those conditions, resulting in a lower tolerance to the otherwise tepid waters. Regardless, I recommend that you wear adequate protection against scrapes. Though we do not have fire coral, the lava formations and coral can be quite abrasive. Several divers ask about wearing gloves over here. I personally don't, because I like the intimacy of contact with the sea, and the better camera control it affords me, but if you feel uncomfortable about what you may accidently touch, by all means wear them.

Hawai'i's Water Temperatures

Month	Average Minimum	Average Maximum
January	71.1	74.7
February	70.3	75.6
March	71.8	76.5
April	73.0	77.7
May	74.7	79.5
June	77.7	81.1
July	78.3	81.1
August	79.2	81.9
September	78.4	81.9
October	77.2	81.1
November	74.5	79.3
December	71.4	75.9

Water Motion

The long, flat ocean waves that gradually rise, then fall, are known as **swells**. They are generated from distant storm systems and cause the surf conditions so famous in Hawai'i. The swells usually outpace the storm systems that created them, arriving several days ahead of the disturbance (if it arrives at all). On the surface, dive boats will ride atop the swell, gently raising up and down, or rocking side to side (see sidebar: Coping With Seasickness). From the beach, the effects of the swell can range from the gentle lapping of the water on the shore's edge, to the spectacular "tubes" that break offshore. Underwater, divers can be most distracted by swells if they are trying to stay in one spot to photograph or study a stationary object. **Surge** is the repercussive effect of the swell caroming off the shore, creating a back and forth lifting motion.

Currents come under the influence of the northern equatorial flow. Waters stream past and through the islands in a westerly direction at 1/3rd to 1/2 khot. The currents can be reversed or reinforced by tidal flows requiring divers to negotiate a variety of horizontal water movement ranging from: dead still waters to an easy light current, from currents heavy enough to make divers hanging on an ascent line look like they are flags flapping in a stiff breeze, to what we call the Tahiti Express - "Aloha nō and away you go". Off some shoreline areas it can be quite dangerous. Always check with your dive guides, life guards, or local experts before getting in "over your head".

El Niño: "The Child"

El Niño (el-neen-yo) is an aberration in the eastern tropical Pacific that results in the periodic warming of the ocean waters. The consequences are baffling to scientists, and sometimes disastrous in their effect. Resultant strong winds travel west along the equator accompanied by a warm water current that displaces the colder, nutrient-rich Humboldt Current. Its eventual arrival off the western South American coast has led to some calamitous results, obliterating the anchovy fishing industry, and pouring torrential downfalls on coastal desert communities. Its arrival has traditionally coincided with the Christmas season, leading to its name, "the Child", in Spanish. Hawai'i experiences some side effects when *El Niños* occur, though not as dramatic. The winter water temperatures tend to maintain the summer level, and eventually rise during the warmer months to an average of five degrees above normal. The opposite effect is known as *La Niña* (little girl), with colder than average winter waters.

The periodic rising and lowering of the oceans is caused by the combined effects of the moon and the sun on the earth's rotation. The high tide to low tide variation in the Hawaiian Islands is negligible, averaging two feet throughout the month.

Coping With Seasickness

Okay, you are on the boat, and realize that you are feeling a little queazy, your brow is sweaty, and you are starting to turn green. First, try looking at the horizon - the far horizon; then breathe deeply, and pray. If all has failed, and you are going to lose it, the worst place to be is inside the head (or marine toilet), where there is no air circulation and the boat's rocking seems much more amplified. The second worst place is inside the boat's cabin (lose it there, and everyone on board will hate you). Try to get to the side of the boat - preferably the one with the wind blowing over your back - and shoot for distance. The clean-up is minimal, the fish love it, and you'll feel a lot better - for a while.

If you are one of the unfortunate, prone to *"mal-de-mer"* when on a boat - or plane - or car, there are a number of remedies to try, like eating something with ginger (Warning: a whole box of ginger snap cookies and four cups of coffee doesn't work), or anything else that might help settle your stomach. There are several over-the-counter drugs you can use, including Dramamine® (the only one that can be used by the elderly and children under 12, as well as adults), Marezine® and Bonine®. Some of these cause drowsiness though, so check the directions for proper dosage and driving recommendations. A relatively new treatment, growing in popularity with the vacation diver, is the prescription Transderm Scop® (pronounced scope - an abbreviation for scopolamine) patch. Check with your doctor about the potential side effects of this particular treatment combined with effects of diving under pressure. Another new item to hit the stands is a wrist strap that applies pressure on nerve points in the wrist. Originally designed to reduce the nausea in chemotherapy patients, it is based on the principle of acupressure. Finally, if all of this fails, you may want to try shore diving.

There is a 90% chance that **tradewinds** will be blowing from the northeast on any given day during the summer, and 50% during the winter months in Hawai'i. They are so predominate that the windward and leeward sides of the islands are named for their vulnerability to the trades. The winds tend to pick up later in the afternoon, which explains why dive charters usually leave so early in the morning.

From October through April the islands can experience a shift in the weather patterns with winds blowing "Kona" (meaning leeward). **Kona conditions** are usually characterized by very strong southerly winds and torrential downpours, and this is usually as inclement as it gets in Hawai'i.

There are over 80 retail and charter dive operations in the state of Hawai'i. Reservations can be made either directly with the companies, or through one of several activity desks located throughout the islands' hotels and tourist centers (a hefty commission (20%) is charged to the dive companies for this service). Boats range in size from six passengers (six-packs) to the limits set by the Coast Guard and the discretion of the charter operator. In picking a boat, the rule of thumb is, the smaller the boat, the faster the trip, but the more uncomfortable the ride in heavy seas. The larger boats are slower, but more comfortable, and usually offer lunch onboard. The personalized service offered by any of the operations is a matter of individual policy.

Section II

Diving The State
An Island at a Time

"The swell which rolls over the reef comes up gently to the edge of the shore . . . A bath in this summer sea is delightful. The water is very buoyant, clear and pleasantly warm, its temperature being about seventy degrees. Once in, I am reluctant to leave it. But can we not come again tomorrow?"
William Root Bliss 1873

Each island in the Hawaiian chain has its own distinctive personality, both above and below the surface of the water. This section is presented to show the different dive sites and inhabitants, each has to offer. Diving any site is a fluid experience, due not only to the life sustaining sea, but also to the transition of marine life. The only constant is the topography. The life within is vulnerable to the demands of nature and its surrounding environment.

All of the islands have their good points as well as their bad. I have tried to be true to that spirit based on my personal experience and that of the professionals I have interviewed. Lava formations have in most cases defined the sites, and inspired their names. Other sites have been named for the predominate resident marine life, or from an inshore landmark.

Though some of the sites listed are diveable from shore, the vast majority are accessible only by boat. The site maps are used to give the reader an approximate location of the site in relation to the nearest point of land and other sites in the locale. It is not the intent that one can find the site services of diving professionals that are familiar with an area before attempting to dive there. Local guides know the waters, conditions, and potential hazards, as they live them daily. Another big plus is that they know the resident marine life intimately. This can be a big boost in the enjoyment of a dive and the productivity of underwater photographers.

Although I have dived extensively throughout the state for several years, I have come to depend upon these professionals for their vast knowledge of their particular area. Several people have given freely of their time, knowledge, and expertise to make this section possible. To them I owe a great debt of gratitude.

Chapter 4

Kaua'i
Beneath the Garden of Eden

Kaua'i is the oldest, and northernmost, of the main Hawaiian Islands. The topographical formations are as weathered and splendid underwater as they are above. The majority of critter life here is the same throughout the islands, but Kaua'i fringes the remote northwest, and is influenced by marine life common to that area, something which is unheard of in the southerly main islands. If you get thrilled by seeing rare and unusual fish, or towering underwater formations, and are able to handle conditions that are sometimes less than perfect, this is the island to explore.

Heavy swells generated from winter storms far out to sea, strong trade winds, and easterlies usually dictate what dive sites around the island are accessible. During the winter months, the south shore is the mainstay of diving off Kaua'i. However, when the conditions are ideal, majestic and wild areas are open to diving that are, otherwise, too hostile to attempt. The North Shore is a page right out of Micronesia underwater, both in formations and unusual critters, but regrettably, access is during the summer only. Since the majority of the diving is done on the south shore, we will start our tour there, and work our way clockwise around the island.

South Shore

The south shore of Kaua'i is protected from the winter swells and northeast trade winds, and as such, is diveable year round. There is rarely a strong current, and most sites are within a 15 minute boat ride from the launch at Kukui'ula Harbor.

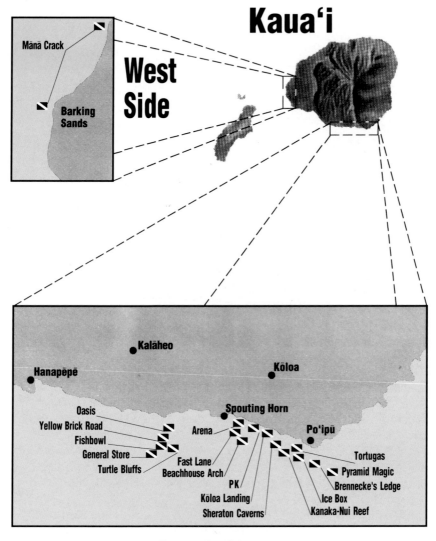

South Shore

A quarter mile south and two hundred yards east of Brennecke's lay two lava fingers running perpendicular to the shoreline. One of the fingers starts at 45 feet and flares into a palm-shaped reef with brightly colored cauliflower coral. The other finger ends in a pinnacle that drops to 110 feet. *Pukas* are filled with *ū̄ū's* (shoulderbar soldierfish), a pair of unusual looking morwong, and a rare Fisher's angelfish can be found. However, it's the schools of pennantfish and pyramid butterflyfish filling the water column that inspired the site's name - **Pyramid Magic**. The outside of this site is known as **Zack's Pocket**, a 70 to 130 foot dive located east of Makahū'ena Point, and named after a Hawaiian boat captain. The bottom is sand and rubble with huge boulders, some as high as 50 feet. There are deep caves in the lava substrata packed with lobster, *ū̄ū's* and common (undulated) moray eels, but are impenetrable because of the small openings. Bring a light to look into the caves, but keep an eye out into the blue, as pelagics and dolphins have been sighted here.

The common longnosed butterflyfish has the longest Hawaiian name - lau wiliwili nukunuku 'oi 'oi.

Brennecke's Ledge is a series of three dive sites along a mile and a half long ledge, located one mile offshore, due south of Makahū'ena Point. The top of the ledge is at 50 feet with cauliflower corals scattered about jagged lava formations. The wall drops three to twelve feet with deep undercuts covered with tube (cup) corals, and home to huge lobster, very large green sea turtles, whitetip reef sharks, and schooling *ta'ape* (bluestripe snapper). The site is vulnerable to strong currents, and not diveable on a daily basis, but has nice coral trees on the south side with longnose hawkfish, and two species of anthias fish.

Looking down at the top of the site, the reef structure resembles an **Ice Box** - hence the name. Located off Po'ipū Beach, the dive starts at 60 feet with an abundance of boulders strewn about in a chaotic array to form small archways and little *pukas*. Lobster and *ū̄ū's* congregate in these recesses.

There is also a ledge structure with a vast amount of marine life. *Mū* (grand-eyed porgy fish) hover midwater, and mantas, dolphin, and on rare occasions, monk seals have been sighted here.

Tortugas is a shallow dive directly in front of Po'ipū Beach Park in 15 to 50 feet. The site is named for a group of four to five turtles, often seen here, though very shy. A 25 square foot area of the reef is believed to be rubbed down smooth by the turtles' consistent presence. It also offers colorful coral and a number of eels.

Kanaka-Nui Reef is a topographical oddity located between Ice Box and Sheraton Caverns. It is a terrace of ledges 40 to 50 feet wide and over a mile long, resembling gigantic stairs, which descends to 130 feet. Boulders are spread throughout the site on a sandy bottom. Take a light and poke around the *pukas* to see *'ū'ū's* and lobster.

Sheraton Caverns, located directly off the Sheraton Kaua'i, is probably the most requested dive site on the south coast. Three large lava tubes, running perpendicular to the shore, are the central focus of the site. There is a small sinkhole with two very small arches, concealing Hawaiian turkey (lion) fish and a turtle the size of a dinner plate. In 35 to 60 feet are the three main chambers, laid out in a "Y" configuration. About four divers could swim abreast through the tubes, with plenty of light being offered through several openings in the ceiling. The base of the "Y" has a lobster rookery, and the western chamber has a school of 20 to 30 surgeon fish, while *ta'ape* cluster in and about the cave structures. The site is known as having "tame everything". Whitemouth moray eels named "Gramps", "Brutus", and "Little Ceasar" compete for attention with the two newest arrivals, juvenile conger eels, and a pair of whitemouths named "Little Squirt" and "Skitzo". Anglerfish have been sighted, as well as very large turtles, and occasionally, a whitetip, but the stars of the site are two small turtles named "Pepe" and "LePue". Always ready for the midday charters, they greet everyone by the swim steps, swimming side by side with the snorkelers, and escorting the divers.

A crown-of-thorns sea star is as menacing as it looks, with venomous spines on its topside.

One of the most important harbors in 19th century Hawai'i is now the most popular shoredive site along the south coast, **Kōloa Landing**. Anchors and chains, remnants of the yesteryear's commercial traffic, are strewn about an open sandy area in 30 feet. A horseshoe shaped reef, with an abundance of coral growth, is the gathering place for schooling *ta'ape*, moorish idols, *'ū'ū's*, parrot fish, and the rare saddleback butterflyfish. Hawaiian lobster and dragon moray eels have also been spotted here. Kōloa Landing can be done as two separate dives, heading east along one reef, then west along the other. The top of the reef is in 10 to 15 feet, and is ideal for intro's, snorkelers, and divers that like lots of light, bottom time, and night diving. Divers should use caution regarding breakers and westerly currents that sometimes sweep the area.

The rare saddleback butterflyfish is most frequently found in pairs.

Two shallow sites close together share terrain and marine life. **PK** is a shore dive located off the birthplace of Prince Kūhiō Kalaniana'ole in a maximum depth of 25 feet. It has ledges with beautiful arches, and the remains of an old wreck. The site is a good shelling area as well. Further west is a boat dive off "Acid Drop" surf break in front of the Hawai'i Beach Resort called **Arena**, inspired by the circular formations. The site is centered around boulders, strewn about the arena that forms a large cave area, and is home to huge lobster. Both sites are located in waters 30 to 40 feet deep.

There are two spots east of Arena: **Fast Lane** is a lava ridge that runs for 300 to 400 yards perpendicular to the shoreline. The top of the ridge is 50 feet wide and starts in 60 feet, slopes then tapers off at 90 feet. Octopus can be found, but the eels are not as accustomed to divers, so it is recommended that you leave the handling to the guides. The eastern site is known as **Beachhouse Arch**, and is large enough to drive a van through. The top of the circular archway is in 65 feet, bottoming out to sand at 85 feet. Look for black coral and slipper lobster beneath the ledges while you are checking out the turtles.

Turtle Bluffs (Hill) is a series of plateaus due south of Manoloa Point. It consists of a rounded sea mount approximately 100 yards square, where turtles are frequently sighted in 50 feet. The mount gently slopes to 65 feet, then drops to 90. Undercuts are frequented by whitetips, while other critters include eels and spotted eagle rays, as well as schools of tropicals usually found as pairs only in other parts of the state.

Directly inshore from Turtle Bluffs is a large, sandy plateau interrupted by a lone pyramid shaped pinnacle that rises from the 35 foot bottom to within three feet of the surface. It stands as a beacon to triggerfish, porcupinefish, pennantfish and butterflyfish, with much the same magnetism as an **Oasis** (Pinnacle Reef) in a sandy desert. Ledges surround the pinnacle the same as the brim of a hat, and are loaded with lobster, moray eels, and turtles. The flats are home to octopus, and serve as patrol grounds for timid eagle rays. A V-shaped aberration in the top of the pinnacle is most likely the scar from an encounter with a 19th century steamer, *Pele*.

The ill-fated ship limped slightly to the southwest, and sunk on a sight now known as **General Store**. Its remains have been spread about with three of its five anchors close to the lip of one lava tube, and the other two further up the ridge. All that is left of the ship - a boiler, heat exchanger, and ship's propeller – are in 85 feet. A horseshoe-shaped ledge in 65 to 80 feet opens seaward with three lava tubes, two on the west side, and one on the east. The wide variety of marine life is found in and around the tubes. Bluestripe pipefish can be seen in two of the tubes along with sponge crabs, lobster, ghost shrimp, and longnose hawkfish in black coral. Hawaiian (sergeant) major fish lay eggs in abundance, and repel potential marauding from threadfin, raccoon and milletseed butterflyfish, while *ta'ape*, pennantfish, and *ulua* swim throughout the site. Pairs of large turtles, ranging from 200 to 300 pounds live here, as well as whitetips and octopus. Rare sightings of manta rays and monk seals have provided the lucky diver a jolt of excitement.

Fishbowl lies directly between General Store and Turtle Bluffs in 40 to 80 feet. It, too, is a lava terrace with ridges and large caves. Moorish idols, turtles and whitetips are common, but fish feeding is the activity of choice for *ta'ape* and several species of butterflyfish.

There was a recent discovery on the inshore side, running parallel to General Store and Turtle Bluffs. A long, narrow, curving path of brightly colored cauliflower coral, in 25 to 50 feet, is bordered on each side by hard substrata. The topography is reminiscent of Dorothy and Toto along the **Yellow Brick Road**. Channels, cut into the substrata by rock boring sea urchins, are both a hiding place and home to several critters. Lobster, eels, leaf scorpionfish, anglers, wrasse, goatfish and milletseed butterflyfish combine to give the allure of the tropics. The place is perfect for photo buffs - you pick the format as anything will work.

West Side

The picturesque Nā Pali coastline provides the backdrop for a number of dive sites along a seven mile stretch known collectively as **Mānā Crack**. The area is conditionally accessible May through September, and offers all the advantages of pristine diving in crystal clear waters. It is about a two hour boat trip past the Barking Sands Pacific Missile Range to the southern tip of the area. A partial barrier reef extends from Nohili Point on the south, through Makaha Point, to Miloli'i on the north. Diving in the northern part has ravines that start at 65 feet and drop to over 100. Sites in the midrange depths include a foreboding crack with a shoulder width entry. Once inside, there are crevices, undercuts and high contrast in the reef structure. Slipper lobster,

Antler coral stand as solitary microcosms of marine life that seek protection in the large branches.

porcupinefish, and tiger cowries are only part of the discoveries to be made here. There are abundant plate and antler corals, and the sand bottom has the texture of granulated sugar. Inside the barrier, the diving is deep.

The south end of Mānā is shallower and more affected by siltation deposits. Though there is less coral life at this spot, there is one very large table top coral, unusual for waters this far north. The exciting aspect to diving new, uncharted territory is the potential for unusual encounters. Blacktip reef sharks, as well as hammerhead sharks and rays, have been sighted in the area.

North Shore

Vulnerable to heavy winter swells, North Shore diving is only available May through September. The topographic structures of the dive sites are huge, and though each site has its concentrated area of interest, it would take several return visits to fully realize the potential. It was on my first dive to the North Shore that I got to appreciate just how special Kaua'i underwater is, leaving me with a burning desire to return.

There are two excellent shore dives accessible from Hā'ena Beach County Park. A pair of tubular-shaped lava formations, in 25 to 55 feet, resemble **Cannons** and are part of a labyrinth west of the beach. Heavy siltation contributes to the poor visibility, but that factor leads to enhanced close up sightings of whitetips and turtles. On the east end of the beach are the **Tunnels**. They are a network of tubes and caves with tops ranging from three to 15 feet, then dropping to 60, with three tall, narrow caverns that contribute to the eerie atmosphere about the site. This dive appeals to all levels, but the best action takes place in the early morning hours (from dawn to 8:00 a.m.), when chances of seeing turtles and resting whitetips is best. Although you can't get lost in the caves, it is recommended that you do this as a guided dive. Rip currents can be quite strong, necessitating an awkward exit downstream. At both sites the sandy bottom is host to frequent sightings of the very rare eastern flying gurnard fish.

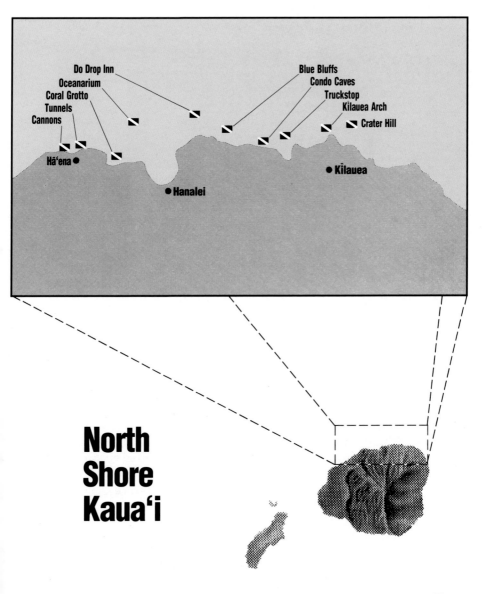

North
Shore
Kaua'i

A beautiful panorama of coral is in the middle of Wainiha Bay just east of Hā'ena Point. **Coral Grotto** has many species of coral known throughout the islands. The topography is laid out on a sloping bottom from 20 to 50 feet deep. It is a good spot for finding large tiger cowries, but not many fish.

The long-handed spiny lobster is one of the several rare marine species found at **Oceanarium**.

In the same way that you cannot absorb all that there is to see and learn about a large aquarium in one visit, **Oceanarium**, northwest of Hanalei Bay, requires several visits to get a feel for all the site has to offer. The formations are mountainous, and loaded with the usual blend of Hawaiian marine life, but accentuated with the unusual and exotic. A horseshoe-shaped cove faces seaward with a resident population of *ta'ape*. Each end of the ridge raises almost into an archway, leaving an eight foot gap between the two sides. To the east of the cove is a peninsula that levels out at 60 feet, then plummets to 140. The bluff is undercut and coated with cup corals and black coral trees. A short distance from the drop-off is a pinnacle that stands as a dive site in itself. Large, rare morwongs can be found here as well as the equally rare long-handed spiny lobster. Visibility averages between 80 and 100 feet revealing other pinnacles in the distance that invite exploration, but there is only so much that you can do on one tank. A large school of the uncommon boar fish has been sighted here as well as devil scorpionfish, anthias fish, conger eels, nudibranchs and occasionally a shark. This particular site is one of my favorites on Kaua'i and merits much return attention.

Continuing east to a seaward point, north of the Princeville at Hanalei Golf Course, is a site named **Do Drop Inn**. The 60 to 110 foot bottom slopes into a short vertical wall. Ledges and rubble are inhabited by eels, triton's trumpet shells, and scorpionfish, while black coral trees with longnose hawkfish can be found along the vertical wall. Unicorn surgeonfish are common in the area, and an eight foot hammerhead has been sighted here.

Blue Bluffs is a 20 minute boat ride east of Hanalei Bay, with a vertical wall from 45 to 110 feet. The top is encrusted with lobe, cauliflower, antler, and porites corals, and the site is good for finding a wide variety of animals, common and otherwise. Fish feeding is practiced here, and a five foot long yellowmargin moray eel has often participated. Play it safe by watching the lead of the dive guides before attempting to interact with the critter. *Pukas* are laden with squirrelfish, shrimp and lobster. A pair of male and female turtles are consistently sighted together, which is unusual as males tend to be loners. Longnose hawkfish usually reside in black coral trees, but they are hard to find at most sites in the state. However, this is not the case at Blue Bluffs and the other north shore sites. Finding the fish in black coral here is the rule of thumb rather than the exception. The Hawaiian turkey (lion) fish is also usually difficult to find, but it is seen often on the lower part of the wall. Sandy flats abut the wall's base, and this is the area to look for eagle and brown sting rays.

Condo Caves is built from nine large lava tubes, some 30 feet high, 30 feet wide and 50 feet long, with the different areas getting rolled into one dive. Several of the tubes invite divers to swim through them, while others have narrow cracks that lead into larger chambers with chimneys in the ceilings. Dive lights are a must. Some ceiling formations resemble stalactites, normally found in ancient limestone caves, and have inspired Condo Cave's description as underwater spelunking at its best. The depth ranges from four to 50 feet, and the marine life runs from the big, to the rare. A school of ten *ulua*, most in the 40 to 80 pound range, and others up to 100, congregate here. Unusual to Kaua'i, is the resident pair of lined butterflyfish at this site. Largest of the butterflyfish family, they are usually found around the southernmost island of Hawai'i. Sleeping sharks are frequently sighted, as well as a pair of eagle rays, one of them old and gnarled.

East of Condo Caves, and seaward of Kalihiwai Bay, is an underwater archway large enough, if you are so inclined, to drive a couple of semis through. The top of **Truckstop**'s arch is at 55 feet and covered with stony coral. The underside has encrusting sponge and cup corals in a blend of orange, yellow, green, reds and browns. Couple this with a number of turkeyfish that live here for a macro photographers delight. The archway is 50 feet wide and drops to 100. Eagle rays and brown sting rays may be seen as well as octopus and a titan scorpionfish named "Sam". The dive can be done as a drift leading to a vertical wall from 45 feet to a white sand bottom at 130. Deep cuts and caves accentuate the wall. One unusual sighting was a transiting school of the big game fish, *mahimahi*.

Moku 'Ae'Ae is a bird sanctuary, 300 yards off Kilauea Point National Wildlife Refuge. On the seaward side of the islet, at 60 feet, is the formation that gives the site its name, **Kīlauea Arch**. The archway drops to 110 feet with caves on either side. Bright, colorful cauliflower corals have established themselves on the substrata, and octocorals abound in the 25 foot shallows. An abundance of surgeonfish grazing in and about the reef. Cuts in the reef, as well as in the small vertical that drops to 80 feet, yield tiger

The venomous spines of the colorful Hawaiian turkeyfish provide protection from unwary predators and handlers.

and checkered cowries, as well as shrimp. The site has a feel for the wild and the pristine, as the lobster are often seen out in the open. Several pelagics may be observed, as well as turtles and sharks. Spinner dolphin and the endangered monk seal, add to the feral excitement of the dive.

A short distance east of Kīlauea Arch is a site rarely accessed, but very special. It necessitates a one hour boat trip when the conditions are absolutely perfect; even then there is usually a surface chop. Most of the time, northeast trade winds and easterlies make **Crater Hill** too rough to dive. Otherwise, it is diving at its best - wild, pristine and virgin. Three archways start at the top of the drop off at 55 feet, and extend to 120. These are cavernesque formations 30 to 50 feet wide, any one of which could be a dive in itself. The temptation would be to succumb to the allure of trying all three on one tank, missing most of the dive offerings, and exhausting the air supply in the process. The uniqueness of these beautiful formations can best be appreciated over several visits. Their ceilings are shared by multihued cup corals and a menu of crustaceans. Thick schools of 'ū'ū' pack the recesses during the day, while 100 pound *ulua* patrol the surrounding open waters. Longnose butterflyfish graze in the corals, and longnose hawkfish rest in the black coral. One six foot specimen of black coral grows upright from the bottom in 90 to 100 feet. The currents that feed the coral also propel divers on an exciting drift dive.

East Side

The last facet of Kaua'i is also weather dependent. Diving the east side of the island depends upon the winds laying down enough to allow comfortable, and safe, surface conditions.

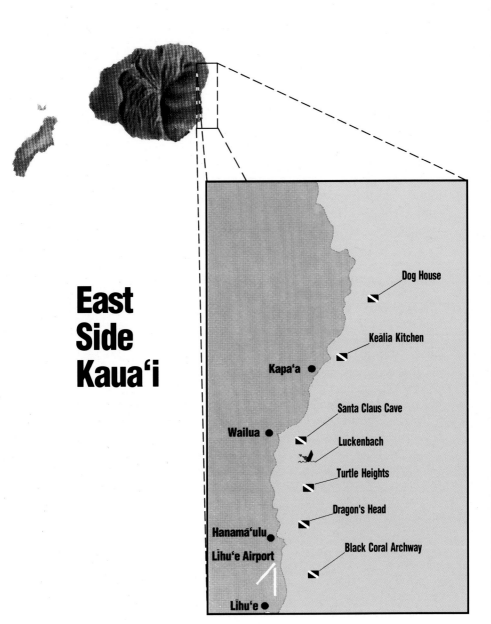

East
Side
Kaua'i

Dog House is seaward of 'Āhihi Point. The bottom topography is a ledge at 75 feet that radically drops off to 110. The site has several types of game fish that serve as the chief attraction to all of the "dogs" or sharks, and if you want to see them, this is the place. Frequently, two to ten medium sized reef sharks, usually blacktips, cruise the area and the divers, for a short time before leaving. Exploring the large antler corals and their resident communities can easily take up the balance of the time.

Keālia Kitchen is a new site located seaward of the lookout south of Keālia. It's diveable about one month of the year conditionally, meaning, it is virgin diving with critters rarely found at other sites. Lobsters walking in the open seem nonplussed by divers, and tiger cowries abound. The bottom is terraced from a range of six to 25 feet; then it drops to 40. Huge boulders rest on the sandy bottom, and are shelter to large schools of 'ū 'ū', groupers, and the rare black longnose butterflyfish.

Directly off Wailua Bay is a ledge at 75 feet that drops to 120. The top of a sea mount, just off the drop-off, has large antler corals and a vast array of fish. It houses an unusual formation that serves as habitat for octopus, lobster, and an inspiration for the site's name, **Santa Claus Cave**. Divers enter a four by six foot opening at the top of the mount, leading through a lava tube 35 feet straight down, and opening into a large cavern 30 feet across and five feet high. A large entryway at the face of the ledge gives it the overall appearance of a fireplace. *Ulua* have been frequently sighted outside the cavern, as well as other transiting pelagics.

On March 4, 1951, the 435 foot freighter *Andrea F. Luckenbach* left San Francisco. Laden with military and commercial cargo, the 8,171 ton ship was heading for Yokohama, Japan, then to Manila, in the Philippines. The ship's captain took sick and was delivered to Honolulu, March 11th. At 8:05 p.m., the *Luckenbach* hit a submerged reef off Kaua'i, damaging her port side. In an attempt to make safe harbor at Nāwiliwili, the ship went dead in the water off Wailua Beach at 11:00 p.m. She drifted inshore, and ran aground at 6:00 a.m. the next day. On August 24th, five months after grounding, she broke in two amidships, but it wasn't for another 20 years before the last of the hulk slipped beneath the surface 300 yards off shore. Today the **Wreck of the *Andrea F. Luckenbach*** lies in 25 to 30 feet, and is little more than scattered wreckage. The boiler room comes to within ten feet of the surface, tubes three to four feet in diameter can be traversed, and the large propeller, with one of its three flukes half buried, is still recognizable after 40 years of submersion. Ten foot high anchors with over 200 feet of chain remain as mute testimony to the ship's survival attempts. After a big storm the site can often yield hidden artifacts, and schooling fish and turtles have taken up residence in the remains.

Due south of the wreck is a ledge in 50 to 55 feet. A drop-off to 120 feet has formed a wall dive with cuts and overhangs, cased by smaller walls. Turtles galore can be found resting under the ledges, and justify the site's name, **Turtle Heights**.

The green sea turtle can be observed and photographed closely, when approached in a non-threatening manner.

Dragon's Head is actually two one-acre pinnacles just off an elaborate ledge system that fringes the shoreline. Both rise to within 60 feet of the surface, and are festooned with black coral trees. The inshore mount is transected by a lava tube starting at 110 and exiting at 80 feet on the seaward side. It opens to a view of the other mount that gives the site its name. A suspended tongue of lava protruding from the south side of the mount resembles the dragon's head, where at 75 feet, its underside breathes a fiery spray of feeding orange cup corals. The mount has a sheer drop to 110 feet, then slopes out of sight, an open invitation to transients. Everything is big here, from the tuna to the turtles, and occasionally a gray shark.

Continuing south is another drop-off from 75 to 130 feet. The dive is done along the wall and necessitates good buoyancy control. An archway, 50 feet across and ten feet thick, remains where the wall collapsed. It is covered with cup corals and black coral trees, deriving the name **Black Coral Archway**. The site is loaded with slipper lobster, hermit crabs, and pufferfish. A large school of *ta'ape* seek refuge from the cruising *ulua*.

Ni'ihau and Lehua Rock

The "Forbidden Isle" of Ni'ihau is privately owned, its 200+ residents tenaciously grasping the vestiges of pure Hawai'i. Its closest point of land is separated from Kaua'i by the Kaulakahi Channel, 17 miles off the southwest coast, and 24 miles from the nearest large boat harbor at Port Allen. Depending upon the type of boat, and the channel conditions, travel time ranges from two to three and a half hours. However, that is only when the winds are flat and the seas are calm - in other words, during the summer months only.

It is during this small, precious window of time, when the least dived sites in the islands are open. Huge, ancient formations are festooned with rare, colorful tropicals. Hawaiian monk seals, near extinction, and found only in the remote northwest, bask lazily on barren ledges. The pelagics we so excitedly dream about at other sites, have yet to taste the intrusion of man, and frequent this area like no other.

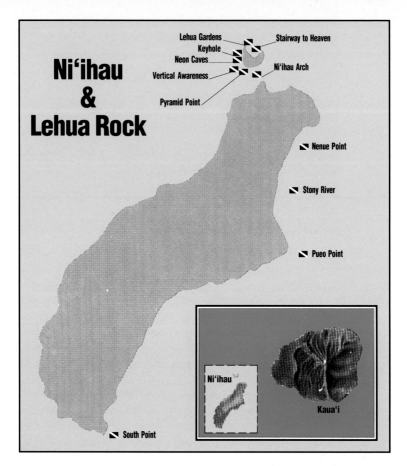

Ni'ihau & Lehua Rock

Lehua Gardens
Keyhole
Neon Caves
Vertical Awareness
Pyramid Point

Stairway to Heaven
Ni'ihau Arch

Nenue Point

Stony River

Pueo Point

South Point

Ni'ihau

Kaua'i

Ni'ihau

The southeast tip of the island is known as **South Point**, with a sloping bottom that ranges from 30 to 90 feet, and blanketed with large boulders. The shoreline wall is interrupted by six foot fissures, with lots of surge fish and sleeping sharks. Corals become secondary to the big critters that are found at this site. Large jacks hang in midwater or cruise the area, and it offers an ideal photographic opportunity for good shark action. When the current is running, the big boys are in; when it's still, the corals and the shallows are worth the effort to get here. This is wild, east side, virgin diving, and you never know what to expect.

Continuing north along the east side, is a ledge line in 50 to 90 feet. **Pueo Point, Stony River**, and **Nenue Point** are similar in their marine offerings with bandit angels, jacks and lobster. It is quite common to see turtles, and whitetips as well. **Ni'ihau Arch** is a series of ridges and valleys, off the northwesternmost point of the island, with large overhangs and a beautiful archway in 35 feet. Again, large is the emphasis with jacks and sharks frequently sighted. The site can drop off deeply as the arch spans the slot between Ni'ihau and Lehua Rock.

A shortbodied blenny waits atop a coral head for passing prey.

Lehua Rock

Literally a stone's throw across the water is the island of **Lehua Rock**. Owned by the State of Hawai'i, it is a much wilder version of the smaller, but more well known, Molokini Crater. Diving here is compared to what Molokini used to offer 20 years ago, before it was "discovered". The large critters include whitetips, blacktips, hammerheads and manta rays. A small depression on the south face of the rock is known as Monk Seal Cove for the numerous sightings of these endangered mammals...

During a drift dive along the west wall of Lehua Rock, Linda Bail was leading a dive group that was having an encounter with an octopus. When it left the puka, it let out a customary squirt of ink, temporarily obscuring their visibility. Linda swam out of the cloud, to find her charges had increased by one - a juvenile monk seal had joined the group and was watching the activities intently. The silver colored seal swam to the bottom of a deep ravine, rolled over and scratched his back on the bottom. He laid there, looking up at a group of gawking divers staring back. Before leaving the area, he stopped to check out each of the divers individually, then departed. The encounter left the group appreciative, but concerned over the seals' potential recovery from their decimated ranks. Existing in numbers believed to be less than 1000 total, they are on the endangered list for the following reasons: sharks which eat them, pollution which poisons them, and their own brutal mating methods that often leaves the female dead.

Vertical Awareness is a stadium sized sea mount 75 yards off the southwest corner of Lehua Rock. At 40 feet, its top is a broad, flat expanse with a network of grooves cut 12 inches deep by rock boring sea urchins. Over the sides, it is a straight drop to 280 feet with black coral trees in the 100 to 120 foot range. A crevice in the wall with a "W" shaped crack opens the mount to a view of large *ulua* schooling in 65 feet. When divers "trespass" into their territory, they swim off; when the divers leave, they return. Three species of anthius fish live in the crevices as well as other rare tropicals, and lobster.

*The bicolored anthias fish is one of three related species found at **Vertical Awareness**.*

Anchoring the boat just off the southwest corner of Lehua Rock, there are two sites along the wall. The one to the right, **Pyramid Point**, is a vertical which drops from 35 to 165 feet. The site is named for the large schools of pyramid butterflyfish that congregate here. *Humuhumu nukunuku ā pua'a* cruise the upper part of the ledge, and when threatened, they seek cover in the grooves cut deep by the urchins. The dive can be run as a drift, poking around all of the nooks and crannies in the wall, and looking for rare tropicals. Attention must be given to the clear blue water, to see what is following the same flowing path. Two large manta rays have been sighted here as well as whitetips and grays. At the end of the dive, outgas time can be spent atop a relatively shallow ledge in a protected cove where the octopus command center stage, and the boat awaits for pickup.

Neon Caves is a large cavern to the left of Pyramid Point. It is 60 to 80 feet wide, cutting into the rock over 100 feet, with lava tubes dispersing from there. Encrusting growth compete for space along the walls of the cave, and lights are recommended to bring out the vivid colors. The cave eventually rises to an above-water chamber, and although the inside is devoid of fish, the outside can provide plenty of excitement. A wide variety of tropicals flit about the walls and ledges, sharks patrol the same area, and monk seals are not unheard of here. As a point of interest, it is not uncommon to see the mammals sunning themselves along the shoreline at any of these sites.

A large split extending through the crater opens almost to the top. From a distance it looks like a **Keyhole**, but it is within the split that the drift dive to Lehua Gardens begins. Shafts of light, filtering through the crack, penetrate the waters beneath to the depths. At the base of the crack, the bottom begins at 40 feet and slopes to 130 feet. Following the wall seaward, and then turning right, climb on the tidal current and the drift begins. The site, from now on, is so similar to Blue Corner, in Palau, it is startling. A look towards the surface reveals a thick school of silver blue baitfish clinging close to the lava's surface. Further down the wall, a large school of *ulua* congregate in shallower waters. A glance into the depths revealed several grays and whitetips pacing the wall until we left. The bottom layout around the point is expansive. The drift seems interminable in length, but nonstop action and beauty are with you the entire way. The dive terminates at Lehua Gardens when the current flows seaward. When it is running towards Ni'ihau, the termination point is the aforementioned Pyramid Point.

Inside the west side of the crater is a substrata of teardrop topography blanketed with fields of octocoral, called **Lehua Gardens**. The dive can be done shallow (25 feet), with a wide variety of rare tropicals, octopus, and *humuhumu's* to enjoy. But the most enjoyable aspect of the shallows are three sinkholes - vertical tubes, six to eight feet in diameter, that dead end, straight down, at 65 feet. The striated walls add to the alienesque atmosphere created by these perfectly circular chimneys. In deeper waters, to 110 feet, pelagic fish are common, as well as grays and whitetips.

Stairway to Heaven is located at the opposite end of the crater. Formidable topographical formations dominate this site in depths of 50 to 130 feet. Large lava ridges are much more barren than the other side, but offer cruising grounds for eagle rays and sharks. Humpback whales and Pacific bottlenose dolphins have been sighted in the crater, rounding out Lehua Rock's showcase of Kaua'i's diving at its ultimate, and Hawai'i's diving as it used to be.

A Pacific bottlenose dolphin rides the pressure wave of our bowplane while in transit to our dive destination.

Chapter 5

O'ahu
Reef – Wrecks and Critters

Diving O'ahu is a blend of offshore lava formations and exciting wrecks, accessible by boat or shore. The modest reef structures do not have a great proliferation of coral growth, but are enhanced by diverse aquatic fauna. A number of ships and barges have been sunk to attract marine life to a relatively sandy bottom. The success of these projects is measured by their popularity as dive sites, and the healthy communities that have been established in a relatively compressed time frame. Visiting divers to O'ahu are faced with the unique problem of contending with congested traffic conditions on unfamiliar roads. Most dive operators respond to these needs by offering hotel pick-ups and transportation to and from the harbor.

South Shore

The south shore of Oʻahu extends from Makapuʻu Point, on the east, to Barbers Point. The majority of sites in this area are concentrated in the Maunalua Bay and along the Waikīkī/Honolulu shorefront.

Oʻahu's South Shore

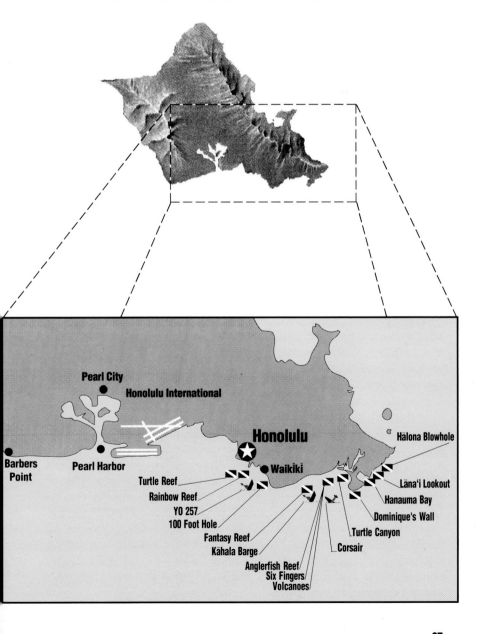

The wave force in **Hālona Blowhole** sends plumes of briny spray airborne, giving it the distinction as Hawaiʻi's answer to Yellowstone's Old Faithful. The dive site there is only accessible about ten days a year due to vulnerable wind conditions and the resultant repercussive surging action. (*Caution:* Do not attempt this potentially dangerous dive unless it is a glass flat day.) A hike down the hill leads to this shore dive entry, and the same beach where *From Here to Eternity*'s "beach scene" was filmed. The dive along the ledge of the coastline is in waters less than 70 feet, with underwater cliffs that extend from shore, that often shelter green sea turtles. Large rock formations are blanketed with lavender octocorals, while some of the lobe coral formations resemble candles of dripping wax. Going too far south leads to an area known as Bamboo Reef (Ridge), named for the number of fishermen attempting to lure *ulua* (jack fish) at this popular fishing spot.

If you're up for a challenge that will get your adrenalin flowing, **Lānaʻi Lookout** beckons. As it is a long walk to the entry point, and like Hālona Blowhole, conditionally dependent, the site is rarely accessed, but it is an above average shore dive. By all means, hire a guide for this dive. Entry is from a reef ledge, where it is a five foot drop into 35 to 40 feet of water. There is a cavern to the right of the entry measuring 60 feet wide, 25 feet high, and cuts 40 feet into the shoreline. A variety of marine life includes whitetip reef sharks and spotted eagle rays. Traveling towards Hanauma Bay, the exit is a quarter mile from the entry.

The idyllic setting of a wide white sand beach, lined with palms, and nestled in a cove that is protected by a small fringing reef, would seem to attract visitors by the droves. **Hanauma Bay** does exactly that - to the tune of 10,000 daily. How to deal with problems of overcrowding has been considered by the state with options from voluntary self-imposed restrictions by the tour operators to bans on commercial tour buses, limits to two thousand visitors daily, and a one day a week moratorium on anyone using the area. Rated the most beautiful beach in the state, Hanauma Bay is the third most popular dive in Oʻahu. Its attraction centers around the protected swimming, snorkeling and diving offered here.

Originally formed as the cone of a volcano, it was eventually breached by the ocean, yet still serves to protect the area from high winds and rough seas. Declared a State Marine Life Conservation District in 1967, the waters are totally protected, and host over 100 different species of fish. Though conditionally dependent, it is usually calm throughout the year. Depths reach 70 feet at the outer point, with bottom reefs and wall formations offering an open invitation to explore. Rip currents can build seaward, and require the experienced judgement of a professional guide. Before you go diving here, make sure you bring proof of certification, or you will be restricted to a sand patch inside the barrier, in less than 15 feet of water. Otherwise, enter off the right side of the sand beach, and swim through a channel in the reef.

*Declared a State Marine Life Conservation District in 1967, **Hanauma Bay** is rated the most beautiful beach in the Hawaiian Islands.*

Palea Point, on the north tip of Hanauma Bay, is a wall dive that starts in five feet and drops to 150 feet. The topography is highlighted by caves and archways loaded with crustaceans and mollusks, and accentuated with colorful corals. Large schools of tropicals and several eels inhabit the site, but keep checking into the blue. Transiting rays and turtles are frequently spotted here.

Swimming towards Diamond Head Crater, along the outside of Hanauma Bay, is **Dominique's Wall**. As a rule, the current runs to the west, so entries must be done off a "live boat" - no anchor. The moving waters slowly carry divers along the wall, starting at 95 feet, then gradually ascending to 35 feet at the Portlock area. It is a great sightseeing dive with ledges that house lobster, and larger transiting game fish, including yellowfin tuna and the rarely seen *mahimahi* (dorado). Novice divers may find the current disconcerting, so it is recommended for experienced divers.

Maunaloa Bay

The five mile wide **Maunaloa Bay** area is protected from the current in relatively shallow water, which is perfect for novice divers. A good variety of marine life and a couple of exciting wrecks can appeal to the most seasoned enthusiasts.

Turtle Canyon is part of a long reef structure in 30 to 40 feet. If you want to see turtles, this is the site. Accessible only by boat, the area is affectionately known as "Turtle International", for all the incoming traffic. Fingers of lava flare seaward, undercut with ledges and overhangs, providing an ideal hiding place for these marine reptiles on an otherwise sand bottom area. As many as 14 turtles have been sighted here, along with fantail filefish, triggerfish and parrotfish.

To the west and seaward of Turtle Bay is a site for experienced divers only. In 1946, a **Corsair** pilot ran out of fuel on a training mission, and ditched the aircraft on a perfectly calm day, creating one of O'ahu's original wrecks. It settled intact in 107 feet. The white sand bottom reflects plenty of light in waters that rarely have less than 100 feet of visibility. With the tips of its blades bent back from the impact, the propeller settled into the sand up to its shaft, while the aft landing hook and taxi wheel are fully exposed, encrusted with a brilliant orange sponge. The port wing is buried almost to the fuselage, but the starboard one remains accessible to the marine community. A large antler coral has established itself just behind the open cockpit, with schools of tropicals swarming this oasis amidst an oceanic desert. Besides the depth, the main drawback is the strong current that picks up within three hours of the tidal shift.

The wreckage of a Corsair, ditched in 1946, provides an oasis for marine life in an otherwise oceanic desert.

Traveling back inshore is another part of an extended reef area in 50 to 60 feet. A full spectrum of tropicals add a colorful touch to the overhangs. Countless goatfish reside beneath the ledges, and the patient observer will frequently be rewarded with nudibranchs and occasionally with an elusive frog fish, from which the site gets its name, **Anglerfish Reef**. This is another area to keep your eyes peeled for manta rays which have a track record of cruising divers here.

Six Fingers (Taco Flats, Big Eel Reef) of lava emanate from a bottom of sand and rubble. The ridges are four to ten feet high with ledges harboring *'ū'ū's* (shoulderbar soldierfish), turtles, and many types of morays, including a six foot long yellowmargin moray eel named "Eric". Spotted eagle rays, pufferfish, octopus, and helmet shells are found in depths ranging from 35 to 50 feet.

A relatively new site discovered near Six Fingers is named for a number of little sinkholes resembling **Volcanoes**. Critter life is concentrated around the lips of the depressions, and include eels, octopus and anglerfish.

Strategically sinking a ship, on a relatively barren sandy bottom, provides an area substrata for the beginnings of a new reef. Once the ship sinks, the reclamation process begins. Marine bacteria condition the hulls by growing a thin layer throughout, and establishing an anchorage for the drifting corals, sponge, barnacles, and larvae. Cauliflower coral is usually the first to take hold, while hydroids seek out interiors and other areas protected from the sunlight. The currents which brought them to the wreck now provide sustenance with passing nutrients. Many species of fish begin to graze, then congregate and finally school about the wrecks, that now can provide a food source and protection. Large predators, using the shelter from the currents, rest in the lee waters of the wreckage.

A yellowmargin moray eel has found a new home on a ship sunk as an artificial reef off Oʻahu.

The **Kāhala Barge** was sunk in 90 feet, a quarter of a mile seaward of the Kāhala Hilton. The retired 200 foot Matson barge resting upright and fully intact, includes a penetrable pilothouse. The barge has always attracted amberjacks, eagle rays, and frequent visits from manta rays and large turtles, while sharks usually move back into the area in the late afternoon. The clear waters are kept clean by the currents, which also add a treacherous consideration when navigating around jagged edges.

Straight inshore from Kāhala Barge is **Fantasy Reef**, an appealing site when the currents aren't running. A setting of lava fingers in 50 to 70 feet are undercut to form archways and ledges, which are home to the myriad of tropicals, crustaceans, big eels, barracuda, and very large turtles.

Waikīkī Beach/Honolulu

Just around the corner from Diamond Head Crater, **100 Foot Hole** is an ancient royal Hawaiian fishing grounds that was accessible only to the *aliʻi* (ruling class). Lying in 70 to 90 feet, it got its name from fishermen, who after being asked how deep it is, would answer, "It's about a hundred feet here." The advent of accurate depth guages has since set the record straight, but the name remains. The site is constructed from a cluster of volcanic rocks tumbled together to form ledges, caves and one large open-

*An eye-to-eye
view of a spotted
(peacock)
flounder.*

ended cavern. One formation, encrusted with cauliflower coral, houses the main tunnel. Within that tube lies an obstructing rock that can easily be traversed. Boats tie off to a naturally formed lava anchorage in 75 feet, just south of the focal point of the dive. Critters abound inside the *pukas*, so bring a light to view the 7-11 crabs, nocturnal fish, lobster, and octopus. There is always a good chance of sighting resting whitetips, two to six feet long. Tuna and amberjacks are often seen cruising the site.

Literally the newest dive site in the state of Hawai'i is the 110 foot long **YO 257** (U.S. Navy designation) **Shipwreck**. Built in the early 40's, the yard oiler served most of her duty at Pearl Harbor. Atlantis Submarines Hawaii, LP, procured the vessel, and sunk it off Waikīkī in August of 1989 as an artificial reef.

The YO 257 has already succeeded as such, attracting yellowmargin moray eels, amberjacks, trumpet and coronet fish, a variety of tangs, and surgeon fish. Sponge crab, spotted puffer fish, and eagle rays are frequently found here, and once a manta ray was sighted lying on the bottom, 10 to 15 feet from the ship, looking up at the divers on the main deck. The ship rests upright in 100 feet. It is a 35 foot descent to the top of the mast, 55 to the top of the pilot house (where the ship's wheel still turns), and 85 to the main deck. Rigging still hangs from its two standing masts and a boom from the foremast (take prudent measures for diving around the wreckage). Six by eight foot panels have been cut from the hull of the ship, which was filled with gravel for stability. The wreck is in beautiful condition with many open areas for easy access, good lighting, and excellent photographic opportunities.

One of the best set-ups is the Atlantis IV submarine bringing passengers to view the wreckage and its resident marine populace. A huge school of *ta'ape* (bluestripe snapper) swim out to greet the sub in anticipation of handouts by the attending divers. (*Caution:* Do not approach the submarine. Maneuvering room is limited, and the thrusters generate substantial turbulence.)

The Wreck of the YO-257

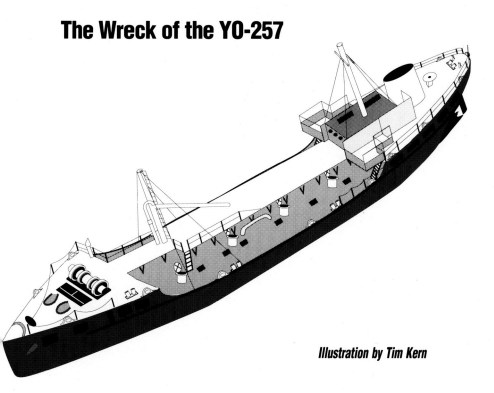

Illustration by Tim Kern

Two sites that are popular with novices lie in close proximity, and in very sheltered waters near Ala Moana Beach Park. Both consist of long fingers of lava extending seaward. Crevices and ledges cut into the lava formations at **Rainbow Reef** blending with healthy coral growth. A wide variety of tropicals respond to diver's handouts. Snowflake, whitemouth, conger and yellowmargin eels, by the anchor site, comprise the eel populace. Porcupinefish, octopus, and a school of moorish idols add to the enjoyment. The excitement comes from the occasional sightings of eagle and manta rays, and turtles.

*The pilot house of the **YO-257** features the ship's wheel, which still turns, and is wide open to allow plenty of light.*

The gentle reptiles are more frequently spotted at **Turtle Reef** just west of Rainbow Reef. They rest in pockets in the side of the reefs, and though the site doesn't offer as extensive a variety of critters, it is almost a sure thing, that more than one turtle will be seen here. Tunnels that cut into the reef are not large enough to swim through, but a light will reveal soldierfish, trumpetfish, lobster, and shrimp living within the safety of the shelter.

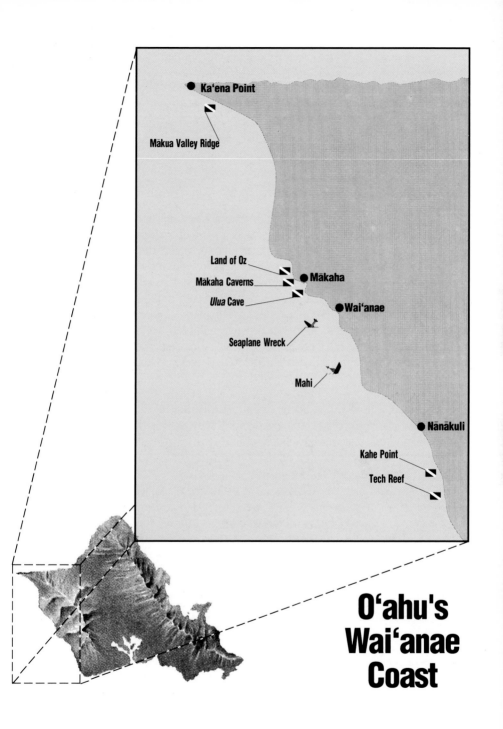

Ka'ena Point

Mākua Valley Ridge

Land of Oz

Mākaha Caverns

Ulua Cave

Mākaha

Wai'anae

Seaplane Wreck

Mahi

Nānākuli

Kahe Point

Tech Reef

O'ahu's Wai'anae Coast

Tech Reef is an off-the-beaten-path shore dive that can be accessed close to the more well known Kahe Point Beach Park. As you are turning into the parking lot for Kahe Beach, follow the old sugar cane railroad. As it veers to the left past a number of campsites, follow it to the end. The best part of this dive is near the shore in 10 to 20 feet. Very large cauliflower corals are built upon a lava substrata, with channels in the coral and lava that provide ideal havens for small fish, and tiger and checker cowries. Sightings of infant turtles and whitetips support suspicions that the area must appeal to juveniles. Because of the shallow depths, there is plenty of ambient light for the photographers, and your bottom time is relatively limitless.

Kahe Point (Electric Beach) Beach Park lies adjacent to the Wai'anae Power Plant. Two exhaust pipes, spaced 10 feet apart, resemble a giant double barreled shotgun, and are the focal point of the dive. The entry point is adjacent to a cooling water pool at the north end of the park. A channel runs seaward, with the pipes on the right, and pockets of coral heads with sandy ravines on the left, that eventually leads through the surfline to clear water in 10 to 70 feet. The pipes contain two sets of subpumps in large round cylinders. They end in 30 feet, and rise to within 10 feet of the surface. A rock barrier, placed in front of the exhaust, helps disperse the three to four knot current generated by the exhaust water, and attracts large parrotfish, moorish idols, butterflyfish, spotted trunkfish, and trumpetfish, that congregate to feed. An old light tower rests on its side, to the right of the pipes, serving as refuge for small prey, and as substrata for cauliflower coral. Besides the tropicals, Hawaiian lobster, cowries, aeolid nudibranchs, pencil and collector urchins can be found. The sand channel is known for marlin spike augers, helmet shells, and cruising grounds for a pair of eagle rays. On one very special occasion…

The conditions were flat, the current slight, and the water temperature in the 80's. That morning, Nick Bierchen and his dive buddy, Michael Parker, saw a large black shadow passing overhead, in visibility of more than 100 feet. With a little foreboding, they looked up to find a school of ten Pacific bottlenose dolphins. For the next ten minutes, they were guests at a private show that would rival anything at a marine life park.

From their ringside seats, 50 feet below, they watched in wonder as the dolphins first jumped out of the water, then dived individually and in teams. They gracefully performed twists, turns and loop-the-loops. In a finale, the dolphins returned to the surface, and walked across the water on their tails. The performance was over all too quickly, leaving Nick and Mike awestruck, and very aware of their own meager limitations in their host's aquatic environment.

The 185 foot **Wreck of the *Mahi*** is the most popular site on O'ahu. It was sunk by Ken Taylor in 1982 as an artificial reef a half mile offshore and 15 minutes from the Wai'anae Boat Harbor. Believed to have been originally built as a minesweeper, the Navy instead used the 800 ton ship in the Bahamas for laying cable, evidenced by a huge adapted bowsprit, which is now habitat to a large yellow head moray eel. Prior to being named the *Mahi*, it was the *Giant II*, and used by a subsidiary of the North American Rockwell Corporation. The Dillingham Corporation purchased the vessel in March of 1968, and leased it to the University of Hawai'i as a research vessel. Although originally positioned facing shoreward, it now lies upright, on a sand bottom, and facing seaward. In 1982, Hurricane Iwa repositioned the ship 180° to its present bearing.

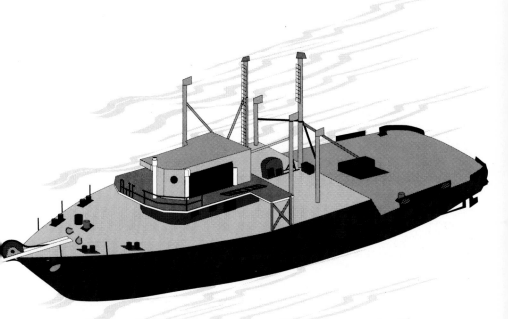

The Wreck of the *Mahi*
Illustration by Tim Kern

Conditions vary from 50 to 100 feet of visibility with light to seasonally heavy surge. There are moorings on the bow, amidships, and stern to protect it from anchor damage. It is immediately apparent how successful it has been in attracting marine life. I have seen a school of at least 20 spiny puffer fish suspended in midwater, facing into the current beside the ship's mast. At 60 feet, the wheelhouse provides a great photographic set-up, with a large porthole ringed with snowflake coral, red and yellow encrusting sponge, and hydroids. On the main deck, the most insistent of the resident critters are the large school of milletseed butterflyfish, and *ta'ape* waiting for handouts. If you don't feed them, they swarm you until either you relent, or another diver enters the scene. (***Photo Tip***: To keep them out of the set-up, take a small mesh bag with bread and tie it off on the main deck, then do your shoot elsewhere.) Two large sections of the ship's starboard hull, and the aft deck's hold cover and hatches have been removed for easy penetration and better lighting.

Donna Stewart-Erhard penetrates one of the aft hatches of the Mahi.

A couple of whitetips, named "George" and "Martha", are occasionally sighted, as well as up to four eagle rays. One charter group encountered a 25 foot long whale shark that swam beneath the stern of their boat and continued on to Ka'ena Point. The docile giant passed within 10 feet of the group that had just begun their descent, giving them a two to three minute thrilling encounter.

North of the *Mahi*, directly off Pōkaʻi Bay, lies a twin engine Beechcraft, the **Seaplane Wreck**, sunk as an artificial reef project. Its bare fuselage lays within a horseshoe-shaped ridge at 90 feet. The horizontal rear stabilizers are missing, the engines and propellers are removed, and the inside of the cockpit has been stripped, except for the instrument panel. A missing window on the pilot's side makes a good photographic set-up. The top of the ridge is at 80 feet, which drops to a rubble base, then slopes to 110 feet. The ledge has small cracks and fissures that are home to crustaceans, tropicals, and yellow margin as well as viper moray eels. A very large school of goatfish reside here, along with pinktailed durgons, milletseed butterflyfish and three different colored leaf scorpionfish. On one dive here an instructor was buzzed by a humpback whale.

A quarter mile off Lahilahi Point is a ledge at 50 feet, where boats tie off the mooring. The top of the ledge has slight coral growth and a few tropicals, but it houses an 80 foot wide cavern that cuts 40 feet into the formation, and is open-ended seaward. The ceiling of *Ulua* **Cave** is encrusted with orange cup corals, and pockmarked with *pukas* that yield discoveries of nudibranchs, anemones, and a large variety of crustaceans. Though the cavern has lots of available light, bring a dive light with you. *ʻUʻu's* take refuge during the daytime, while tropicals seem to view the world in a topsy turvy manner as they patrol the cave's ceiling swimming upside down. The cave is a good site for finding cowries. It bottoms out over 80 feet outside the formation. One of the highlights here is reputedly the largest yellowmargin moray eel on the Waiʻanae Coast, named "Franz". He shares his home, at the left side of the cave's entrance, with an unlikely companion, a slipper lobster. Do not feed here - two to three intermediate sized yellowmargins get aggressive at even the thought of food.

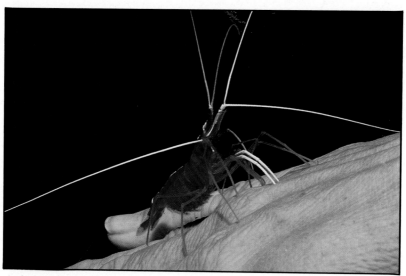

A cleaner shrimp gives Kathy an impromptu manicure.

A series of overhangs, archways, and lava tubes set the foundation for a shallow water dive 100 yards off Kepuhi Point. The most immediate impression is made by the large school of *ta'ape* that cluster near the main entrance to **Mākaha Caverns**. Reacting in tandem to the movement of the divers, the fish clear the entrance of a cavern formed by the V-shaped merging of two open-ended lava tubes. Covered with fragmented coral, shells, and rocks, the topography is very flat, giving the spacious room a more geometric, man-made look. Outside, the site spreads over a large area. Working seaward, the coral thins out, but the pockets are home to octopus, and several species of eels. The site also has five resident turtles, adding to the already abundant photographic opportunities. These are, in turn, accentuated by transiting dolphins and an occasional manta ray.

Further north along the same ledge system, is the **Land of Oz**, named after a hard-core Australian diver, Ozzie, who insisted on diving in adverse weather conditions, which led to the discovery of this site. It's essentially the same type of dive as Mākaha, except the tubes and archways are smaller, but more plentiful. Not having the *ta'ape*, or much else in the way of marine life, the topography is the main drawing card. The reef formation runs parallel to the shore in 20 to 70 feet. A ravine runs perpendicular to shore, then its south side turns into a wall which drops to a cave at 65 to 70 feet. Besides a variety of tropicals, it is a good site for lobster and sighting turtles.

Immediately north, along the Kea'au Ledge, are a couple of sites with variations on the same basic topography, that inspire their names – **Outside Mākaha, Tube Two** and **Four Arches.** The sites range from 20 to 70 feet, and almost always yield octopus to the sharp-eyed searcher.

Traveling towards Ka'ena Point on Farrington Highway, just past Kāneana Cave, is a finger of lava that extends seaward. Entrance to this shore dive is on the left side of the ridge. Even when the waters appear calm, avoid the right (windward) side, as the swell can catch divers unaware, and deposit them atop the sharp reef. With the exception of snakehead cowries, there is not much to see along the ridge. The site becomes more visually alluring further away from the shoreline. Much damage from the impact of divers on the site gives way to a flat bottom topography that slopes to the main point of interest, a channel extending due west, and known as **Mākua Valley Ridge**. A 250 foot swim will lead to two small pinnacles that stand as a gateway on either side of the channel. From there, continue along the gutter to a collapsed lava tube that resembles an amphitheater. The top of the depression is at 33 feet and drops to a rubble bottom at 45. One of the highlights to this site is the numbers and varieties of shells that can be found, including leviathan, groove tooth and checker cowries. There are an abundance of mitre shells as well as chinese horns, and occasionally a helmet shell. (**Author's note:** Despite a distressing trend to collect live specimens, I strongly recommend taking only the dead, empty seashells.)

North Shore

The North Shore extends from Kaʻena Point on the west, to Kahuku Point on the north. There are several sites along this coast including one of the most popular, but conditions are very weather dependent, and usually accessible during the summer months (May through September) only. This is the winter home of the Bonzai Pipeline - renowned in surfing circles for its legendary swells and offshore breakers, but when the water is flat, several operators fix their sites on the North Shore.

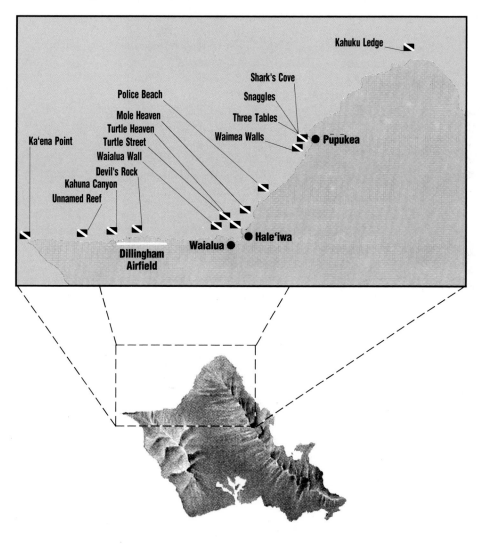

Ka'ena Point is the northwestmost point of O'ahu. It is a 45 minute to one hour boat ride from Wai'anae Harbor, necessitated by its inaccessibility from shore. Because of the predominate rough conditions and its remote locale, it offers some of the more pristine diving on the island. The sloping shoreline drops to 20 feet and levels out before dropping again to 45 feet. Black lava boulders are the predominate building blocks of the site, interlaced with a scattering of lava foundations and coral. The drop-offs are undercut with overhangs, caverns, and a profusion of *pukas* - several large enough to hold a number of divers. Take a light to search around as spiny and small slipper lobster seek refuge in the shallows, along with the multi-spotted 7-11 crab and several types of shells. The normally rare leviathan cowry abounds here along with its larger cousin the tiger. At the point, the bottom drops off to 130 feet, and is a good sight to look to the blue for passing travelers. (***Warning***: Use some discretion here, as the current can become very strong at times.)

Around the corner from Ka'ena Point, just past Army Beach, is a site a half to one mile offshore, that has yet to be given a name. **Unnamed Reef** is a series of ledges running perpendicular to the shoreline with channels of sand in between. A cluster of small caverns, in about 60 to 70 feet, are home to a variety of lobster, tiger cowries and triton's trumpets. Where tritons can be found, rest assured there is a community of the poisonous crown-of-thorns sea stars. Whitetips have been sighted resting in the caves, and blacktips are occasionally seen patrolling the formations.

***Kahuna* Canyon** is five miles west of Hale'iwa Harbor near Mokulē'ia. It is a site for for "*kahunas*" – everything is enormous. A massive bowl-shaped crater begins at 90 to 100 feet and tops out in 35 feet. The seaward half of the formation is missing, making the site very easy to navigate. Around the eastern side, the crater runs into a chasm, with large walls rising from the sea floor to form an underwater "Grand Canyon" extending 200 yards towards the shoreline. The walls are cut with caves and large *pukas*. Everything seems so huge – parrotfish, unicorn surgeonfish, *ulua*, amberjacks and yellow

A triton's trumpet snail makes a feast of a crown-of-thorns sea star.

headed moray eels. Octopus are easy to find as well as slipper and spiny lobster, 7-11, sponge and swimming crabs. Immediately after the area reopens from the winter storms, the site is a bountiful harvest of dead and empty cowries, augers and mitres. Visibility typically runs from 80 to 100 feet, and a look into the distance often catches a glimpse of a passing shark.

At the east end of the Dillingham Airfield, 15 minutes from the Hale'iwa Harbor, a finger of the Waialua Wall extends seaward. A large wash rock rests on that plateau in 20 feet, approximately a half mile offshore. **Devil's Rock** rises four to five feet above the surface marking the position for diving in varied topography. The inshore side of the rock is a sheer drop to a sand bottom at 70 feet. The frequent turtle sightings are indicative of all the sites along the North Shore area. A couple of vertical cracks, five to ten feet wide, on each side of the wall, hide lobster, but are good for shelling, including tiger cowries. Excellent snorkeling is available to nondivers around the wash rock, which is nicely encrusted with healthy corals. The seaward side drops to over 90 feet, and is an active area for dolphins during the summer months, and whale sightings during the spring.

To the east is a three mile long drop-off known as **Waialua Wall**. The vertical varies from 10 to 80 feet, and displays a wide variety of colorful Hawaiian corals. In the shallows, the rock shelves are blanketed with octocorals, and from 30 to 70 feet crevices and caves break into the wall. Take a light to look for shells and lobsters, and keep your eye out for turtles usually seen there. The bottom is mostly coral rubble amidst boulders, and habitat to large schools of goatfish and *ta'ape*.

A half mile off the west end of Kaiaka Bay is a coral reef in 25 to 30 feet. The site has a variety of overhangs and arches. On top of the shelf is a large crack that is 60 yards wide by 100 yards long, where a school of 15 to 20 porcupinefish reside. At its center, several formations rise into arches, tubes and caves. The residents of the formation, and the topographical aberration give the site its name, **Turtle Street**. Six very tame turtles provide an excellent opportunity to photograph the gentle creatures, and the site is nestled with lots of *pukas* - good grounds for lobster.

Turtle Heaven is directly inshore, half the distance from Turtle Street. The reef rises to within 10 feet of the surface. At some point during its creation seismic activity split the formation, leaving a valley 100 feet below. The wall is a vertical drop and its counterpart is 100 yards further inshore. This dive is concentrated along a 200 yard stretch of the seaward side of the wall. Its top has abundant tropicals, colorful coral, arches and overhangs. Little *pukas* can be found through one side of the wall which leads to the Turtle Street site. The valley itself is known as **Hale'iwa Trench**, and subject to heavy siltation. About 20 yards off the wall is a large coral mount that seems to be part of the original structure still standing. The pinnacle is 100 feet across and rises to within 35 feet of the surface. A dozen turtles rest on the mount and are very comfortable around divers.

Mole Heaven is named for the species of cowry shell that can be readily found on a shore dive off Hale'iwa Beach Park. The site is best accessed by swimming out from Jameson's Restaurant, to the green #3 buoy on the starboard side of the channel. There is a surface layer of poor visibility (two to three feet) that clears to about 60 feet at the six to 10 foot level. The site is a labyrinth of channels, with walls that run from 25 feet, to within three feet of the surface. They are 12 to 15 feet across, and separated by a silt bottom, with the offshore end tapering to a width of one diver. The site is best dived working in towards shore. A matrix of *pukas* are filled with tiny lobster and a number of tiger cowries. Though inaccessible during the day, everything comes out at night for good photographic subjects in shallow waters.

Further north on Kamehameha Highway is a site that is best done from a boat. A series of lava fingers, worn smooth by the heavy wave action, but with beautiful rock outcroppings, run seaward from **Police Beach**. Small fish and shrimp hang out in the sand bottom channels that separate the fingers. Though depths range from 15 to 85 feet, the best diving is in 40 to 70 feet. During the daytime, two small caves house the largest turtles at the site, and at night, textile cones forage the bottom in search of food.

The east side of Waimea Bay marks a site accessible either from shore or by boat. The same lava flow that produced the land formation, continues underwater with three fingers that radiate seaward. The fingers start at 25 feet, with a healthy community of encrusting corals, then a drop to 60 feet. Known as **Waimea Walls** (Point), the main area of interest is along the base of these drop-offs. A tunnel transects the middle projection two thirds the distance from the shoreline. The ceiling of the lava tube is canopied with snowflake coral, while cracks in the tunnel's walls house nurseries of 20 to 30 juvenile lobster. Whitetips are frequently seen near the tunnel, along with turtles, and occasionally eagle rays. The bottom breaks down to rubble and stacked boulders, yielding shells as well as sightings of *ulua*. It can be accessed by a 200 yard swim from the Three Tables site, but it is easier from a boat. Protected from the strong trade winds by Kalalua Point, the waters are usually calm, allowing for a good anchorage in 15 feet, directly on top of the site.

There are three popular shore dives at the Pūpūkea Beach County Park in Waimea, where showers and rest room facilities are available right at the site. A walk down an embankment leads to the beach entry, and some of the nicest cavern formations in the islands. These are long lava tubes in a small area, and with efficient air consumption, a diver could scout all three sites on one tank. The substrata is mostly devoid of coral, as heavy winter surf has pounded the formations clean and smooth.

Three Tables is named for a trio of flat rocks running perpendicular to shore, which break the surface, then max out in 40 to 50 feet. Lava tudes are on the right side of the tables and a nice wall to the left, with interesting boulders and some coral. Occasional sightings of sharks, rays and turtles spice up the dive, but tropicals, octopus, eels and parrot fish are the regular staple. This is a popular night diving spot with lobster being the main attraction.

Adjacent to Three Tables is a site that's okay during the day, but best experienced at night. Enter **Snaggles** from a small cove in back of the fire department. After a 20 yard snorkel along the wall, drop to 25 feet and follow the wall for about 300 yards. There are several lava tubes and arches which are good spots for lobster. Four to five foot long morays live here as well as several parrotfish. The site leaves off at the entrance to the second most popular site on Oʻahu, **Shark's Cove**, right off the Sunset Beach Fire Station. There are a couple of sources for its name: from the air, the rocks forming the cove look like a shark, or the cove looks like a shark took a bite out of it. Whichever name you choose doesn't really matter since sharks do not frequent this area. The site ranges from 15 to 60 feet with lots of arches and open ended lava tubes, allowing much light penetration and easy access [Please note the sidebar in Chapter 1 - Diving Hawaiʻi's Caves Safely]. The main caverns are all in 30 feet or less. Large boulders are interspersed with sand and lava formations in the shallows, and large schools of convict tangs, and baby mullets. The "elevator" is a hole 10 feet in diameter, allowing a descent to 20 feet, then exits through one of three different tubes. One is 40 feet long and four feet in diameter - 90° to the left. The other two are almost interconnected, and exit straight into the sea. The top one is in 10 to 15 feet, and the bottom one in 20. One tube allows divers to come up into an enclosed dry chamber large enough for three to four people. (*Caution: I strongly recommend using an experienced guide as an escort. It is easy to get disoriented and lost in some spots – especially the "elevator".*)

The northernmost tip of Oʻahu marks a relatively inaccessible site that can only be dived when the conditions are perfect, which is rare. Depending upon the speed of the boat, transit times from Haleʻiwa Harbor can range up to two hours to the site, three quarters to a mile offshore. Again, because of its inaccessibility, the area is unspoiled. **Kahuku Ledge** runs parallel to shore at 70 feet, then plummets in a sheer drop to over 160 feet. Yellowfin tuna, openwater jacks, and the other resident fish abound. There is a proliferation of lobster and tiger cowries, as well as a healthy population of crown-of-thorns sea stars, and their chief predator, the triton's trumpet snail.

Windward Side

Some of the very best diving that Oʻahu has to offer is on the windward side of the island, between Kahuku and Makapuʻu Points - but it comes with a price. The sites are relatively unspoiled and not over fished because they are rarely dived, but most of the sites need a boat for access. Vulnerable to the predominate tradewinds during the summer months, and affected by the north swell during the winter months, the surface conditions can get rough and uncomfortable. Even during a calm day the swell can be so bad that the underwater world can be less than desirable. But when all of the conditions are right…

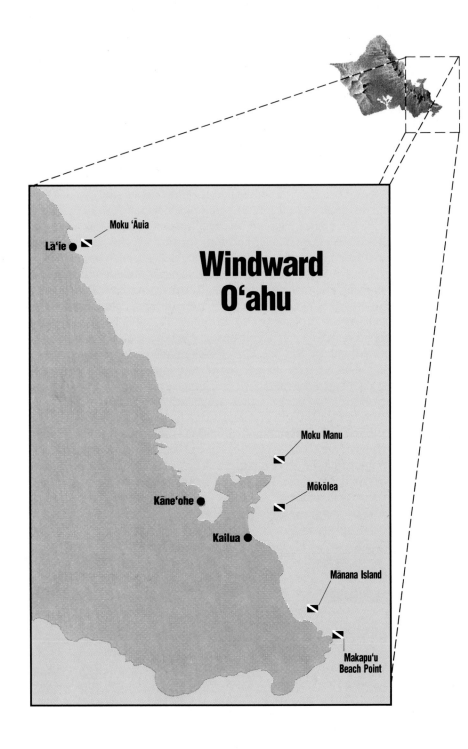

Moku ʻĀuia

Lāʻie ●

Windward Oʻahu

Moku Manu

Mōkōlea

Kāneʻohe ●

Kailua ●

Mānana Island

Makapuʻu Beach Point

Near the Mormon Temple, in the coastal town of Lā'ie, is a tiny offshore bird sanctuary called **Moku 'Āuia** (Goat Island). It is about 100 yards wading through shallow waters to the island, then a descent along its seaward side in 40 to 45 feet. (**Warning:** Because the island is a bird sanctuary, it is *kapu* - Off Limits.) There are small *pukas* throughout the site, loaded with reticulated cowries, lobster, 7-11 and sponge crabs. A multitude of fish parade by the islet as schools of goatfish work the bottom for food. The fragile violet shell is a very rare mollusk, that attaches itself to a floating raft of bubbles, and can often be found washed up on the beach.

Moku Manu (Mow-coo ma-New) is a two island remnant of the Ko'olau volcano, over 500 yards off Mōkapu Point, between Kailua and Kāne'ohe. Because the site is not dived

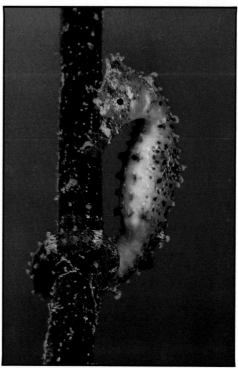

Rumors circulate of seahorses in Hawai'i, with most originating from the Kāne'ohe Bay area. This specimen was taken from deep water and shipped to the Waikīkī Aquarium. (Photo courtesy Mike Severns © 1989. All Rights Reserved)

frequently, it is a rich environment of plentiful, and large, marine life, including parrot, goat, and unicorn fish, *ulua* and tuna. *(Caution: Currents sweeping along the coast can venturi through the pass between Moku Manu and Mōkapu Peninsula, building to a point where safety becomes the paramount consideration.)* Diving can be done around, between, and away from both islands, with over five sites to choose from, the wind conditions are usually the determining factor. One of the most popular approaches is to bring the boat inside a cave between the two islands. Divers drop over the side, and descend 90 feet to the bottom. The cave is pitch black inside, and cuts into the islands approximately 50 yards, tapering to a point. Bring a light, as there are some lobster inside, and plenty of nocturnal fish. Coral grows vigorously outside the cave and around both of the islands. About 200 yards off the south side of the island is a sand channel in 60 feet, home to several skittish turtles - at least they are during the daytime. At night, they stay constant companions, following the beam of the diver's light path throughout the dive. Another 100 to 200 yards out are large channels with caves and overhangs. The seaward side of the north island has a skirting shelf at 30 feet that drops to 90, then plummeting to 200 plus feet further out. Lobsters make their home in lava tubes along the drop-off, and *pukas* are the residence to several moray eels, including yellowmargins and whitemouths. As usual in areas with a drop-off, keep your eyes peeled to see what swims by.

Due south of Moku Manu, half the distance to Kailua, is a speck of a rock named **Mōkōlea**. The islet is a seabird sanctuary, and nearly white from the droppings, which have inspired its more commonly known name. The spire can easily be circumnavigated on one tank in 35 to 70 feet. The walls of the caves that cut into its foundation are festooned with lobster. Outside the *pukas*, a community of cauliflower coral thrives, along with isolated stands of antler corals. It is not uncommon to see whitetips here, and the site has fish galore, with several very large parrot and unicorn fish, as well as plentiful *ulua* and *'ōpelu*.

Near Sea Life Park are two more seabird sanctuaries, **Mānana** (Rabbit) **Island** and **Kāohikaipu Island**. From shore, they look close enough to be tempting to swim to, but in reality, it would be tough. The water is shallow (20 feet) all the way to the island, with good coral formations and shelling, but the best diving is done from a boat, either off the seaward side of Mānana, or along a ridge at 40 feet that runs between the two. The islands are close enough together to be spanned on one tank in depths between 40 and 70 feet. There are overhangs on the ledge with good coral encrustation and plenty of lobster. Triton trumpets, helmet shells, and several species of cowries comprise the shell inventory. The seaward side of the larger Mānana Island slopes to 100 feet with several openings along that face of the drop-off.

There are a couple of *Big Cautions* at this spot:
- There is a current named the Moloka'i Express (when currents are named, they usually need to be reckoned with), that whips around Makapu'u Point. It usually brings in clean waters, but can take unsuspecting divers along with it.
- The other warning has to do with the marine life. The site has an explosion of tropical and game fish, which in turn, have attracted an equally healthy community of sharks, including whitetips, grays and tigers. *Tiger sharks have a history of attacks on humans at this site, and are not to be ignored. Divers are urged to leave the water if they are sighted in the vicinity.*

Another site near Sea Life Park is an easy shore dive off **Makapu'u Beach Point**. Before you begin, look to see if there are surfers at the beach. If so, forget the dive, as the conditions would be less than appealing. If not, the dive starts at the right, where the beach turns into the rocky shoreline. The site bottoms out at 45 feet with a sandy bottom and coral outcroppings. It is an out-and-back dive along the lava slope to the point. Trumpetfish lead the community of Hawaiian tropicals that hover near the nooks and crannies.

Kathy eyeballs a big cigar starfish on a sponge encrusted lava wall.

Chapter 6

The Maui County Basin

The islands of Maui, Lāna'i, Moloka'i and Kaho'olawe were initially formed as one big island. Over time, as the land masses separated and receded, the shallow basin filled with sea water to form the four islands known collectively as Maui County.

Maui has one great advantage over the other islands. During inclement weather, there is always a safe haven for boats in a storm. Operators on Maui only lose about five diving days a year due to bad weather.

Diving directly offshore Maui is relatively limited, compared to the offerings at Lāna'i or Molokini, so "inter-island" charters are the key. Nevertheless, there are some popular sights worth mentioning.

Maui

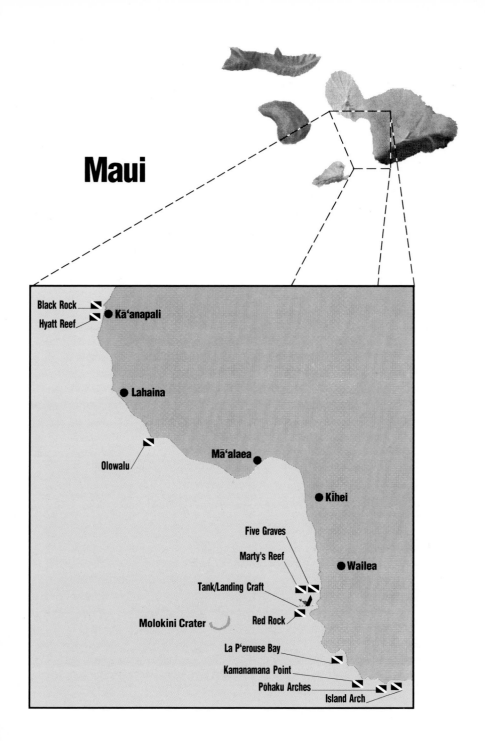

Black Rock
Hyatt Reef
● Kāʻanapali

● Lahaina

Olowalu

Māʻalaea ●

● Kīhei

Five Graves

Marty's Reef

● Wailea

Tank/Landing Craft

Molokini Crater

Red Rock

La Pʻerouse Bay

Kamanamana Point

Pohaku Arches

Island Arch

West Maui

The Sheraton Maui Hotel at Kāʻanapali is built upon a large lava formation that interrupts the long passageway of white sand beaches at the resort complex. The diving around **Black Rock** appeals to beginning, intermediate, and night divers because of the shallow depths, easy shore access, and diverse marine life. The foundational rock formation continues underwater in a wrap-around vertical wall ranging from eight to 25 feet. Rubble at its base leads to a flat sand expanse at 32 feet. Divers can enter the water from either side of the rock, and swim a few yards to large schools of tropicals and a few scrawled filefish. They are acclimated to human presence, and always looking for a handout. The site has leaf scorpionfish, and lionfish for good macro opportunities, and resident eels, including "Mongo", a large yellowmargin moray. At night, the site unveils Spanish dancers, conger eels, shells, lobster and other crustaceans. Spotted eagle rays have been sighted here including one that gave birth before the eyes of a startled, and frustrated, videographer who left his camera home.

Located off the Hyatt Regency Maui, just south of Black Rock, are fields of densely packed finger corals, interspersed with sand channels, in depths ranging from 15 to 55 feet. What makes **Hyatt Reef** so exciting is the constant presence of green sea turtles that have become fearless of divers, providing an excellent opportunity to photograph these large, gentle reptiles. Seaward, the density of the coral breaks down to rubble and huge antler corals. Octopus, pufferfish, shells, eels, and an occasional anglerfish are found with regularity. Sand flats abut the coral at 55 feet, and set the course for transiting eagle rays.

The combination of the abundant and diverse marine community in shallow waters off the Hyatt Regency Maui has made it one of the most popular boat dives from West Maui.

Several sites dot the coastline along Lahaina including; **Wahikuli**, **Māla Wharf, Lin Wa Mooring, Puamana**, and **Transformer**. They are meager in comparison with the rest of Maui's offerings, but popular as local and intro dives.

The cars that line the roadside along the sandy beaches at **Olowalu**, five miles south of Lahaina, announce its popularity among snorkelers. The boats that seek haven there, when the conditions everywhere else are blown out, attest to its popularity with divers. Large fields of finger corals, built up as much as ten to 15 feet from the surrounding sand bottom, are scattered about in a haphazard array. It is easy to lose your bearings, and usually requires a trip to the surface to find the dive boat. It is a good site for crown-of-thorns sea stars, pufferfish, and turtles. The coral abruptly ends at 40 to 50 feet, where the sand bottom slopes to 180+...

Instructor/guide Dave Fleetham had the day off and was doing an afternoon dive off Olowalu with two friends. On the first part of his dive, he was shooting macro photography in deeper water beyond the coral fringes. Unexpectedly, a manta ray swept by, so Dave returned to the boat, chagrined about the mismatched format on his camera. The dive guide, working with the intro divers, surfaced, and yelled to the boat that there were seven rays around them. Dave grabbed his friend's camera, set up with a wide angle lens, and swam to the area now abandoned by the intro group. He redove to 40 feet and hung midwater looking seaward. Turning around, he saw a column of the gentle pelagics heading straight towards him. Just a few feet from him, the first ray banked to the right, the next one to the left, the next to the right, etc. - nine in all, putting on an underwater exhibition of hydrodynamic maneuvers before leaving. Dave turned to see them once again in 30 to 35 feet, swimming in tight circles. Time soon ran out, and he had to return to the boat. When he arrived, the dive guide said there were four more with the group on the other side of the boat. It is important to note that the divers left the rays, not vice versa.

Mākena

Five Graves is dived extensively on a daily basis, and is a favorite night dive, so the guides know the site intimately. It can be done either as a boat dive or from the shore (marked by five Japanese graves off Old Mākena Road). Two points of lava extending seaward, and perpendicular to the shoreline, frame the area. The site is replete with caves, lava tubes, and *pukas*. Facing seaward, the left hand ridge is broken by a passage close to the shoreline. Another swim-through on the seaward side of the long ridge, has a chimney through the top with a small black coral tree. Swimming through a break in the ridge, then back along the coast immediately leads to a small cave with a square window in its ceiling. This is not a spot to dive with surf conditions. A concave formation outside the cave is known as the "toilet bowl" for the uncontrollable swirling action of the water in heavy surf. Further along the shoreline leads to a bubble cave that opens to an

This anglerfish blends in perfectly with its surrounding motif.

above water chamber, and can accommodate up to 12 divers. The rock formations, scattered about the shallow, sandy bottom between the two ridges is known for its turtles, while patient searching can also yield exciting discoveries of anglerfish, leaf scorpionfish, nudibranchs, and conger eels.

Directly seaward of Five Graves, a quarter mile offshore, is **Marty's Reef**. A circular to oval shaped patch reef blends plate and antler corals on a 60 foot flat bottom. Octopus are frequently found, and occasionally leaf and devil scorpionfish. A variety of tropicals include milletseed butterflyfish and a large school of *ta'ape* (blue lined snapper). Territorial trumpetfish follow divers around in an interactive demonstration of camouflage versus photo set-ups, while yellowmargin moray eels offer another subject to photograph close-up. The sand bottom is home to large, foraging helmet shells. The dull, encrusted topside of their shell belies a smooth, colorful surface beneath the sand.

South of Marty's Reef are two artifacts that can at least whet the appetite of wreck diving enthusiasts. A half mile boat ride off shore will access divers to the **Tank and Landing Craft**, located on a bleak, sandy bottom in 60 feet. After having been picked clean by divers, the dilapidated remains of the tank are habitat to a large number of goatfish, as the body and turret are all that remain of the hulk. The landing craft rests upright in about 55 feet of water, 100 yards due south of the tank. With its tracks intact, and some 30 caliber ammunition strewn about, the craft is in a little better shape than the tank. Milletseed butterflyfish congregate around the wreckage along with big resident eels and an occasional leaf scorpionfish. Done together as a drift dive, they provide plenty to see, and offer ample wide angle photographic opportunities.

Several pinnacles and ridges rise to 85 feet from the 110 to 120 foot bottom, to form the arena of a spectacular dive southwest of the tank and landing craft. Deep crimson sponges encrust the widespread verticals and mounts, and give the site its name, **Red Rock**. Orange/red anglerfish and large, red titan scorpionfish hold to the color motif, while barracuda, whitetip reef sharks, eagle and manta rays provide the electricity for this dive. Black coral trees with resident long nose hawkfish are found along the walls at 100 feet. *Ta'ape, m ū' s* and eels round out the marine life. Keep in mind that the site is deeper than those normally offered, and don't forget to bring a light to fully realize the color.

La Pérouse Bay, named after the French explorer, evenly bottoms out at 60 feet with a ridge running seaward, midway in the bay. The top of the ridge comes within ten feet of the surface, and is covered with extensive coral formations that are interlaced with a proliferation of red slate pencil sea urchins. Several small caves, full of nocturnal fish, invite poking around. Goatfish abound here, and it is a good site for spotting barracuda, turtles, triton's trumpet snails, and crown-of-thorns sea stars. The seawardmost point of the ridge tapers to a sandy bottom at 70 feet where manta rays have been seen cruising by. There is a school of spinner dolphins that could be considered residents, with their high pitched whistles about the only contact divers have with them in-water.

Kanaio Area

Kamanamana Point (Pinnacle Point) is just before the western boundary to Kanaio Beach. The end of an *'a'a* lava flow left its mark with several pinnacles along a sloping bottom to 25 feet. It drops off to the 50 foot mark, then tapers to sand at 60 feet. Lobster, *ta'ape*, and Achilles tangs can be seen on any dive here, with usual sightings of turtles, and occasionally an eagle ray.

Pōhaku (stone) **Arches** is a wash rock area east of Pinnacle Point. The topography of the site looks like a cavern in structure, but is actually three interconnecting archways in waters 35 to 70 feet. Tube corals and sponges line their undersides, and lobster can sometimes be found.

A quarter mile northeast of the site is a rectangular rock that rises 40 feet above the water's surface from the bottom 25 feet below. It houses a 20 foot wide archway that starts at the surface and extends to the bottom, giving **Island Arch** its name. Large boulders, worn smooth by the heavy surge action, are scattered about the shallows. The sites are remarkable for their utter lack of siltation, and the view of the shoreline is stunning - a barren lava flow showing no evidence of civilization: no construction, roadways, or buildings. Both sites have a similar variety of critters that are not often found in other areas: whitespotted surgeonfish, saddleback butterflyfish, and a good variety of coral reef life evident in the deeper waters.

Molokini Crater

The "Valley Isle" of Maui is dominated by the imposing 10,023 foot Haleakalā. A recent survey conducted by the University of Hawai'i's Sea Grant program, lists **Molokini Crater**, part of a chain of vents for that now dormant volcano, as the most popular dive site in the state. Molokini is a breached tuff cone located in the 'Alalākeiki Channel midway between Maui and Kaho'olawe. Travel times to the crater range from 20 minutes out of Kihei, 45 minutes from Mā'alaea Harbor, to over an hour with some of the larger dive boats out of Lahaina.

Protected from the winds by Haleakalā, Molokini usually offers calm waters. Early morning departures to the crater are necessitated by the northeast trades that pick up in the afternoon, but diving the crater is worth the effort. Molokini's unusually clear waters set the stage for a showcase of Hawai'i's unique and exciting marine life. Visibility averages 100 feet, but ranges from a low of 60 to frequently over 150.

Molokini Crater has been designated the state's most popular dive destination by the University of Hawai'i's Sea Grant Program, based on the average number of divers that access the site daily.

A State Marine Life Conservation District, Molokini's resident populace is protected from fishing, hunting, or collecting. The critters are so familiar with the divers' presence, they either go about their daily existence, or share interaction through fish feeding, eel petting, and encounters with transiting pelagics.

Molokini's exposed land mass is crescent shaped, rising 160 feet out of the water. At the northernmost point underwater, the edge of the crater drops to 35 feet, gradually slopes to 70, then plummets to over 300. Lava

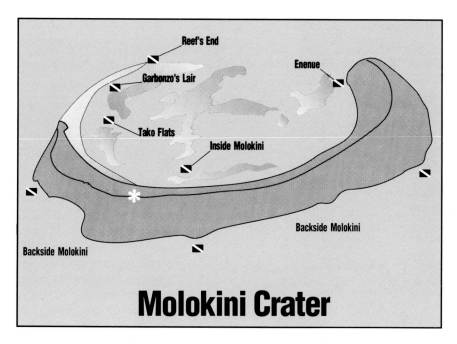

Molokini Crater

slabs, large boulders and antler coral form an arena called **Reef's End**. The most immediate impression is the number of fish that live at this sight. Schooling butterflyfish in the hundreds may be found in species such as pennant, pyramid, raccoon and milletseed. The hard-to-find saddleback, reticulated, and oval butterflyfish are usually seen as mated pairs. *Mū's* hover mid-water facing into the current, while *ulua* casually swim through the populace looking for food.

The lava slabs, strewn about the dive site, and stacked in a haphazard manner, serve as a focal point for schooling *ū'ū's*, goatfish and several moray eels. Spanning the area between the site and the sand channel (where most of the dive boats drop anchor), is a large rubble field. At initial glance, the rubble has no visual allure, and divers usually swim directly over it, thus missing out on a wide variety of invertebrates, including rough-spined, long-spined, and pebble collector urchins. Octopus can often be found in the rubble as well, but discrete guides leave them alone at this site. *Ta'ape* will aggressively attack the tips of the octopus' tentacles, damaging the shy critters.

Giant manta rays are frequently sighted swimming over the sand channel, their mouths agape to feed on plankton blooms. These gentle pelagics, when not intimidated, are often attracted to divers' bubbles, and will give either a heart-thumping, close encounter, or a lesson on the joys of flying underwater.

Located next to Reef's End, inside the crater, is **Garbonzo's Lair**. A large lava and coral formation, ringed by rubble, sits in 45 feet, and is the focal point of the site. Interlaced with scores of slate pencil sea urchins, the

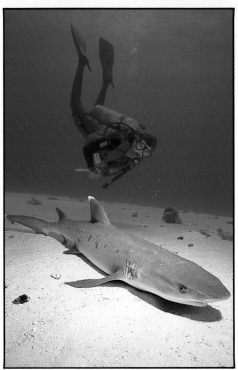

lair is the sometime home of a local celebrity - a very large yellowmargin eel dubbed "Garbonzo". We have been treated to a pair of ornate and colorful dragon moray eels that have taken up residence here, offering an opportunity to photograph an otherwise rarely seen species.

Two other rarities were sightings of a manta ray hovering over the lair while cleaner wrasse darted about its gills, and a large eagle ray hotly pursued by two smaller ones. The male latched onto the larger female and coupled 10 feet in front of us, as the pair rapidly glided out of sight.

Tako Flats is located at the inside end of the sand channel. It derives its name from a Japanese expression for octopus, due

*A whitetip reef shark at **Reef's End** gets a close inspection by Instructor/Captain Bill Moore.*

to their frequent sightings. The area is relatively level at the inside rim of the crater, and covered with rubble. Large antler coral decorate the inside fringes of the reef, where pufferfish, moray eels, pincushion starfish and other invertebrates abound. The sand channel also serves double duty as a runway for manta rays cruising the area.

The inside rim of the crater is often densely lined with snorkeling charters, there for half-day excursions. It often gives the appearance of a large parking lot with counts up to 30 or more boats. The snorkelers are usually segregated from the dive charters. Nevertheless, knowing what dive group you are with, and an approximate surface locale of your boat, will help avoid confusion. The snorkeling boats either anchor or use the moorings within the area called **Inside Molokini**. Dense buildups of finger coral, and the chance to feed the myriad of fish in shallow waters are the area's main attractions.

The side of the crater, opposite Reef's End, is called *Enenue*, after the gray lowfin chub that meet the boats at anchor. The base of the crater's wall levels off to a very wide shelf at 50 feet, then plummets to a sand channel over 130 feet down. At 40 feet, huge boulders mark the focal point of the site's favorite activity - fish feeding. A school of milletseed butterflyfish insist that all newcomers feed them. If you don't have food to offer, they will either go to someone who does, or provide escort service through their territory.

At Molokini Crater there is a whitetip known as 10:30 Charley. It is usually one or more of several five foot females that reside in the deeper waters at Enenue. *Around 10:30 every morning, after the first wave of divers has had a chance to harass the area's octopus, the sharks start patrolling. Their refined sense of smell is demonstrated as they sniff out hiding place after hiding place for a solitary, and terrified octopus. On occasion they find the right rock with an unfortunate octopus. The shark props it pectoral fins on anything to get leverage, then uses its shovel shaped head to burrow under the rock. With a thrust of its tail upwards, the relentless predator upends the boulder (some unbelievably large), and with a flurry of tentacles, ink, and a gray blur, the*

A resident pair of ornate dragon moray eels have given divers an excellent opportunity to observe an otherwise rarely seen specimen.

victor is off with the spoils, tentacles hanging from both sides of the mouth. Any other shark in the area follows in close rapid pursuit, for morsels that might get away. The successful shark thrusts its head from side to side and rakes the octopus across its tiny teeth, and with a final thrust the octopus is history.

Continuing seaward along the shelf leads to a turnaround called "The Point". Surprise encounters are always a possibility. It is here I had my first whale shark encounter, as well as an incredibly close sighting of a manta ray. (**Caution:** Currents often pick up, and can get deceptively strong. I recommend using discretion, and staying with the guides before venturing out too far.)

One of the most requested, but rarely dived sites, is **Backside Molokini**. The aforementioned current gently carries divers along a wall that is pockmarked with *pukas* and cauliflower coral, and is transected by deep crevices that can yield any number of different finds. It offers divers a chance to see large black coral trees, often inhabited by longnose hawkfish, in relatively shallow depths. Up and down the wall, octopus and several species of nudibranchs can be found, while schools of pennant, pyramid and milletseed butterflyfish congregate at 50 feet. Large whitetips cruise the 60 to 70 foot depths. By looking out into blue water, there is always the possibility of sighting rays, schooling tuna, or dolphin. In 1988, customers

A pair of octopus prove to be a handful for the author.

with one of the Lahaina operations were treated to an encounter with six humpback whales that cavorted with them for over thirty minutes.

The outside crater wall radically plummets to 350 feet, and does require good buoyancy control skills. The visibility at Molokini is usually so clear that depths become deceptive, and a diver not paying attention to the instruments can find himself exceeding the recommended safe diving limits imposed by the no decompression tables. Because of the current, drift dives are conducted as "live boat" dives - the boat drops the divers off, follows the progress by their bubbles, then is there for pick-up when divers ascend. Transitions in and out of the water usually have to be fast, necessitating a certain degree of self reliance. Backside Molokini is also more exposed to the elements. Wind and swell can make this site undiveable, when the inside might remain relatively unaffected. Regardless, this site is very special and we always deem it a special treat to dive here.

Molokini Crater has been fascinating divers for years with its unusual diversity of colorful marine life, charming them with close interaction, and exciting them with thrilling pelagic encounters. Its reputation as the state's most popular dive site is certainly well deserved.

Kaho'olawe

The uninhabited island of Kaho'olawe is used by the military for live bombing and shelling exercises. As such, the surrounding waters are off limits, save for rare occasions when the military opens them for fishing and other recreational use (about two weekends per month). The island is also in direct line with the tradewinds, making it vulnerable to high surface chop, so Kaho'olawe does not get dived very much. This translates into exciting, pristine adventures the few times during the year when it is accessible.

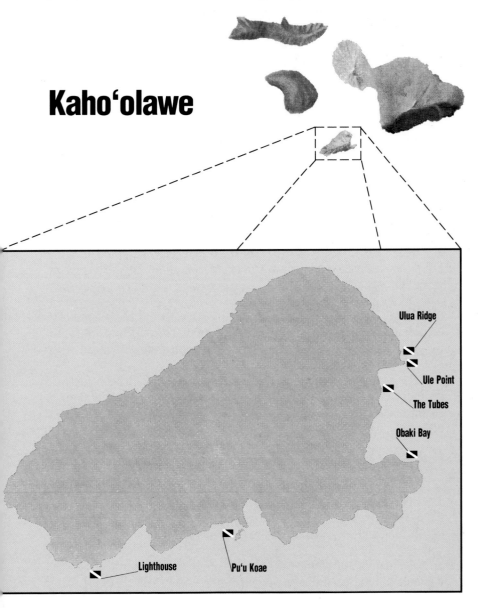

Kaho'olawe

Ulua Ridge

Ule Point

The Tubes

Obaki Bay

Lighthouse

Pu'u Koae

Three hundred foot deep Kanapou Bay is located on the eastern end of the island. Its northern tip is known as **Ule Point** (Hole In The Wall, Derby). A twenty foot long cave, large enough for two divers to swim abreast, passes through the point. The site has unusual tropicals, large *ulua*, and the ever present possibility for pelagic sightings. One hundred yards north of Ule Point is *Ulua* **Ridge**. The formation connects to the shoreline wall at 40 feet then slopes seaward to 60, then 80, and finally dropping to 110. Contoured on each side, it is notable for the large black *ulua* that congregate there. An equal distance on the other side of Ule Point, are **The Tubes** that open at 35 feet. About four divers could fit into the entry room where three tubes extend inshore to a dead end. Although it is an excellent spot for collecting sea shells, it is also an easy place to get lost, and I highly recommend not going in without the escort of a dive guide familiar with the area. Outside of the cave, the bottom drops off radically.

Obaki Bay, on the opposite side of Ule Point, is relatively protected from the trades. Large schools of *'ōpelu*, and their respective predators cruise the corals over the sloping bottom. At 80 to 90 feet, a school of garden eels face into the current. Sightings of hammerhead sharks confirm its pelagic potential.

Pu'u Koae is a small rock island midway along the south shore. Diving here is done primarily along the west side of the island. It is a sheer wall that drops to 100 feet, where boulders continue on a sand bottom to 200. A few yards further out, fathometer readings confirm depths exceeding 430 feet. A large school of curious unicorn surgeonfish, *ulua*, and rare butterflyfish highlight the marine life. A cave starting at 50 feet and dropping to 70 has lobster on the inside and anthius fish at the base of the entry. The inshore side of the island has been heavily damaged by bombing practice, so there is little to see except a lot of ordnance - HANDS OFF. Quite often local residents will be seen rooting around the shoreline for the *'opihi*, a shellfish considered a delicacy (meaning "inedible" to most of us). Do not follow suit by going ashore. The island is a bird sanctuary with nesting whitetail tropic birds, and as such, is protected.

The first point of land east of the **Lighthouse** marks the site of a shoreline drift dive with lots of *pukas* to poke around. It can be done in shallow to intermediate depths, and leads to a protected cove for a live boat pickup.

Lāna'i

Most diving charters to the island of Lāna'i originate from Lahaina. Travel time ranges from 45 minutes to one and a half hours depending upon the speed of the boat, the surface conditions on the 'Au'au channel, the site destination, and what kind of distractions might be encountered along the way.

The majority of diving off Lāna'i is done along the south coast, with a couple of sites on the western and eastern sides. The shoreline walls, surrounding many areas of Lāna'i, are so precipitous, they look like the island was shaped with an icing knife at the time of its creation. Formations of ridges, pinnacles, lava tubes and caverns, provide the topographic setting for interesting and varied underwater exploration.

Lana'i

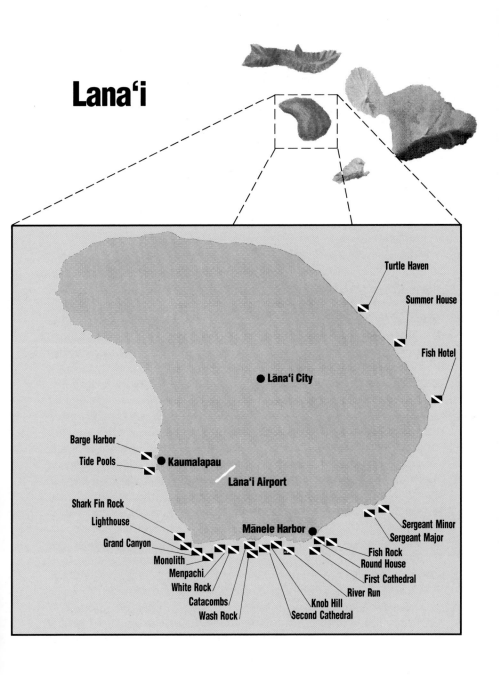

Barge Harbor is the popular name for Kaumalapau Harbor on the island's west coast. All of Lāna'i's supplies are shipped from O'ahu, and the pineapple is shipped out from here. It also marks the spot for interesting cave and wall diving. Because it is the furthest site from Lahaina, it is rarely accessed, remaining pristine and undisturbed. An overview of the site looks like three gigantic porch steps. The top of the terrace starts at 15 feet, then incrementally levels out at three different depths to its base, 95 feet below. A large school of *ta'ape* cruise a field of boulders which radically slopes to 130+, and ends at a fine sand bottom. A large archway marks the northern border with a cave at each end of the arch. The walls are honeycombed with tubes, in a variety of sizes, ranging from a tight squeeze for one, to accommodations large enough for four abreast. They are usually packed with lobsters of every variety known in the Hawaiian Islands. When poking around the walls, don't forget to look out into the blue for pelagics.

Just south of Kaumalapau is **Tide Pools**. This shallow water dive is interesting for its unusual topography. Lava tubes and archways cut into the shoreline wall in 10 to 50 feet of water. It is highlighted by one very large, long channel with lots of open ceiling area that is amenable to good photographic lighting. The rubble apron gradually descends to a flat sand bottom at 60 feet.

The southwestern tip of Lāna'i has two sites that serve as havens when the south shore is blown out, and offer excellent diving in their own right. **Shark Fin Rock** is named for the tip of an offshore ridge that rises above the surface and resembles - well, you know. Boats anchor on an inshore ridge that runs parallel to the shoreline in 15 feet at it shallowest. A large school of milletseed butterflyfish compete with *nenue* for divers' hand outs. The predominate formation is the exposed ridge running perpendicular to the shoreline, and gradually descending to deeper water. At the seawardmost point, it is always good to take a long look into the blue...

I was concentrating on shooting a pair of lionfish at 90 feet, when I heard the sharp metallic tap of my dive buddy's knife on his tank. I looked over to see him flapping his arms up and down signaling a ray. I couldn't see it, so I went back to work. Within minutes, the tapping resumed. I was shooting macro, and was irritated by the continued interruption. I looked over to the right to see him signaling more emphatically. I gave him the okay, but this time he pointed towards my other shoulder. When I looked to my left, there, hovering three feet away, was a giant manta ray with a wing span of 10 feet, seemingly intent in watching what I was doing.

The dilemma was in deciding what to do. I couldn't photograph it, so I just held my arms out to my side, inhaled, and gradually floated up a couple of feet. The ray slowly banked off, and swam seaward, out of sight. Within a few seconds, it returned, banked to the left and continued the game for about 20 minutes. Running out of air and available bottom time, I regretfully returned to the boat. The ray followed me back and circled below the boat, thrilling the charter passengers. I changed tanks, grabbed my wide angle set-up, and jumped back in. As soon as I re-entered the water, the ray led me back to the same spot, every once in awhile dropping headfirst towards the bottom, and displaying its full underside. I spent another 20 minutes witnessing this harmless giant's enjoyment of swimming freely in the wild.

The main ridge at Sharkfin is paralleled by two smaller ones to the south. The site is good for finding many eels, octopus, and an occasional turtle and whitetip.

Hawaiian turkey(lion)fish are found at both sites around the southwestern tip of Lāna'i.

The beacon at Palaoa Point marks the site known as **Lighthouse**. The major focus of the dive is along the wall that hugs the shoreline, from the surface to 35 feet. A cave at the midway point is a favorite rest stop for whitetips basking in the warm, fresh water vents. Further south is another dubbed Volkswagon Cave because you can just about squeeze a VW van into it. The tube extends inshore about 40 yards to a dead end. The bottom is layered with silt which can be easily disturbed, but avoidable with good buoyancy control. Usually a guide will go into the cave and coax a whitetip out to the divers waiting at the entrance. From the wall, there is a field of boulders, some small, others huge, that house a wide variety of fish, octopus and invertebrates. The site's northern boundary is a large granulated sand field with huge boulders and crown-of-thorns sea stars. A Henshaw's eel resides in the channel that gradually slopes to over 100 feet.

Around the corner from Lighthouse is a 15 foot wide break in the vertical wall that runs along the shoreline. The site is vulnerable to a south swell, resulting in surge and reduced visibility, but when it's clear, the formations are quite dramatic. The top of the wall is in 10 feet and drops to a base at 55. The formation cuts a 40 yard trench into the shoreline, bringing to mind the **Grand Canyon**. Inside the ravine, there are many *pukas* open for exploration. Octocoral and yellow encrusting sponge coat the inshore wall, and Hawaiian sergeant (major) fish valiantly defend their purple egg patches also encrusting the area. To the left of the main entrance is an inverted V-shaped crack from 55 to 40 feet divers can swim through. Outside the canyon is a healthy coral community on the apron, where crown-of-thorns feed on cauliflower corals. The bottom slopes to the depths, but the main area to explore is along the wall. An abundance of fish inhabit the midwater range - parrotfish, butterflyfish, surgeonfish, and pufferfish. One unusual sighting we had was a surface-feeding milk fish at a cleaning station.

Menpachi, on the south coast of Lāna'i, is misnamed for the shoulderbar soldierfish ('ū'ū) that live in its cave. A large lava tunnel starts at 60 feet and extends shoreward, opening to a ridge on the right with several archways. Some scattered wreckage was left from filming an episode of *Charlie's Angels* several years ago. The site will always yield spotted pufferfish, an occasional octopus, and is good for shells.

Shoulderbar soldierfish ('ū'ū) are a nocturnal species frequently found inside caves and beneath ledges during the daylight hours. They are more commonly called "menpachi" by guides throughout the state.

Directly seaward from Menpachi is a sea mount rising from the 120 foot bottom to within 40 feet of the surface. The main focus of the dive at **Monolith** is the foot of the pinnacle that levels out at 100 feet and extends seaward. A three foot black coral tree gives refuge to a longnose hawkfish, and a large school of garden eels live in the sand west of the ridge, at 90 to 100 feet. The star of the site is "Stretch", a very large and friendly yellowmargin.

Traveling east from Menpachi is **White Rock**, an inshore cove that is a good haven from the surge of the south swell. There are two distinct areas to dive in waters of 55 feet or less. The wall that hugs the shoreline eastward, is rife with tubes, *pukas*, spotted pufferfish, and shells. A ridge to the west has a very photogenic break in the center for a well lit, shallow water set-

Harlequin shrimp are small, delicate and ornate crustaceans that hide in the recesses of coral branches and crevices.

up of underwater topography. A small cave is lined with yellow encrusting sponges, and another tunnel transects the ridge. The rubble field between these two areas is a poke-around diver's delight. Lionfish, leaf scorpionfish, harlequin shrimp, helmet shells, and octopus reveal themselves to the patient and the fortunate.

A pinnacle that breaks the surface of the water at low tide is known as **Wash Rock**. The main focus of the dive is the ridge running perpendicular to the shoreline just east of the site's namesake. The seaward end of the pinnacle, at 60 feet, has a large lava tunnel that can easily fit six divers abreast. The site is renowned for its whitetips, moray eels, and an occasional turtle. A school of *ta'ape* hover midwater towards the seaward side while the inshore end of the ridge has a lattice work of lava that frames a great photo set-up. The flats between the main ridge and the pinnacle have several very large antler corals loaded with their respective communities of juvenile tropicals and crustaceans. The pinnacle itself can be easily circumnavigated in a few minutes, but warrants much more time for poking around and exploring. A few tight pockets are good collecting spots for shells, and other finds include the unusual anemone crab as well as octopus.

Directly inshore of the site's main ridge is a series of tubes, caves and overhangs at the foundation of the shoreline. Its topography is reminiscent of **Catacombs** and gives this site its name. Spiny lobster abound here, but the caves can get quite narrow. Lights are recommended.

The two most requested sites on Lāna'i are huge caverns remaining from the island's formation. **Second Cathedral** is located just to the east of Wash Rock. A large pinnacle, rising from 55 to within 15 feet of the surface, is the outer shell to a hollowed-out interior. Large openings allow

137

Second Cathedral is one of two most requested dive sites at Lāna'i.

a lot of light, and offer plenty of exits, but I still recommend bringing dive lights to seek out the critters inside. A small black coral tree, that is white from lack of sunlight, hangs from the overhead. The inside walls are loaded with crustaceans and invertebrates, and can easily take up an entire dive seeking them out. The ceiling is lined with orange cup corals, and *pukas* with reticulated cowries, and an occasional yellowmargin. A number of tubes offshoot the cavern, making the site a topographical delight. Divers are recommended to exit with no less than 1000 p.s.i. in their tanks for safety. The outside of the pinnacle has a black coral tree at 35 feet, wire coral curling out from the formation, and is skirted with rubble. A school of *ta'ape* hover by an adjacent ridge, and a whitemouth moray eel, named "Elwood", actively seeks divers for a handout. When not threatened, Elwood can be picked up, making him a great photo subject. Nevertheless, he has teeth, and knows how to use them.

A series of randomly placed ridges, interlaced with archways, caves, and tubes, is highlighted by a U-shaped formation, capped by a large table rock, and is known as **Knob Hill**. The site ranges in depth from 30 to 55 feet. Several antler corals accentuate the ridge that serves as habitat to eels, octopus, a variety of starfish, and the usual collection of tropicals. The outermost ridge runs parallel to shore, with a whitetip often found resting beneath an overhang. A large barracuda hovers midwater on the seaward side of the ridge, and the site is good for finding shells. The west side of Knob Hill is bordered by a white, granular sand field, and has an occasional helmet shell. The "knob" is a table rock formation sitting atop the inshore U-shaped ridge. It has a colorful crawl space, lined with yellow and orange encrusting sponges and cup corals. It is best to stay out of the small enclosure on days with a heavy surge.

East of Knob Hill is a series of ridges running parallel to the shoreline. When the current from Kaho'olawe is deflected to the west, it gets strong enough to make divers hanging on the descent line look like flags flapping in a strong wind. Thus it is named **River Run**, and only dived when the waters are still. Depths vary from 45 feet to much deeper, but the focal point of the dive is centered around the ridges. The highlight is a Javanese moray eel, common in the South Pacific, but unusual for these waters. We estimate it to be over six and a half feet long with a girth of six to eight inches, but we haven't gotten close enough to measure it yet, nor do we intend to.

A large pinnacle above the surface is segregated from the main body of land and known as Sweetheart Rock, after a Hawaiian Romeo and Juliet legend. On the eastern base of the pinnacle, is a site known as **Round House**. The name comes from a mount that has a number of openings to small tubes and caves at its base, and gives the overall impression of an old-time building used to turn and redirect the old steam locomotives. The most interesting part of the site is the shallow water formations that appear like something resembling the birth chamber in the movie *Alien*. Large, ribbed, striated hollows give an otherworldly effect to an interesting maze.

"Elwood" is a friendly whitemouth moray eel that resides at **Second Cathedral***.*

First Cathedral is the other popular cavern at Lāna'i. Light entering the cave through a lattice work of openings in the wall, coupled with a large, altar-like rock at the center of the floor inspires the site's name. The opening is at 45 feet with a couple of exits at the other end. The two tiered exit, to the right, has a large community of *'ū'ū's* in one of the recesses, while the other side has a rather unique exit called the "toilet bowl". It is a small circular opening that, when the surge is heavy, concentrates the water flow, creating a strong suction that can "flush" the diver out of the cave. Guides forewarn divers when it is too strong to attempt, and if you are lugging photo equipment, you may wish to use one of the alternate exits. Once outside, there is much to explore. Traveling eastward along the ridge leads to a break, with large boulders forming a triangular swim through. Going in the opposite direction is a huge archway that couples a large ridge to a small pinnacle.

Fish Rock is a lava ridge that runs perpendicular to shore and is named after the many tropicals that blanket the formation. The entire ridge is covered with cauliflower coral. A small overhang, at the shoreward side, often shelters a turtle. Continuing seaward, on the eastern side, is a chimney that, in heavy surge, can be dangerous to the unsuspecting. It is best to do this site as close to the bottom as possible on rough days. The seawardmost end of the ridge drops to over 70 feet, and is a great area for finding spotted pufferfish. Other critters at fish rock have included anglerfish, octopus, eels, banded coral shrimp, and Spanish dancer nudibranchs.

A group of three ridges running side-by-side, perpendicular to the shoreline, is known as **Sergeant Major**, named for a large populace of the resident damselfish. The site offers a variety of marine life in 45 feet. The eastern ridge has a cave with an occasional resting turtle. The center ridge is transected by a lava tube large enough for a diver to pass, and is connected to the third ridge by an archway. A long, narrow lava tube dead ends at the base of the third ridge, and often shelters a whitetip or a turtle. Octopus, dragon wrasse, leaf scorpions, pufferfish, and bluestripe pipefish complement the large community of tropicals that thrive here. Pelagics make frequent visits to Sergeant Major, including eagle rays and giant mantas.

About a hundred yards to the east of the site is another group of ridges known as **Sergeant Minor**. A long lava tunnel starts at the seawardmost side of the main western ridge. Its entrance is at 50 feet and can accommodate four to five divers swimming abreast. The tube has several species of lobster, and sometimes a whitetip taking an undisturbed breather. A small cave and a break in the ridge leading to another one, are often good spots for sighting turtles. The inshore formations of Sergeant Minor are off the beaten path and very special. They are open ceiling chambers with many tropicals and a photographer's challenge and delight.

Three sites, on the east side of Lāna'i, merit mentioning. All of them have similar underwater topography: formations of dense packed finger and lobe corals interrupted by channels that run perpendicular to the shoreline. Their bottom actually consists of calcified alga leaves that have the consistency of uncooked oatmeal flakes. The sites are usually sought as a haven from Kona winds, and by beginner divers, but they pale in comparison to Lāna'i's otherwise superb offerings.

Fish Hotel, off Club Lāna'i, is named for an eight by 25 foot pinnacle that houses a large community of tropicals, in 30 feet of water. Keōmaku marks the site known as **Summer House**. The bottom slopes from 20 to 70 feet and is good for finding turtles. **Turtle Haven**, off Kalakala, is the best of the three for locating the endangered reptiles in 35 to 40 foot depths.

Moloka'i

To date, the only charter operations running trips to Moloka'i are from Maui. It is a 50 to 60 minute boat trip from Lahaina to the island of Moku Ho'oniki off the eastern shore of Moloka'i. This is another area rarely accessed, because of its vulnerability to the trade winds and strong currents, so when it is available, it is very special.

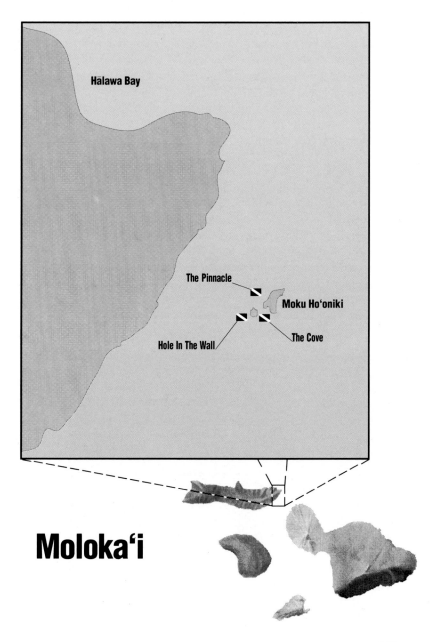

Off shore of the north side of the island is a sea mount known as **The Pinnacle**. The bottom has an irregular slope and the mount rises from 60 feet on one side, 110 on the other, to within 30 of the surface. At the 85 foot mark, a small swim-through houses slipper lobster. Though the populace of tropicals is sparse, this is a great spot for shells and anglerfish. Its offshore location is ideal for a check out of transiting pelagics including gray, hammerhead and whale sharks.

An opening above the water on the west side of the island justifies the name **Hole In The Wall** for the next dive site. Boats usually anchor atop a shallow, flat bottom, that gradually rises to within 20 feet of the surface, then drops off seaward in a vertical wall. This is a great spot to just stop and look into the blue for passing pelagics. Hammerheads, as well as grays, are frequently sighted here. The bottom slopes radically to 120 feet, scattered with lava slabs, boulders and ordnance. Large schools of pennant and pyramid butterflyfish pass in the midwater range, while further up the wall countless tropicals blanket the protective topography. The *pukas* are rife with discoveries including large tiger cowries. Returning to the boat, look around the shallow flats for octopus, eels, and pufferfish.

The Cove, of the south face of the island, provides a protected anchorage, and a popular dive for fish feeding and poke around exploration. The shallows are in 40 feet, where milletseed butterflyfish and *nenue* await divers for a handout. Antler corals make pretty photo set-ups, and the lava formations are hiding places to octopus, slipper lobster, and shells. The inside of the cove gradually slopes to 55 feet before dropping off to 85, then leveling out to a more gradual drop to the depths. The site is cased by large lava formations and boulders. The western end hooks around the corner to Hole In The Wall, while the eastern side leads to deep water, and unpredictably strong currents.

With the ability to hold its breath up to two and a half hours, the green sea turtle often tucks beneath a small ledge for a snooze.

Chapter 7

Off The Kona Coast of Hawai'i

The "Big Island" of Hawai'i is the southernmost in the island chain, and while all of the islands boast their dive offerings as the best, the Kona Coast has much to substantiate its claim. Protected from the trades by Mauna Kea (13,796 feet) and Mauna Loa (13,680 feet), the lee waters are, for the most part, glass smooth. Visibility consistently runs from 100 to 125 feet, and often exceeds 150. These idyllic conditions are vulnerable to a shift in winds and passing tropical storms. When the weather does change, there are few places to hide, so operators can lose from five to 15 days a year due to conditions, and depending upon what type of boat they are running.

Lava formations provide the setting for underwater exploration, habitation for Hawai'i's marine life, and an arena for close encounters with critters normally only dreamed about. For me, the most exciting part of Hawai'i's diving menu is the opportunity to encounter pelagics that frequent the area. Hawai'i borders the abyssal drop-off, and is in the path of transiting whales, rays, tuna, and the largest of all the fish in the seas - the whale shark.

Whale sharks are the largest of all the fish in the sea, reaching lengths up to 45 feet.

Many enriching dive sites can be easily accessed from shore, but most necessitate a boat, and are within 15 to 30 minutes travel time from the harbor or pier. These transit times can come alive with escorts by both bottlenose and spinner dolphins, and rare sightings of false and pigmy killer, melon-headed, and short-finned pilot whales.

The west side of the island, known as the Kona Coast, is an 85 mile stretch that extends from 'Upolu Point on the north, to Ka Lae Point at the southern extreme, offering over 40 different dive sites to choose from.

The northernmost is **Black Point**, a series of cutbacks and canyons that start at 10 feet and extend to 70. The shallows are comprised of extensive reef growth with the usual populace of tropicals, eels and several green sea turtles. At 30 feet, a black coral tree grows on a vertical wall, and is inhabited by a longnose hawkfish. A group of large *ulua*, has been frequently observed congregating in one of the caves, and an occasional whitetip reef shark can be found there. The wall bottoms out at 120 feet, and is a good spot for finding shells.

South of Māhukona is **Horseshoe Canyon** (Sarcophagus Cave). This network of caves is highlighted by a 100 foot long lava tube, formed when molten lava cooled on the outside, leaving behind a hard shell. As the lava flow decreased, and eventually died out, the tube remained. It extends inshore to an above-water chamber, where up to seven divers can surface into a pocket well lit by sunlight penetrating its several cracks and openings.

Black Point Too is a series of three dive sites, two considered deep, offshore from Māla'e Point. The northern site is lava substrata with good coral formations that slopes seaward to the sandy bottom at 100 feet. A series of caverns on the south side includes one tube running inshore 60 feet, with its entrance at 50 and the exit at 20 feet. Good for yielding shells on the inside, its outside walls are populated by a healthy coral community. A vertical chimney in another tube yields a good selection of Hawaiian tropicals and eels, including the unusual conger.

Keikei Caves is located just north of Waiakaʻilio Bay in 30 to 80 feet. A coral covered lava finger extends perpendicular to the shoreline, with innumerable caves on each side of the formation. The site is rich with pyramid and raccoon butterflyfish, pufferfish and eels. There are at least four major caverns with enormous plate corals starting in 30 feet and dropping to 60 feet. The caverns cut into the shore up to 80 feet, often host green sea turtles, and invite exploration. The "kitchen sink" is a large opening under a ledge that drops down 10 feet into a tube which, in turn, extends seaward into a large cavern, with numerous exits.

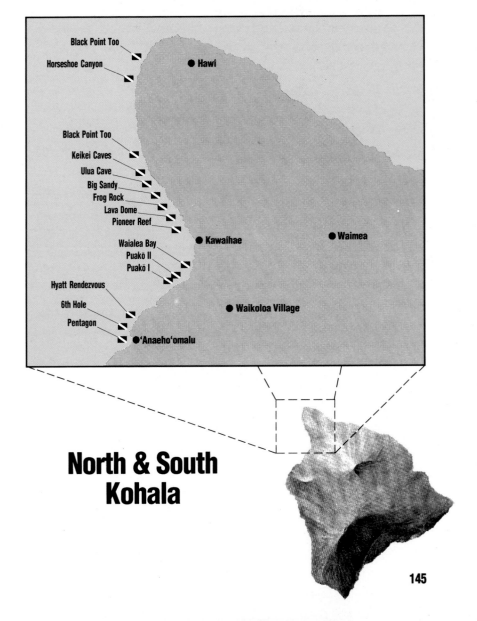

North & South Kohala

The spotted pufferfish is also called a velcro fish for the feel of its skin.

Ulua Cave is located 100 yards off a point of land a quarter mile north of Kohala Ranch. The dive is named for the large cavern that always has a congregation of *ulua*, and sometimes a whitetip. Facing southwest, there is abundant cauliflower coral growth on its exterior, the top of which is at 35 feet, with a 40 foot archway, walls, and ledges at the exit of the cave. Turning right from the ledges, the irregular bottom slopes from 50 to 60 feet where it meets a gradually sloping sand bottom. Raccoon butterflyfish, bandit angelfish, and lobster highlight the ever present tropicals. Current can be fairly strong depending upon the tide. When the weather starts to get less than desirable, a small bay just south of *Ulua* Cave, is a good spot to seek safe haven. With rarely any current, the large sand patches make for a safe, nonintrusive anchorage, and have given the site its name, **Big Sandy**. A finger of lava extending seaward is the focus of the dive. At the edge of the site is a short vertical wall off the large coral laden mound. This is a good spot for seeing tropicals, eels, turtles, and every so often, dolphin.

South of Big Sandy, **Frog Rock** is named after a large rock that bears a facial resemblance to "Kermit" - you'll just have to see it. A series of caverns to the south of the noted rock has a healthy coral community in 20 to 50 feet. Conger eels, turtles, and an occasional whitetip complement the community of tropicals. Warbling, high-pitched whistles heard while diving announce a resident school of spinner dolphins cruising the sites along this area of the coast.

Continuing south, **Lava Dome** (Bells Reef) is a large mushroom shaped dome, covered with coral. Nearby is a large amphitheater shaped formation with an inside depth at 60 feet, opening to a sand floor at 80 feet. There is a good establishment of tropicals, eels and frequently turtles. Garden eels have settled into the sand bottom at 80 to 100 feet.

Captain Cook first discovered the Hawaiian Islands in the late 19th century. His ship anchored near the Kawaihae harbor in an area now known to divers as **Pioneer Reef**. Two coral mounds, each the size of a city block, are separated by an alley that heads seaward. The shallow mound is in 35 feet, sloping to where the reef drops to over 110, then levels off at a sand bottom. Turtles are always sighted here, as well as several very large moray eels, and often a transiting ray.

Waialea Bay has a shallow dive that can be done as either a boat or a shore dive. With most of the time spent in the shallower waters, it is an average experience for the seasoned diver, but an enjoyable one for the novice. The floor of the bay is covered with small corals, and a large reef running through its center.

In 1859, a lava flow poured into the water at a point on the Kohala Coast, now known as the Village of Puakō. Three quarters of a mile south of the Puakō Boat Ramp is a dive area located at the end of the ancient lava flow. The top of the flow is richly covered with coral

Arc-eye hawkfish can be seen on practically every dive waiting in the limbs of cauliflower or antler coral.

outcroppings that are constantly tended by tropicals. Divided into two distinctive dive sites, **Puakō II** is the northernmost, and accessible from shore or by boat. The depth ranges from 35 to 100 feet. Divers never quite know what to expect, which makes this dive so interesting. On any given dive, turtles or spotted eagle rays may grace the area. A community of garden eels live in the sand flats. **Puakō I** (Ruddles, Ins and Outs), drops into a wall richly covered with corals. The site is alive with moray eels, pincushion starfish, and dramatic drop-offs, in 40 to 80 feet. Honeycombed with crevices, there are a lot of "ins and outs" to explore. Most of the caves and archways are in the 10 to 20 foot zone, where turtles are frequently seen. Past the end of the lava flow is a seemingly endless field of coral with a couple of archways, and a favorite spot for finding shells and octopus. Accessible by either boat or shore, caution should be taken as a strong rip current can get a little tricky at this site.

The **Hyatt Rendezvous** (Mauna Lani Caves, Turtles) is an interesting site for one phenomena - 10 to 15 turtles that gather and rest atop a huge mount while their shells are being cleaned by wrasse. The large pinnacle measures 75 feet long and 300 feet in circumference, rising from a 40 foot bottom to within 15 feet of the surface, with a healthy coral growth on top. A maze of lava tubes and archways, inland of the pinnacle, are fun to swim through, explore for lobster, and offer good photographic opportunities.

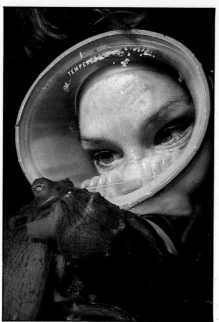

Endearing encounters with octopus are a common occurrence for divers in Hawai'i.

The site is accessible by boat only and located directly in front of the Mauna Lani Resort.

Around the corner and south of Hyatt Rendezvous, there is another unique dive site, but for reasons other than marine life. The **6th Hole** tee shot, of the Mauna Lani Golf Course, is bordered by a cliff dropping to the ocean. There are two ways of approaching the green. One is by teeing off along the fairway to the right, requiring two shots to the green. The other is shorter, by driving the ball directly to the green from the tee - over the water! Several attempts by would-be Arnold Palmers and Lee Trevinos, have resulted in a flurry of golf balls deposited on this most unlikely of dive sites. Besides the treasure trove of Top-Flites™, the area is good for Hawaiian tropicals, moray eels, cowry shells, triton's trumpets and helmets along a sand bottom in 20 to 60 feet.

Although primarily a shallow dive, one of the most popular sites is off the channel of 'Anaeho'omalu Bay, with a central lava structure 200 feet in diameter rising from 25, to within 15 feet of the surface. The coral encrusted lava formation has five openings, thus, the name **Pentagon**. In one of the adjacent caves rests a four foot whitetip, and a skittish six to seven footer that will move to the rear of the cave, and out of sight, when disturbed. A short swim north reveals a 100 foot long lava tube running east to west. The tube is completely enclosed, can fit three divers abreast, and has a room adjacent to it. To the south is a series of archways that invite exploration. There is also a drop-off to a coral and sand bottom at 100 feet. In late afternoon, the chances increase of seeing spotted eagle rays.

Kīholo Bay is a boat dive south of Pentagon surrounded by black sand beaches and lava cliffs. It is a sheer drop-off to 60 feet, where boulders are littered about the sand bottom. The surface of the rock is rubbed smooth by the sea, and resettled with a thriving coral community. This serves as a focal point for a myriad of marine life. Lobsters and other crustaceans, as well as octopus and other mollusks seek refuge in the shelter of the huge stones.

Getting closer to the Kailua area is **Plane Wreck Point**. The remnants of a twin engine aircraft were sunk in 115 feet off Keāhole Point. Squirrel fish and other Hawaiian tropicals have taken up residence within the wreckage, providing excellent photo opportunities.

Preferring to be left alone, docile whitetip reef sharks rest beneath ledges.

Part of the lava flow from the 1801 eruption of Mt. Hualālai entered the ocean immediately south of a spot called Mahai'ula. The bottom topography is classic evidence of an old reef area covered by lava, then reestablished with new growth and repopulated. Two sea mounts are the center-

North Kona

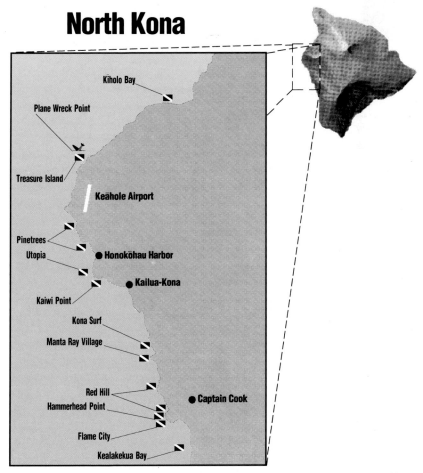

Kīholo Bay

Plane Wreck Point

Treasure Island

Keāhole Airport

Pinetrees

Utopia

● Honokōhau Harbor

● Kailua-Kona

Kaiwi Point

Kona Surf

Manta Ray Village

Red Hill

Hammerhead Point

● Captain Cook

Flame City

Kealakekua Bay

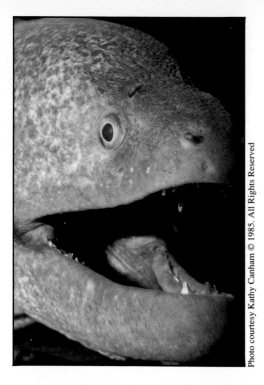

Follow the lead of an experienced dive guide before attempting to interact with a yellowmargin moray eel.

piece for this dive, with a long inventory of marine life inhabiting them. The mount to the north is on a black sand bottom, and has small *pukas* stuffed with *ū'ū's*, slipper lobster, and sponge crab. When divers first enter the site, the initial impression is – "We're going to dive here"? – but then the hunt begins around **Treasure Island**. A list of the critters found includes - two triton's trumpets, spiny lobsters, razor wrasse fish, flounder, four spot butterflyfish, leaf scorpionfish, and a pettable yellowmargin eel named "Long John Silver". After the dive, and all of the discoveries, the impressions are always changed – if you like a diversity and a profusion of marine life, this spot is great.

The **Pinetrees** area, two miles north of Honōkohau harbor, is a series of 10 to 12 dive sites that represent a microcosm of Kona Coast diving. A cluster of pine trees marks a projection of land at Wawahiwaʻa Point that is surrounded by waters rife with lava formations, and is also the home of a gregarious green sea turtle – this is "Piggy Country".

Golden Arches is the northernmost site at Pinetrees. Two archways and a pinnacle rise from the 55 foot bottom to within 15 feet of the surface. A patient diver, with a good set of eyes, can locate a wide range of otherwise very hard to find critters, including lionfish and the rare anglerfish.

Next is **Pinnacles**, several peaks, archways, overhangs and lava tubes are inhabited by tropicals, dragon eels, and seasonal fire gobies. *Mū's* serve their sentinel duty hovering in mid-water. Octopus and anglerfish are commonly found in the 50 foot waters, and there is a very large and equally friendly whitemouth eel residing among several not-so friendly yellowmargin and yellow head moray eels.

Tag Anyone? Meet Miss Piggy

As the boat dropped anchor on the dive site at Pinetrees, we were met by the most unlikely of greeters, a threatened green sea turtle, affectionately known as Miss Piggy, who has no inhibitions around divers. I never thought reptiles could have a personality until I witnessed this juvenile's friendliness, curiosity, and playfulness.

Admiral Scruffy is an appropriately named terrier with a reputation of her own in the diving community. When out on the dive boat, she perks up at the very mention of the turtle's name, so conversation is usually a spelled out "P-i-g-g-y" in whispered tones. When the turtle approaches the boat, the game is on. Scruffy leaps at the apparent position of Piggy, and paddles furiously to-

"Admiral Scruffy" and "Miss Piggy" share in a game of tag with each other.

ward her playmate. The turtle, naturally maneuverable in her aquatic environment, easily glides out of reach of Scruffy's paws. It is a quick circular loop, a close pass, and Piggy tantalizes the dog to keep chasing her. Scruffy chases - she's almost on top - Piggy dives and gets away. Scruffy starts back to the boat, and Piggy teases her back into the game. When the dog boards the boat Miss Piggy constantly cruises by with rapid passes until Scruffy can no longer fight the temptation, so in she goes and the game resumes.

When the divers enter the water, Miss Piggy is quick to make eyeball-to-face mask contact looking for a handout. She then provides escort and modeling services for the simple price of a piece of squid. No pay - she moves on, and believe me, Miss Piggy is worth the price of admission. Her modeling acumen has placed her on the BBC television series *Last Frontier*, by John Stoneman, and in a couple of prize winning photographs.

Besides her human-like behavior, the fact that Piggy initiated contact with the divers makes her truly special. On July 2nd, 1987 some guides were trying to lure a *mū* into taking squid from their hands. Miss Piggy happened onto the scene, snatched the squid from their fingers, and ate everything else they had to offer. You should know by now how the name came about. She became an instant hit.

Though looking like an average turtle, if Piggy's behavior doesn't give her away, her research tag will. She willingly submitted to the tagging for her usual fee of squid, and can now by easily identified cruising a four mile stretch of sites between Kaloko and Keāhole Points.

A Photogenic Opportunity

Miss Piggy is a photogenic opportunity to witness a turtle who doesn't realize that she is a turtle. With all of the publicity, she has gotten to be more of a "Smokey the Bear" symbol in educating divers in their proper conduct with her reptilian cousins. When over-stressed, as in the case of a diver trying to hitch a ride, turtles require more oxygen and tire easily, which may lead them to drowning from thoughtless interaction of this nature. So, hands off - they are a threatened species, and it's against the law to harass them in any way.

The ubiquitous Miss Piggy

Suck 'em Up Cave is named for a long lava tube, 15 to 20 feet high and 10 feet wide, that tapers to a small opening. When the surge is active, the resultant action exemplifies its name. L'il Abner and Daisy Mae, tame and toothless conger eels, share the site with pufferfish, octopus, and pyramid butterflyfish. The site is a favorite night dive area of local guides.

Skull Cave lies adjacent to Suck 'em Up. A pair of lava tubes along the wall resemble the eyes, where divers swim in through one, and out the other. On the tubes' ceilings, cup corals, mute in their daytime pastels, open at night to feed in an explosion of oranges, greens, and browns.

Lead City is named for innumerable fishing leads that pepper the bottom. A large archway highlights the site. An influx of cold, fresh water invades the still salt waters of Freeze Face Cave with hazy rivules from the temperature inversion. In the open, the bottom gradually slopes from 25 to 45 feet, then drops off.

In the summer of 1988, Jim Light and Dan Bergen got to experience what they described as high drama on the open seas. Serving as instructor/ dive guides, they were taking a dive charter to a nearby site off Kailua-Kona. Bottlenosed dolphins were escorting their boat, and all aboard were anxious to slip into the water with them. When the boat stopped, everyone put on their snorkeling equipment and slipped over the side. Once they were in the water, the excitement really began. A school of false killer whales was chasing a mahimahi. The fish was stunned by the clicking of the whales (a normal hunting technique), and swam to the divers beneath the boat for refuge. Whenever the fish would venture away from the group, the whales would make a pass or lunge at it, but to no avail. At one point, the fish swam into Jim's arms for protection.

Finally, as time necessitated moving on, the group had to exit and continue the charter. Unfortunately for the mahimahi, it could not follow the divers, and as soon as the last one exited, the fish became a vulnerable target. One of the whales immediately grabbed it, and shared it with the rest of the pod. There was no competition; it was a community effort. The cold realities of life and death in the marine world were brought to witness by a very fortunate group of divers.

One mile north of Kailua, right at Kiawi Point, is an area vulnerable to currents and surge, thus rarely dived. Three pinnacles at **Utopia** hide spiny pufferfish, 7-11 crabs, tiger cowries and triton's trumpets, but instead of poking around, the most effective way to enjoy the action is to find a place to

Professional dive guides consider an encounter with a hard-to-find anglerfish a special treat.

stop and just watch. The depths range from 20 to 100 feet with heavy coral encrustation. Teardrop butterflyfish, rare reticulated butterflys, and assorted tangs complement the activity of tropicals found at every site. Tiger cowries have been observed nesting, and sergeant major fish valiantly defend their egg patch. Pyramid butterflyfish and *nenues* swim in the midwater range, where there is always the chance to see big jacks, up to 100 pounds, swim by. Titan scorpionfish, trumpetfish, and cleaning stations add to the viewing pleasure.

The dive site known as **Kiawi Point** (pronounced Kee-ah-vee), is located south, around the corner from the point of land it's named after. Unlike Utopia, this Kiawi Point is very sheltered from the northwest swell, and one of the most frequently dived sites off Kona. Four small caves and three archways hug the shoreline area in 20 feet of water. All of the caves measure less than 20 by 20 feet, one of them hosting as many as five whitetips at a time. The archways are separated from the caves, and the topography is home to many different critters. Flame angelfish, leaf scorpions, pipefish, and harlequin shrimp have all been discovered here, while other rare sightings include reticulated butterflyfish, and unicorn fish at a cleaning station, being given the "once over" by juvenile saddle wrasse. The bottom is interspersed with lobe coral out to the drop-off, where a flourishing community of finger coral follows the contour in a radical slope. At this point look into the blue – there is a steady flow of jacks in the

Oval butterflyfish are not so common, and are usually found scouring the reefs in sets of two.

area, along with frequent sightings of manta rays. Although hammerhead, gray, and whale sharks are uncommon, this is the site you are most likely to find them.

On the north side of Keauhou Bay, a dive site with innumerable pinnacles is accessible only when there is no swell. A large number of unusual butterflyfish (oval, reticulated, saddleback) are in the 70 to 80 foot range. Yellow tangs hunt for food and seek out shelter in the finger corals that cover the drop-off zone. The site is particularly noted for the high percentage (50 to 60%) of encounters with giant manta rays. The nearest landmark to the site is the **Kona Surf** Resort on the opposite side of the bay. Another site located directly in front of the resort, has a mediocre reef formation and resident fish populace, but is more well known for the exciting pelagics that come in to feed at **Manta Ray Village**. When the waters are calm, and there is no moon, four to six manta rays will take advantage of the plankton that are attracted by the hotel's lights, in the early evening hours.

Red Hill is another concentration of several dive sites, located along a one mile stretch between Keikiwaha and Keawakāheka Points. Constructed of ridges, lava tubes, caverns and archways, the diverse topography is home to a wide variety of marine life. **Ridges**, **Paradise Cave**, and **Amphitheater** are inspired by the topographical formations that highlight the respective sites. The 120 foot **Long Lava Tube** is adjacent to Amphitheater and runs perpendicular to the shoreline. Before entering the seaward side of the tunnel, divers pay their respects to a friendly conger eel named "Cecil". Beams of sunlight penetrate an overhead opening, but bring a light – the discoveries are diverse and abundant. Divers willing to make the sacrifices necessary to do a night dive are immediately rewarded

Delicate ghost shrimp tuck into the recesses during the daytime, but emerge when the sun goes down.

with sightings of spiny and slipper lobster, a pair of delicate ghost shrimp, and the always captivating Spanish dancer nudibranch.

Two outcroppings of lava, south of Long Lava Tube, are very long steep ridges that extend seaward between 15 and 80 feet. One of the ridges at **Driftwood Caverns** is more predominate, and both have an abundant growth of finger corals surrounding them. Archways in the shallower areas support a rich populace of fish, while turtles and mantas are frequently sighted in the deeper waters.

Adjacent to Driftwood Caverns is **The Dome**, a 100 by 50 foot inverted bowl adjoining the shoreline wall. Three entries, one on each side, are large enough to admit a submarine, opening to the interior of appealing soft corals and sponge. A 15 to 20 foot high cathedral ceiling allows plenty of light penetration and caps a housing complex of frilly aeolid nudibranchs, grouchy 7-11 crabs, and docile conger eels. Manta rays frequently frolic in the Red Hill area rounding out a showcase of Kona's best.

Hammerhead Point is named for these oddly-shaped sharks that are often spotted here. Though occasional sightings of the pelagics are exciting, the rich population of fish that are found on every visit please the most discriminating divers. Colorful yellow and Achilles tangs, unusual pufferfish, and rare butterflyfish accentuate the large populace of the more common pyramid butterflys. The site is on the Kealakakua Bay side of the point, just outside the Marine Life Conservation District. Heavy currents can sweep its sheer ledges that rise from 140 feet to within 30 feet of the surface.

Flame City is part of the Marine Life Conservation District just north of Kealakakua Bay. It is named for the several rare flame angelfish found in residence, but they are not the only rarities here. Saddleback, oval, and

Graceful giant manta rays will often provide a close interaction with nonaggressive divers, or will bank away and leave if threatened.

reticulated butterflyfish flourish under state protection. This also means that the dive has to be done from a "live boat" - no anchoring. Six scenic arches cut into the shoreline along with a small canyon, 25 feet at its deepest. A thriving coral community covers the 10 to 45 foot range with finger coral and individual lobe coral heads clustered all the way down the drop-off. Lined, teardrop, blue lined, and longnose black butterflyfish challenge photographers to go for the great shot, as well as endemic bandit angels and gold striped sailfin tangs sharing in that task. Three sizes of triton trumpets decorate the site with their patterned shells, and keep the destructive crown-of-thorns sea star populace in check. Tucked in from the northwest swell, dives at Flame City are almost always capped off with sightings of turtles, mantas or eagle rays.

Historic **Kealakekua Bay** is a state Marine Life Conservation District framed by a backdrop of 300 foot high cliffs. A relatively shallow shelf supports barrel sized lobe corals interlaced with dense packed finger coral, which gradually, then radically, drops through 90 to 140 feet, making the site popular with snorkelers and scuba divers alike. The drop-off sports large communities of fragile plate coral, rare to the Hawaiian Islands, but reminiscent of the type commonly found in the South Pacific. Parrotfish, black longnose butterflyfish, flame angels, oval butterflyfish, bird wrasse and spotted pufferfish complement the tropicals that insist divers feed them when entering the water. Belying the fierce reputation his "cousins" have earned, one gargantuan yellowmargin moray eel named "Orville", has a gentle disposition that has become legendary since he was first discovered in 1975. This scenic bay was the site where Captain James Cook was killed in 1779. A solitary white obelisk stands as a memorial to the famed British explorer.

South Kona

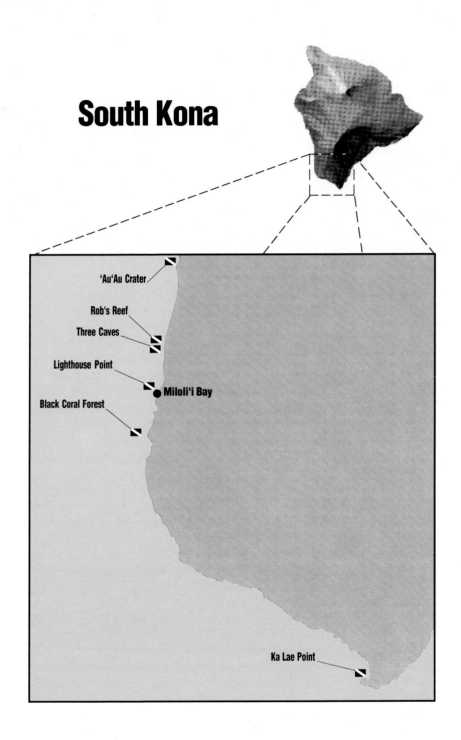

'Au'Au Crater

Rob's Reef

Three Caves

Lighthouse Point

Black Coral Forest

Miloli'i Bay

Ka Lae Point

The black sand bottom at 'Au'Au Crater leads to a precipitous drop-off.

'Au'Au Crater is to me the most unusual dive for underwater topography. A small tuff cone, severed in two with the seaward half fallen into the sea, marks the site of volcanic and primitive underwater terrain. A small shelf, hugging the shoreline, is blanketed with black sand and supports huge boulders. Two pinnacles break the surface of the water, and serve as a platform to fishermen that want to use the area for some close to shore, deep water fishing - and deep it gets. Within 100 yards of the shoreline, the water plunges to over 600 feet. Splitting the shelf is a rift that left two vertical walls plummeting to the depths. The site is still relatively sparse of marine life, without the usual populace of tropicals. However, it is an open invitation to transiting pelagics, substantiated by sightings of mantas and eagle rays.

A great system of lava tubes, just north of Three Room Cavern, sports a cathedralesque cavern called "Skull Cave". Once inside, look back through the opening, and you'll understand how it got its name. Four foundational pinnacles rise to within 20 feet of the surface, and are surrounded by thick finger corals at the site called **Rob's Reef**. The ledges are a sheer drop to a sloping wall, where a theater of blue water presents a pelagic show of whale sharks, and a seasonal glimpse of whales that tend to come into the shallows.

Continuing south to Laeokamimi Point are three dive sites with large caverns that are located along the shoreline walls. **Three Room Cavern** or **Three Caves** is the centerpiece. It is a short swim from the shallow anchorage to the cave's entrance at 35 feet. The inside of each of the three chambers is lined with light, yellow sponge. On one of our dives the guide pulled out a 10 inch Spanish dancer, the largest species of nudibranch in the world. These crimson beauties are mesmerizing to observe, its bright red color, and undulating swimming motion brings to mind exotic flamenco dancers, thus the name. Connected to the room furthest from the entrance

Though normally a deep water fish, this very rare Tinker's butterflyfish accepts a hand-out.

is an opening to a 100 foot lava tube. The access can get very narrow (one at a time), so if you are claustrophobic, better try from the outside. North from the entrance to Three Caves is another opening to the tube at 25 feet. To the south of Three Caves is **Two Story Caves**, a 50 x 30 foot chamber with a hole in the center of the floor that leads into another large cavern. Five species of lobster have been seen here: target, spiny, mole, slipper and Hawaiian, as well as crabs, cowries, and a species of anemone.

    Lighthouse Point is a site located on the north side of Miloli'i Bay, named for the onshore beacon. A ridge, running perpendicular to shore is the centerpoint of search for harlequin, ghost, and banded shrimp, 7-11 and hermit crabs, and leaf fish. Washrocks break the surface, and an archway sits at 40 to 45 feet, its walls covered with red, yellow and orange encrusting sponge. Though the site has a shallow anchorage, it drops off rapidly. The bandit angelfish, endemic to Hawai'i, is found here as well.

    South of Okoe Bay is **Black Coral Forest** named for the profusion of soft coral growth at the site. Starting at 85 feet, coral normally found in much deeper water grows to diameters of six to eight feet with the "forest" thickening as the depth increases. A strong current carries the planktonic rich nutrients to feed the corals that serve as home to longnose hawkfish, bandit angels, and the extremely rare Tinker's butterflyfish.

    Last but not least, is **Ka Lae Point** (South Point). Framed by a cove of high vertical cliffs, this is the southernmost point in the United States. With waters that range from 15 to 140 feet plus, the site presents a diversity of topography and marine life. Densely packed finger corals are home to the many species of tropicals. Huge boulders were strewn about, and now serve as haven to eels, hermit crabs and more tropicals. The slope quickly drops to a sandy bottom inhabited by a large populace of garden eels. They hold to the security of their tubes with their tails, and while fully extended, they sway to the beat of the ocean awaiting food in the passing current.

Spanish dancers, one of the world's largest nudibranchs, "dance" in an undulating motion in midwater.

Section III

Outgassing
Things to do Between Dives

"One perfect, rapturous, intoxicating,
supreme vision of beauty."
Isabella Bird 1881

Since most diving charters return by mid-day, plenty of time is left for relaxing, beaching, or touring. There is a seemingly endless number of activities and destinations to choose from when planning out your free time.

This is by no means a comprehensive guidebook to all of the islands. It would take several volumes to accomplish that task. The recommendations were selected on a purely subjective basis with a few guidelines.

They either appeal to the visitor because of their:
- natural beauty,
- historical significance,
- or their ties to Hawaiiana.

And, it doesn't cost an arm and a leg to experience them.

As most visitors rent cars, maps and guide books are a must. The maps that I use are published by the University of Hawai'i Press, by cartographer James A. Bier. They serve as topographical guides as well as road maps with listing of all of the islands' highlights. They are readily available at most book, convenience, and gift stores. I also recommend "The Essential Guide To . . ." series of guidebooks published by Island Heritage, and available through the same outlets.

Caution: Because of the times that we live in, theft is a problem, and contents of rental cars are a prime target. The safest prevention against loss is to not leave anything of consequence inside your vehicles and trunks, locked or not.

Chapter 8

Kaua'i and Ni'ihau

Kaua'i

Lehua Rock

Ni'ihau

As our helicopter lifted from the tarmac, music filled the gaps between our pilot's narration about the history and the points of interest passing beneath us. We flew over ancient construction sites attributed to the fabled Menehunes, then vast fields of sugar cane, on our way to one of the geologic wonders of the state. The helicopter seemed to labor as we approached the lip of a ridge, then easily swept into the chasm of the Waimea Canyon. It was a tear between trying to take in the entire vista that just unfolded before us, and collecting our hearts that were left somewhere back on the ridge. The panoramic expanse was only an introduction to what was ahead of us. Approaching the coastline, we looked down to see the wide sandy beaches of Barking Sands, then into the distance at the "Forbidden Isle" of Ni'ihau. Showing a skilled hand at maneuvering in tight spaces, our pilot brought the craft to within feet of ribbons of water that cascaded hundreds of feet from the streams above. The Nā Pali coastline captivated our view. As we continued north, verdant cliffs were stacked one against the other in one of the most spectacular displays of nature's handiwork. Hanalei Bay (home of "Puff, The Magic Dragon") was next on the flight, and our turning point for the beginning leg of our return. One last thrill was flying into an overcast, mountainous region that opened to a wall of 14 different waterfalls, canopied by the low hanging clouds that nourish the wettest spot on earth – Mt. Wai'ale'ale. This 50 minute "E-ticket" special opened views to us made naturally inaccessible by the inhospitable topography, and served as our bird's eye introduction to one of the most beautiful islands in the world.

Overview: Kaua'i

Nickname	The "Garden Isle"
Area	553.3 square miles
Coastline	90 miles
Highest peak	Kawaikini – 5,243 feet
Population	48,400 (12/31/89 estimate)
County seat	Lihu'e
Airport	Lihu'e
Distance to Honolulu	102 miles
Agriculture	sugar
	taro

Nowhere in the Hawaiian Islands is the allure, romance and embodiment of the Polynesian South Pacific more exemplified than on Kaua'i. This small, plush, emerald green island is the northernmost and oldest of the main Hawaiian Islands. Eons of time and erosion have sculptured this island into an eclectic blend of flat agricultural plains, mountainous backdrops, and feral rocky coastlines that are interrupted by pristine sandy beaches.

Blanketed by thick tropical foliage, the "Garden Isle" has attracted, then awed its guests with visual wonders that have inspired the creative talents of painters, writers, photographers, and the movie industry.

The aromatic plumeria blossom (pua melia) is often the flower of choice by lei makers. (Photo courtesy Paul Grulich © 1978. All Rights Reserved)

Vivid red bracts of a Red Ginger (Ostrich Plume Ginger) make the plant idea in tropical floral arrangements.

Man has done little to mar the Eden-like beauty of Kaua'i. Development has been constrained by relatively strict guidelines, leaving the island free of towering commercial and resort edifices, and distributing both the local and transient population. The main airport is in the town of Līhu'e, and the resorts are concentrated around three different locales: Princeville/Hanalei to the north, Kapa'a/Wailua to the east, and Kōloa/Po'ipū along the south coast.

There is one main horseshoe-shaped highway that almost, but not quite, circumnavigates the island. The mountainous terrain leading to the Nā Pali Coastline has set the parameters on this 90 mile long artery, and is a good starting point for our tour. We will begin at the northernmost point and work clockwise around Kaua'i to its other extreme.

Filmed on Kaua'i

The natural wonders offered on Kaua'i have not gone unnoticed by Hollywood. A wide variety of backdrops can be found easily accessible on this relatively small island. The azure blue Pacific is contrasted by the white sandy beaches, towering volcanic terrain cut deep with lush valleys, and are offset by pastoral settings of farmland and serene rivers. The first and third "Indiana Jones" movies were filmed in part here, as well as *King Kong*, *Blue Hawai'i* and *South Pacific*. The television miniseries, *Thorn Birds*, drew from the natural resources of Kaua'i, and the opening sequence of *Fantasy Island* ("Zee plane, boss, zee plane!") is a footnote to the tourist attractions. In fact several of the points of interest are punctuated by the guides - "filmed on Kaua'i".

The Kalalau Trail offers beautiful panoramas of the Nā Pali Coastline along its 10.8 mile path.

The best vantage point for viewing the **Nā Pali Coastline** is by helicopter, but it is by far not the only one. Though the magnitude of the 2,700 foot high cliffs can be realized to the fullest from above, there are alternatives that are more intimate, yet more limiting in scope. This 25 mile-long stretch of coast can be seen from inflatable boats that cruise along nearshore waters, and reach beaches and parks that are otherwise inaccessible by foot. Pick as calm a day as possible to do the trip, and don't pack anything that you are afraid of getting wet. Hiking trails lead to overlooks of the canyon, the coastline, and waterfalls. The 10.8 mile Kalalau Trail leads first to Hanakāpī'ai, then to Hanakoa, and finally ends at Kalalau Valley. The hike is wet and muddy, and can be slippery in spots, but the views and photographic opportunities are definitely worth the effort.

The demands of the 22 mile round trip are too rigorous for a single day's outing, but camping is possible. If shorter distances are more within your range, the two intermediate stops at Hanakāpī'ai and Hanakoa are amply rewarding. Beaches along the Nā Pali Coastline are alluring, but potentially hazardous, so heed the warning signs that are posted.

Three geological aberrations just past the start of the Kūhiō Highway are the **Waikanaloa and Waikapala'e wet caves** and the **Maninihole dry cave**. Extending several hundred yards under the ledge, the lava tubes are well worth exploring. Bring a light as the available daylight at the entrance is soon lost. Continue east, past Hanalei and the Princeville resort area, and look for signs leading to -

Kīlauea Point National Wildlife Refuge

The Kīlauea Point National Wildlife Refuge is one mile off Kūhiō Highway on the northernmost point of Kaua'i. The 160 acre refuge was established in 1985, attracting seabirds, marine critters, and between 600 to 1000 people daily to its panoramic shoreline. The most exciting part of visiting the refuge is the seabirds and the marine life. Brown boobies, great frigate birds, the American golden plover, and albatross have all been "watched", while over 700 red footed boobies nest here, as well as black footed albatross, and wedge-tailed shearwaters.

A Laysan albatross patiently nests in the security of the Kīlauea Point National Wildlife Refuge.

Whales (in season) and turtles are frequently sighted, and one of the most endangered marine mammals in the world, the monk seal, was discovered birthing and nursing a pup on the offshore island of Moku 'Ae'Ae. A resident school of spinner dolphins has recently come under scrutiny. Considerable efforts are being pushed to legislate minimum distances of 1,200 yards, to prevent harassment of the playful sea creatures. When their natural behavior is changed by enthusiastic boaters, swimmers, and snorkelers, it's termed harassment, and generates the fears that the public is literally loving the animals to death. Besides offering sanctuary to the wildlife, the refuge has an ongoing program of restoration and protection of the coastal plant community. To date, five different endemic plants have been successfully re-established. From the admissions gate, where a small fee is charged to anyone over 16, a pathway leading to the lighthouse is highlighted by large placards pointing out facts and information about the temporary and permanent critters at the refuge. The dominate lighthouse was erected in 1913 to assist the trans-Pac fleets through the Hawaiian Archipelago. It was managed by the Coast Guard, and eventually shut down, but it has since been modified to run again. Located next to the lighthouse, the visitors center is staffed by some of the over 200 volunteers at the refuge. It offers a modest gift shop and free binocular rentals. Another service available is the Crater Hill Hike, offered every Tuesday and Thursday as a guided tour to some of the more remote sections of the preserve. Up to 15 people can register for this one and a half hour excursion to breathtaking scenery, and close observations of seabirds, native vegetation, and great photographic opportunities. The newest addition is the Environmental Education Center, with a multimedia presentation designed to heighten the public's awareness of wildlife conservation. A series of educational brochures has been produced on some of the individual wildlife that visits the refuge, written separately for adults and children at the fifth grade level. Hours are from 10:00 a.m. to 4:00 p.m., Monday through Friday. More information may be obtained by writing: Kīlauea Point National Wildlife Refuge, P.O. Box 87, Kīlauea, Kaua'i, HI 96754, or by calling (808) 828-1520.

*The twin cascades of
'Ōpaeka'a Falls are
viewable from a roadside
vista off Route 580.*

As the Kūhiō Highway turns south, continue through the villages of Kapa'a and Wailua to the Route 580 turnoff. The route follows parallel to the Wailua River, with a number of scenic pulloffs, including one a couple of miles up the road for the **'Ōpaeka'a Falls.**

After taking in the view, hike across the street to an overview of the **Wailua River.** This 19.7 mile waterway is the only navigable fresh water river in the state, and is regularly traveled by tour boats leading to the **Fern Grotto** – a cavern overgrown with the soft ferns and plants, that create a tropical backdrop for weddings, and one of the most popular tourist attractions on the island.

Līhu'e is the commercial center on the island. The old public library building now houses the **Kaua'i Museum.** Permanent displays of the history and geology of the island, as well as its flora are presented through ancient local artifacts, arts and crafts, and multimedia, and are augmented by temporary exhibits. The museum is located at 4428 Rice Street, near the main Post Office. Admission is charged.

There are resorts being built throughout the state that are a cut above the normal rooming accommodations, and are now being categorized as "super resorts" - places that are interesting enough to tour without necessarily staying there. Aside from being high ticket hotels, they are becoming a destination stop in their own right, and as such, the **Kaua'i Lagoons Hotel** qualifies. Spread over 800 acres along the Kalapaki Bay, the resort boasts

Tour boats regularly ply the waters of the Wailua River enroute to the Fern Grotto.

50 acres of lagoons with Venetian launches and a garish fountainhead. The grounds can be toured by way of a carriage drawn by Clydesdales, Percherons or Belgian draft horses. There is an exotic wildlife populace to see on the premises as well.

Kūhiō Highway turns into Kaumuali'i Highway at Līhu'e to continue the drive around the island. Turn south onto Route 520 to access the K⁻oloa/ Po'ip⁻u tourist area. The road is immediately canopied by a covering of swamp mahogany trees (**Tunnel of Trees**), that border each side of the road like military cadets with swords drawn in tribute to a classmate's wedding. The coastline is usually protected from winter's inclement weather, and the beach fronts' several resorts, hotels and condominiums. Boogie boarding, snorkeling and diving are actively pursued at this natural gathering place. Continuing west along the coastal drive leads to **Spouting Horn**, one of several blowholes found throughout the islands. Its easy access and 40 foot high geysers of spray are a magnetic attraction to camera buffs and tourists.

Route 50 continues west through Hanapēpē to the town of Waimea where Captain Cook first landed in the Hawaiian Islands in January of 1778. Nearby, the ruins of **Fort Elizabeth** is the only reminder of the Russian's attempt to expand their realm to the islands, Alaska, and the northwest United States. Built in 1816, it was a short lived and unsuccessful expedition. *Menehune* Road leads to an ancient irrigation waterway, marked by a bronze plaque, and known as the ***Menehune* Ditch** *(Kīkī a Ola)*. The construction of this seemingly inconspicuous rill is attributed to the legendary *Menehunes*...

Hawai'i's "Little People"

On Kaua'i, as well as on the other islands, many feats of ancient construction are attributed to Hawai'i's legendary *Menehune* - the little people. Akin to Ireland's leprechauns, the *Menehune* are described as thickset and hairy, growing between two and three feet tall, and having deep gruff voices that sound like the low growl of a dog. At night they would come to the lowlands, from their forest homes in the mountains, to work in great numbers on building projects (fish ponds, *heiaus* (temples), roads, etc.), having to complete the projects in a single evening's time. Though there are many ancient remnants found throughout the islands, and no records to account for them, to date, no one can lay claim to ever actually seeing the little people, so thus they remain, the legendary *Menehune*.

There are two options to follow at this juncture. From Waimea, follow either Waimea Canyon Drive or Kōke'e Road north. Whichever choice you make, take the other route on the return leg of the drive. Both routes are scenic and lead to the **Waimea Canyon** lookouts. Take your time, and plenty of film as this is one of the natural wonders of the state. Mark Twain has been credited with describing the site as the "Grand Canyon of the Pacific". The gorge drops 2,750 feet and is 14 1/2 miles long. A round trip drive to the canyon from anywhere on Kaua'i is less than a half day, so this should be one of the "must sees" of anyone's visit to the island. However, don't let the canyon, as gorgeous as it is, be the final destination of the excursion.

Continue north and upcountry to Kōke'e State Park. Several roadside turn-offs lead to photogenic vistas, and near the end of Kōke'e Road, the **Kalalau Lookout** opens to one of the most beautiful panoramas in the state – the Kalalau Valley - 4,000 feet below. As beautiful as the scenery is here, it is often socked in by low laying clouds that collect around the summit of nearby **Mt. Wai'ale'ale** (why-ollie-ollie). With 485 inches of annual rainfall, this extinct volcano that formed Kaua'i is now known as the wettest spot on earth.

The 2,750 foot deep Waimea Canyon has been described as the "Grand Canyon of the Pacific".

Overview: Niʻihau

Nickname .... The "Forbidden Isle"
Area .... 73 square miles
Coastline .... 45 miles
Highest peak .... Paniau - 1,281 feet
Population .... 202 (1987 estimates)
County seat .... Lihuʻe, Kauaʻi
Distance to Honolulu ..... 152 miles
Agriculture .... sheep
                               cattle

In an archipelago of islands that have been developed into one of the leading tourist destinations in the world, and where that industry is the single leading source of income, the "Forbidden Isle" of Niʻihau stands as an enigma. Privately owned by the Robinson family, the 20 mile long by five mile wide island is inhabited by native Hawaiians, who have tenaciously held onto the language of their ancestry, and resisted the influences of the world around them. Niʻihau lies 17 miles southwest of Kauaʻi, in that island's rainshadow. Averaging between 20 to 40 inches of annual rainfall, Niʻihau nevertheless boasts the state's largest natural fresh water lake - the 182 acre Halālaʻi.

English is taught on the island's only public elementary school by law, but native Hawaiian is still the spoken tongue. The island is off-limits to outsiders, and restricted to guests by invitation only. All of the residents are employees of the Robinson family, working the sole industry of the island, raising cattle and sheep, or in one of the family's related businesses. As isolated from civilization as Niʻihau has always been, at times the island and its people have gotten caught up in the events of history, no matter how involuntarily…

December 7th Reached the "Forbidden Isle"

On the Sunday morning of December 7, 1941 most of the 180 residents were walking to church at west coast village of Puʻuwai, unaware of the history that was unfolding on Oʻahu. Two Japanese fighter planes flew over the island, smoke streamed from one of the planes as its engine sputtered. They circled the village a few times, then headed north seeking out their home carriers. At 2:00 p.m. one of the planes, sporting the rising sun insignia on its wings and fuselage, returned, after its crippled companion aircraft had crashed into the ocean. It buzzed the island for about 15 minutes, then landed, crashing through a wire fence, and stopping about 75 feet from the home of Hawila Kaleohano. Kaleohano ran to the plane, ripped open the cockpit cowling, and pulled the pilot out of his seat, breaking the restraining harness in the process. As the pilot fumbled to get his papers and a revolver, the Hawaiian grabbed his papers and gun. The islanders summoned a Mr. Harada, employed by the Robinsons for the last year, to interpret their interrogation of the intruder. The pilot said that he had flown in from Honolulu, only later revealing the truth about the attack, then claiming he was the sole survivor of the attack force, and suggesting that he should settle on Ni'ihau. The locals decided to hold the pilot under guard until Mr. Robinson would arrive on his scheduled weekly trip with supplies. Five days after his arrival was overdue, a fire was lit in the mountain facing Kaua'i - a prearranged signal to communicate that there was trouble on the isolated island. The pilot and interpreter, his newfound collaborator, plotted to seize what guns they could, grabbing a double barreled shotgun and revolver that had been stolen from the Robinson ranch.

After terrorizing several of the villagers, the pilot and interpreter went from home to home threatening to kill anyone who would not help them find the now hidden papers previously secured from the pilot. The terrified villagers hid the women and children in caves in the hills. Then six of the men took Ni'ihau's whale boat and rowed 16 hours before reaching Waimea, Kaua'i to seek help. Those six were loaded aboard the Coast Guard lighthouse tender, *Kukui*, with their whaleboat, and a contingent of soldiers to rescue the island's residents, and take the pilot into custody.

Back on the island, the pilot and interpreter/ally had salvaged a pair of machine guns from the aircraft, and had taken them to the village, but while they were ransacking a house, two of the islanders stole the machine guns and ammunition. After searching all night, the Japanese had found the pilot's pistol and map of O'ahu in a Mr. Hawilas house. They burned the home, then destroyed the aircraft.

At 7:00 a.m. Saturday, Beni Kanahele, 51, and his wife sneaked back to get some food, and were caught by the Japanese. Beni told the interpreter, in Hawaiian, to take the revolver away from the pilot, but he refused, saying he feared for his life. Beni grabbed the pilot and tried to wrestle the gun away, so the interpreter grabbed his wife threatening to kill her with the shotgun. The pilot shot the massive Hawaiian three times with the revolver, but Beni grabbed him by the one leg and his head (the same as he daily handled the sheep at the ranch), and threw the pilot against a stone wall, crushing his skull and killing him instantly. The interpreter loaded two shells in the shotgun, pointed it at his own stomach, and despite a lunging attempt by Beni's wife to prevent the act, he committed suicide.

The wounded native was evacuated to Kaua'i, and required a month to recuperate. The day that World War II ended, Beni Kanehele was awarded the Purple Heart and Medal of Merit. The hero of Ni'ihau recovered, and returned to the quiet life he and the other villagers had carved out for themselves on the "Forbidden Isle".

Chapter 9

O'ahu is The "Gathering Place"

O'ahu is the third largest island in the Hawaiian chain and the central hub of commerce, education, culture and tourism. Known as the "Gathering Place", 80% of the state's population lives here, with the majority residing in the city of Honolulu. It serves as the introductory point to Hawai'i for most of the state's six and a half million annual visitors, and is loaded with activities for the family and single traveler alike.

Honolulu is a full-fledged international city where the old meets the new in a confluence of cultures. The blend of traditional Hawaiian, Polynesian, Oriental, Filipino and Mainland America are evident in the island's architecture, landscape and foods. Epicurean fantasies range from fast food stops to continental cuisine. Practically every fine eatery offers a fresh catch from the sea, and a real, old-fashioned lū'au should be experienced at least once.

Waikīkī Beach has become synonymous with tanning, boogie boarding, and Diamond Head Crater. Running parallel to Kalākaua Avenue is Waikīkī's famous, long and spacious, white sand beach; a favorite for strolling, swimming, and sunbathing, or just people watching. It is renowned for its high-rise hotels, tourists' shops, and a seemingly endless night life. At present, 33,000 rooms (with more under construction) are located within a block of the main thoroughfare, and comprise 90% of O'ahu's hotels. That leaves the greatest part of the island open for its magnificent scenery.

O'ahu

Honolulu

Overview: O'ahu

Nickname .... The "Gathering Place"
Area .... 607.7 square miles
(military bases and training areas comprise 26% of the total
land space of O'ahu)
Coastline .... 112 miles
Highest peak .... Ka'ala - 4,020 feet
Population .... 844,300 (12/31/89 estimate)
County seat .... Honolulu
Airport .... Honolulu International
Distances to interisland airports in miles:
Līhu'e , Kaua'i 102
Kapalua, Maui 81
Kahalui, Maui 01
Moloka'i 53
Lāna'i 74
Kailua-Kona, Hawai'i . 170
Hilo, Hawai'i 216
Agriculture .... Sugar
pineapple

173

At night, Waikīkī and Honolulu stay alive for visitors with restaurants and nightclubs, or strolls along Kalākaua Avenue, or Waikīkī's famous beach.

Looking at **Waikīkī** today, with its high rise hotels, and wall-to-wall boutiques and tourist shops, it is hard to believe that this area was at one time a marshy floodplain. Construction of the Ala Wai Canal diverted the streams that fed this one time prime agricultural resource, allowing its exploitative development into the now bustling tourism center. The most visible of its natural attributes is the long stretch of wide sandy beach that runs practically non-stop, from one end of Waikīkī to the other, bordering parks, hotels, resorts, beachside cafes and restaurants. Its shoreline is gently lapped by the crystal blue waters of the Pacific that combine to draw beach-goers by the thousands every day. Navigating a walk along the beach, and

Driving Around O'ahu

After arriving at Honolulu International Airport, claiming all of their luggage, and renting a car, visitors leave the airport for their destination on O'ahu. It becomes immediately apparent that there is a major problem to contend with – dealing with the traffic. With 80% of the state's population concentrated on its third largest island, and sporting one of the major metropolitan cities of the Pacific, without the benefit of a popular mass transit system, the traffic situation is to say the least – congested. There are more cars per capita on O'ahu, than anyplace else in the world. Add to that the numbers of rental cars (almost every visitor or family gets one), and the potential for tie-ups, delays, and outright jams, multiplies. To help with traffic flow, several streets throughout Honolulu and Waikīkī have been designated "one-way". Traffic cones are placed during rush hour to ease congestion, and avoiding travel between 6:30 to 8:30 a.m. and 3:30 to 5:30 p.m. will help. With a little patience, navigating O'ahu's highways can be a scenic, pleasant experience.

trying in the process not to step on someone, can be a challenge. Despite this maze of humanity, children lay claims to patches of sand to construct simplistic castles with their buckets, and surround them with briny moats to protect against imaginary invaders (at least that's what I used to do with them). Some people have never outgrown their fantasies and have turned their castles into an artform…

Sand Sculptors

Look at the size of the crowds gathered around the creations, and you'll see just how popular sand sculpturing is. It's a shutterbug's delight with the public often getting into the act to be immortalized with the soon to fade creation.

The fun of turning a lump of wet sand into an "impenetrable fortress" has forever fascinated the youthful beach-goer. Sculpting the same medium into an impressionistic or surrealistic character requires talent, the ability to work fast, and the detachment of knowing that within a couple of hours it will revert back to its original nondescript surroundings. Tides and wind wait for no artist, so time is the utmost consideration. Sand sculptors work with very simplistic tools: buckets of various sizes, kitchen tools, a piece of Formica™, a toothpick for detail work, and a straw to blow away the excess sand. When a portion is completed, it is sprayed down with a mixture of watered down Knox Gelatin (often with food coloring to tint). Artists can be found along public beaches, and in front of several large resorts that have hired them to entertain the public.

Free-lancers will leave a hat out for donations, in hopes of supporting themselves, while refining their art until a resort notices them, or the next mainland sand sculpturing competition rolls around.

At the east side of Waikīkī, beyond the crush of the hotels, retail stores and shoppers, and sunbathers, is the 170 acre **Kapiʻolani Park**. Wide grassy expanses are rimmed by shade and coconut trees, providing an open expanse for picnics, kite flying, jogging, several community activities, and an unobstructed view of Diamond Head Crater. The park provides a suburban setting for several attractions.

Beach Access

By law, all beaches are public. Beach access signs can be seen intermittently along shoreline drives to mark spots that are obscured by residential and commercial properties. Those owners are required to provide a right of way, yet in real life, it doesn't happen that way, with some of the nicest beach property owned by private resorts. To avoid embarrassing and mood breaking confrontations, just ask local shops on each island where the best spots are to use the beach. All of them have several readily accessible beaches that are little used, and many of the locals know how to find them.

The **Honolulu Zoo** is a modest facility spread about 42 acres at the park's west end. Over 300 species of animals are displayed, as well as a small petting zoo for the children. Hours are daily from 8:30 a.m. to 4:30 p.m., and Wednesday evenings during the summer months. For more information call 923-7723; admission is charged.

Though there are numerous floor shows throughout the islands featuring performers in local costume and dance, most all of them are at night, and next to impossible to light properly for photographs. Since 1937 Kodak Corporation has met that need by sponsoring a Polynesian program, in an outdoor setting, during the daylight hours. This hour-long demonstration is free and open to the public Tuesdays through Thursdays, at 10 a.m., at the Waikīkī Shell across from the Honolulu Zoo. Featuring performers in Hawaiian and Polynesian garb, the **Kodak Show** is as much entertainment as a photo opportunity. Guests are allowed to come onto the field for close-ups during a break in the show, and later invited to participate in an impromptu hula lesson. For more information call (808) 833-1661.

On the ocean side of Kalakaua Avenue is the Waikīkī Aquarium featured in Chapter 3.

Honolulu

Hawai'i boasts one of the most prestigious institutions in the Pacific arena for its study of Hawaiian and other Pacific Island cultures. Three hundred thousand tourists and residents visit the **Bernice Pauahi Bishop Museum and Planetarium** every year. Built in 1890 by Honolulu businessman Charles Reed Bishop to honor his wife, the facility has distinguished itself in botany, zoology, entomology, and publishing, as well as having amassed one of the most extensive collections of artifacts from throughout the South Pacific and Hawai'i. Bishop's wife was the last descendant of King Kamehameha before the Hawaiian Islands were annexed into the United States. The state has honored the Bishop Museum, designating it the official Hawai'i State Museum of Natural and Cultural History. Several buildings in the complex are used for public displays, research facilities, and storage and preservation of the collections. One of the highlights of their collections is displayed in the three story main gallery. Capes, headdresses and leis were made from the feathers of island birds which were captured and plucked live to afford the ruling *ali'i* this finery. An ancient Hawaiian house made of *pili* grass stands under the 50 foot long skeleton of a sperm whale. The most recent addition is the Harold Kainalu Long Castle Memorial Building, which has essentially doubled the museum's display and collections area. A high-tech planetarium, rotating museum displays sponsored by the Smithsonian, school programs, on- and off-island field trips, and craft demonstrations, delight first time visitors, and keep the residents returning. The Archives Department includes over 750,000 photographs, covering 150 years of Hawai'i's history, the Entomology Department has amassed the third largest insect collection in the United States, and the Marine Research Department has one very special prize. *(See page 179)*

The Bishop Museum is spread about an 11 acre tract at 1525 Bernice Street. Hours are from 9 a.m. to 5 p.m. daily, and admission is charged. (808) 847-8200

The everyday sights, smells, flavors, and culture of the Orient come to life in Honolulu's **Chinatown**. The culture is expressed in its architecture; everything else in its market place. The area is bordered by King, Nu'uanu, and Beretania Streets, and the Nu'uanu stream. Tours are available through the Chinese Chamber of Commerce (808) 533-3181, and the Hawai'i Heritage Center (808) 521-2749. Bring a camera, but respect the privacy of the shoppers and the vendors.

At the time of its construction in 1926, the 10-story **Aloha Tower** was the tallest structure in the islands, but it has since been dwarfed by the surrounding high-rises. It now stands as a monument to a bygone era, and a reminder of the renovation promised the Honolulu waterfront. Once used as the harbor control tower, it now offers a clear view of the Honolulu Harbor from its 10th floor observatory (8:00 a.m. to 9:00 p.m.). The tower looks down upon the **Hawai'i Maritime Center** and the adjacent *Falls of Clyde* (featured in Chapter 3). Every December, recreational and world class runners from around the world congregate in the wee morning hours in front of the Aloha Tower, to compete in the annual **Honolulu Marathon** for $40,000 in prize money, including $10,000 each to the top male and female finisher. There are typically over 10,000 participants, from the weekend joggers to world class athletes, in ages ranging from seven to 83. Individuals, runners' clubs, military units, oriental tour groups, and others in outrageous costumes join in for a morning of fun and grueling accomplishment. The community comes out in force to support the runners and cheer them on throughout the course and at the finish line at Kapi'olani Park.

Built for King Kalākaua and his wife Queen Kapi'olani in 1882, the **'Iolani Palace** was only used for 10 years until the monarchy was deposed in revolution. The building became the seat of the provisional government, and later the legislature, where it remained in that capacity, until the State Capitol Building was completed in 1969. Called the "crown jewel" of Hawai'i's historical buildings, the 'Iolani Palace is the only royal palace in the United States. Forty five minute guided tours are a must, and offered every Wednesday through Saturday, 9:00 a.m. to 2:15 p.m. Much memo-

Still ruled by a monarchy, Hawai'i's seat of government moved from Lahaina, Maui in 1845, to Honolulu, which, in turn, became the official capitol in 1850. The royal family was very enamored with the British, who with France and the United States, were actively pursuing an expansionist policy in the Pacific. England's own monarchy intrigued Hawai'i's counterparts, greatly influenced their dress, architecture, and landscaping, and is still evident in the state flag of Hawai'i, which is partly comprised of the Union Jack. However, the missionary and business interests in the islands, convinced the reigning king (Kamehameha IV) to maintain close ties with the United States, eventually leading to the overthrow of the monarchy by a coalition representing the sugar conglomerates. A provisional government was established in 1893, and on August 12, 1898 the islands were annexed as a territory of the United States. In 1919, under continued pressure from island businessmen, the first bill for statehood was introduced to the 65th Congress, by Prince Kūhiō, a delegate to Congress from Hawai'i. It died in committee, along with the subsequent resolutions. The issue was put on hold during World War II, and resumed immediately afterwards. Delegates from Hawai'i continued to exert intense pressure on Congress through the Hawai'i Statehood Commission; a state constitution was drafted, and elections were conducted in Hawai'i to choose governing officials and representatives to Congress. With the acceptance of the Territory of Alaska as the first non-contiguous state in the Union, the final argument was eliminated, and on August 21, 1959, after waiting longer than any other territory for admission to the Union, the proclamation was signed by President Dwight D. Eisenhower, and Hawai'i became our country's 50th - the "Aloha State".

rabilia is displayed in the Victorian setting. Contact (808) 523-0141. Admission is charged.

The first monarch of the islands is memorialized in the **Statue of King Kamehameha I**. It stands facing the palace, across the street, in front of Ali'iolani Hale. June 11th is set aside annually to honor the king, with a parade, and for a few days following, the statue is adorned with flower leis reaching 30 feet. This is a replica of the original commission, which was lost at sea off the Falkland Islands enroute from Paris. Subsequent salvage operations recovered the original, that now stands near Kamehameha's birthplace on the "Big Island" of Hawai'i.

The importance of the missionaries' role in shaping the destiny of the Hawaiian islands could only be understated here, and it only seems fitting that a tangible part of their lives would remain with us today. The buildings that comprise the **Mission Houses Museum**, at 553 South King Street, are the originals that were prefabricated and shipped from Boston, then served the 19th century mission leaders in their calling. The complex is managed by an organization whose membership are descendants of those missionaries, the Hawaiian Missions Children's Society (808) 531-0481. Furnished in period pieces, several of the museum's artifacts were owned and related directly to the mission's work. Hours are from 9:00 a.m. to 4:00 p.m., and admission is charged.

Megamouth

One of the newest and most interesting specimens in the icthyology collections department of the Bishop Museum was, until 1976, never known to have existed. On November 15 of that year, the AFB-14, a U.S. Navy research vessel from the Naval Ocean Systems Center, in Kaneʻohe, Oʻahu, was on station 25 miles northeast of Kahuku Point, Oʻahu. The water depth was 15,000 feet, and in order to remain stationary in the shifting winds and currents, two parachutes were deployed at 545 feet as sea anchors. Upon completion, as the chutes were being hoisted on deck, one had a most unusual shark entangled in the drag line, with a bulbous head, a four foot wide mouth, and rubbery lips. With difficulty, the 14.6 foot long shark was boarded. Upon returning to the harbor, they called in Dr. Leighton Taylor from the Waikiki Aquarium. It was immediately ascertained that this shark was an altogether new discovery. When transfer of the carcass was to take place by hoist, the tail fin snapped off and its body plummeted into the harbor. After a team of divers retrieved the shark, it was preserved, studied, then remanded to the custody of the Bishop Museum.

*The newly discovered "Megamouth" (*Megachasma pelagios*), a deep water filtration feeder, is a 14.6 foot long shark, whose discovery generated a great deal of excitement in the scientific community (Official US Navy photo courtesy of the Naval Ocean Systems Center © 1976)*

Some other facts were determined about this phenomenon, now known as "Megamouth". The new shark has been classified as *Megachasma pelagios* meaning large, yawning hole (or open mouth) of the open sea. It weighed 1,653 pounds and was an adult male. It is believed the females can grow to 30% larger by the characteristics of other shark species. The mouth contained 236 rows of teeth and its stomach contents revealed a deep water species of shrimp. It is also believed the shark has bioluminescent tissue in its lips to help attract prey at the dark abyssal depths, a huge tongue, and gill rakers to help filter plankton. Megamouth is only the third known species of sharks that is a filter feeder; the other two are the basking shark and the whale shark, both surface feeders. Rubbery fins and flabby musculature leads to the belief that the discovery is a slow, weak swimmer.

Exactly eight years after the first discovery, a second one was caught in a gill net five miles east of Avalon, California. Also a male, this 14.7 foot long specimen was snagged at 125 feet by the commercial vessel *Helga*. Its discovery extended the known range of the shark from Hawaiʻi to California, and is now on display at the Los Angeles County Museum of Natural History. In August of 1988, a third male specimen, 16 feet long, was discovered swimming feebly in the surf off Perth, Australia. The range of distribution now seems limitless, but their numbers remain unknown. Two of the biggest questions arising from the discovery of Megamouth are: How much is being inadvertently caught and discarded as junk fish that no one ever knows about? And, what else is still out there that is yet to be discovered?

Across the street from the Mission Houses, at the corner of King and Punchbowl Street is the coral block and wood **Kawaiaha'o Church**, built in 1842 under the patronage of King Kamehameha III. The church served as the site of religious as well as state ceremonies, and was the church home to some of the later royals until the fall of the kingdom.

Vistas

From the Pali Highway exit of the H-1 freeway, travel north four and a half miles to the **Nu'uanu Pali Lookout**. The turnoff leads through a canopied rain forest to a gap in the mountain range. [Note: If you are driving a convertible, either keep the top up, or be prepared to raise it quickly. The same rains that nurture the forest will not discriminate when it's watering time.] The site has some historical significance as scene of the 1795 Battle of Nu'uanu. Kalanikupule's defending forces were driven up the valley to the *pali* by Kamehameha's followers. Rather than face death at the hands of the victorious invaders, several chose to jump. It was the final battle that led Hawai'i on the road to integrating with the world around it. There are two reasons for coming here: the view of the windward side of the island is rated as one of the best vistas in the state, and the strong trades sweep up the sheer windward face of the mountains, and venturi through the pass. Anything worn and not secure can be swept away in the gale.

The Courts of the Missing display the names of 28,745 men missing in action from World War II.

Nearby, the **National Memorial Cemetery of the Pacific at Punchbowl** is a poignant reminder of the realities of war. The inside crater of an extinct volcano is the final setting for 30,000 graves dating from World War I through the Vietnam War. At its entrance, the registrations office has an exhibit honoring and citing the Medal of Honor internees. At the opposite side of the grounds is a 30 foot statue of Columbia that represents a mother overlooking her lost children - a roll call of 28,745 servicemen missing in action. Their names are etched in stone, listed in the "Courts of the Missing". The famed correspondent Ernie Pyle is buried here, as well as the Challenger Astronaut Elison Onizuka, a native of Hawai'i. A platform overlooks Honolulu, and is usually loaded with tour buses, limousines, and rental cars at O'ahu's number one tourist attraction.

The statue of Columbia figureheads the memorial, representing a mother overlooking her lost children.

The National Memorial Cemetery of the Pacific at Punchbowl is a poignant reminder of the realities of war.

From the base of the drive leading out of the cemetery, continue straight onto **Tantalus Drive**. This starts a trek through eucalyptus and banyan trees, beautiful homes and breathtaking scenery. The drive eventually turns into Round Top, then goes by **Puʻu ʻUalakaʻa Park**, a state wayside offering another vista of the city of Honolulu and Waikīkī. The drive eventually stops on Makiki and leads back into the city.

Diamond Head Crater is probably the most well known natural landmark in the state of Hawaiʻi. It looms above Kapiʻolani Park, and the high rise hotels of Waikīkī Beach. A drive to the inside of the crater parks visitors next to a trail, which leads to the summit, and a panorama of Honolulu, Waikīkī Beach, and the distant Pearl Harbor. On the other side is an equally dramatic view of Koko Head and the Hawaiʻi Kai development. The climb is seven tenths of a mile one way, and not meant for the faint of heart. There are many steps and a couple of long dark tunnels, so bring a flashlight. Hours are from 6:00 a.m. to 6:00 p.m. Other crater hikes include Koko Head and Koko Crater.

The summit of Diamond Head Crater offers a stunning panorama of Waikīkī, Honolulu and a distant Pearl Harbor. Kapi'olani Park is in the foreground of the shot.

South Shore

Starting at Diamond Head Crater, and traveling east on Kalaniana'ole Highway, takes you first through several residential areas, and the Hawai'i Kai development along Maunalua Bay, then to several attractions featured in other chapters. First to Hanauma Bay, 12 miles from Waikīkī, then to Hālona Blowhole, both featured in Chapter 5.

O'ahu Goes To The Movies

Though many think of Kaua'i when the islands' film industry is mentioned, O'ahu has provided the backdrop for several movies, television miniseries and popular shows. Because of Hawai'i's pivotal role in the Pacific Theater of World War II, several films have related to that era, including: *From Here To Eternity*, *Tora,Tora,Tora*, and *In Harm's Way* to mention a few. The movie, *Hawai'i* was filmed here, and O'ahu is the home of the old *Hawai'i Five–0* series ("Book 'em, Dan–O"), and Tom Selleck's *Magnum P.I.*

Get your camera ready and be prepared to pull over at the many roadside stops. The scenery features unusual lava formations weathered in striated patterns along the coastline. The next stop is **Sandy Beach**, a favorite spot for body surfing. Continuing around Makapu'u Point leads to **Sea Life Park**, featured in Chapter 3. The balance of the highlights will be listed traveling counterclockwise around O'ahu.

Windward Side

There are a couple of attractions near Kāne'ohe that are off the beaten path, and thus overlooked by mainstream tourists. **Ho'omaluhia** is a 400 acre natural preserve that features educational programs dealing with the flora and fauna of the area, and traditional craft demonstrations. A visitors center has information about the facility and applicable permits. From Kamehameha Highway turn onto Luluku Road between Kāne'ohe and Kailua. Hours are from 9:00 a.m. to 3:00 p.m. daily.

Valley of the Temples Memorial Park is the pastoral setting for the **Byodo-In Temple**, a replica of a 900 year old Japanese temple. Offset by a two acre reflecting pool, the structure is a photographer's delight. Located off Kahekili Highway, hours are daily from 8:30 a.m. to 4:00 p.m., and admission is charged.

The contemplative setting of the Byodo-In Temple reflects the influence of the ancient Orient in Hawai'i

Continue northwest on Kamehameha Highway to **Sacred Falls Park**, a mile south of Hau'ula. A 2.2 mile hike leads up the Kaluanui Stream to an 80 foot waterfall, in the lush tropical foliage of the valley. Despite the fact that this is one of the island's most popular trails, check the *mauka* weather conditions. Heavy rainfalls can lead to treacherous conditions from falling rocks and flash flooding.

Waimea Coast

Sunset Beach is home to thunderous winter breakers that attract surfing enthusiasts from around the world. Part of the renowned **Banzai Pipeline**, the beaches from Sunset to Hale'iwa are safe, on calm days during the summer, but can be deadly to the inexperienced during the winter months. When the waves are at their peak, the shoreline drives, and any other available parking spot, are crowded with the curious watching to see attempts at riding these behemoths.

Pūpūkea Beach County Park is the site of Shark's Cove, O'ahu's second most popular dive spot. The beach park is enjoyable before or after the dive, or as a destination in its own right.

The northwestern extreme of O'ahu is known as Ka'ena Point, and is not accessible by standard vehicles. Do not attempt to take a rental car to the point with the feeling that if you break down, it isn't your vehicle. The rental companies warn visitors not to try, and if the vehicle gets stuck, or breaks down, the resultant charges can be excessive.

Double back along Farrington Highway to cross the center of O'ahu towards Pearl City. The drive leads through fields of sugar cane and pineapple. Dole Corporation has set up a pavilion for tasting, shopping, and taking a close look at the succulent plants in the fields. Continuing south, the drive leads over the hills of Aiea, looking down upon Pearl Harbor. It was the same path the Japanese zeros took on their initial approach.

The smouldering superstructure of the mortally wounded Arizona *remains the most vivid image of the Japanese attack on Pearl Harbor. (US Navy Photo - Hawaii State Archives - Admiral Furlong Collection)*

December 7th, 1941

In the early morning hours of that fateful Sunday morning, a 33 ship task force from Japan had arrived, undetected, at a point 200 miles north of Oʻahu. A pair of incidents should have tipped the Americans that something unusual was on the horizon. At 3:45 a.m., the minesweeper *Condor* was patrolling outside the entrance to Pearl Harbor, when they sighted what they believed was the periscope of a submarine, and called in the destroyer *Ward* to investigate. For less than three hours the ship had no success, until the sub's conning tower was exposed by the early morning daylight. The destroyer sunk the submarine, and relayed a message to headquarters of the action. At 6:00 a.m., the six Japanese carriers turned into the wind and launched the first wave of 183 planes (torpedo, dive and horizontal bombers, and fighters). A couple of minutes past 7:00 a.m., a large mass of air targets registered on the primitive Army radar scope set up near Kahuku Point, on the opposite side of Oʻahu. The contacts were plotted, and eventually reported to Fort Shafter, but dismissed by the duty officer as either aircraft maneuvers from the U. S. carriers, or an incoming flight of B-17's due in from San Diego that morning. At 7:15 a.m., the second wave of 167 planes (horizontal and dive bombers and fighters) took off from the Japanese carriers. The attack on the U.S. Pacific Fleet at Pearl Harbor commenced at 7:55 a.m., as the radioman for the Japanese Attack Group Commander signaled the task force that the surprise attack had successfully begun - *"Tora! Tora! Tora!*...(Tiger! Tiger! Tiger!)"

The grounded aircraft were to be destroyed first to prevent a counter attack or defense, so, simultaneous attacks were committed at other strategic military bases on Oʻahu: Hickham Army Air Field, Ford Island Naval Air Station, Schofield Barracks, the Naval Air Station at Kāneʻohe, Wheeler Field, and smaller fields at ʻEwa and Bellows.

More than 90 ships were at anchorage in the harbor that morning, but the primary targets were the eight battleships at their moorings that completely surrounded Ford Island, in the middle of the harbor, called "Battleship Row". In the first five minutes the *Utah*, then used as a target vessel, had taken two torpedo hits, and within 12 minutes had bellied up, a complete loss.

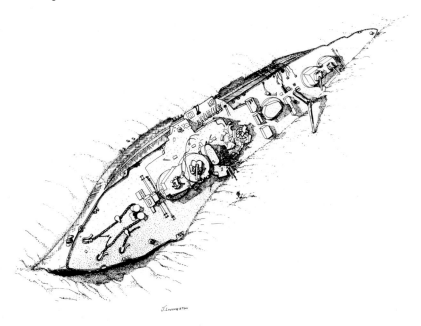

The remains of the USS Utah. *(Illustration by Jerry Livingston - courtesy USS Arizona Memorial National Parks Service)*

The *Oklahoma* was hit by three successive torpedoes, and capsized to the point where her masts hit the mud, then she took two more hits. As the men tried to escape the ship they were strafed, and the death toll climbed to 415 from that ship alone. Moored directly in front of the *Arizona*, the *Nevada* was the only battleship to get underway during the attack, despite suffering a torpedo hit in the bow section. For fear of sinking at the entrance, and blocking the balance of the fleet in the harbor, the ship was ordered to beach herself, and did so on the shallow hard sand bottom at Waipiʻo Point. The *Arizona* took five torpedoes in her port side. An armor piercing bomb penetrated to the powder magazine, that, in turn, set off a chain of explosions, including the main forward battery magazine. The concussion from the explosion forced the two gun turrets and the two conning towers to drop twenty feet below their normal positions. The *Arizona* was down in less than nine minutes, taking 80% of the ship's complement of men with her.

The wreck of the USS Arizona *from the bow perspective (Illustration by Jerry Livingston - courtesy* USS Arizona *Memorial National Parks Service)*

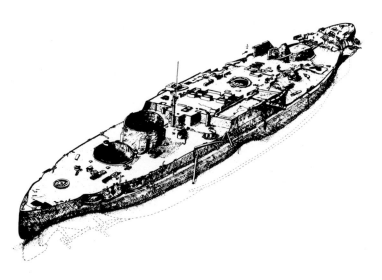

The wreck of the USS Arizona *from the stern perspective (Illustration by Jerry Livingston - courtesy* USS Arizona *Memorial National Parks Service)*

Total time of the attack was one hour and fifty minutes, and by 1:00 p.m. it was all over. With all but 29 of the attacking planes retrieved, the task force changed course and departed. In their wake, they left 2,403 Americans killed, 1,178 wounded, 188 aircraft destroyed, and 18 ships damaged. Despite the success of the surprise attack by the Japanese, the toll was not a fatal blow to the American Pacific Fleet. The Japanese goal was to immobilize the fleet for at least six months. The American aircraft carriers were out to sea on maneuvers, and played no part in the action; the fuel depots and shore facilities were either untouched or damaged slightly, and only three of the ships were damaged too badly to eventually return to service. The *Oklahoma* was floated and sold for scrap, only to sink at sea while being towed back to the West Coast. The *Utah* and the *Arizona* remain where they settled - permanent reminders of a date that was to be etched into the soul of humanity.

The #1 gun turret on the USS Arizona *(photo courtesy* USS Arizona *Memorial National Parks Service)*

Today, the solitary white platform that straddles, but does not touch, the rusted hull of the *USS Arizona* stands out against the green waters of the harbor and the backdrop of Ford Island. A marble plaque is carved with the names of the 1,177 sailors and marines that died in the surprise attack - 1,102 of whom are entombed in the wreckage below, and stands as a sad reminder of a bloodier era.

The shuttle boats transport visitors to the Arizona *Memorial which straddles, but does not touch the wreckage below.*

Because much of the *Arizona's* superstructure had been dismantled and cut away during the war, many questions remained unanswered about the condition of the remaining hull that still served as a tomb for so many men who lost their lives that December 7th. In 1983, the Submerged Cultural Resources Unit was tasked with mapping and photographing the remains of the *USS Arizona*. With the assistance of the U.S. Navy's Mobile Diving and Salvage Unit One, the *Arizona* Memorial Association, and the National Park Service staff, the SCRU conducted a 10-day on site assessment of the wreck. This led to the 1984 mapping survey, over a three week period, and many discoveries, including the No. 1 gun turret, believed to have already been salvaged, but found intact, as well as a large number of unexploded five inch shells directly beneath the memorial structure. They were immediately removed by the Navy Explosive Ordinance Disposal team.

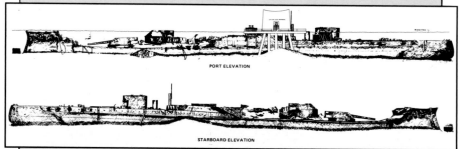

Portside and starboard profile of the USS Arizona *with the placement of the memorial (Illustration by Jerry Livingston - courtesy* USS Arizona *Memorial National Parks Service)*

New tasks emerged from the preliminary studies: to construct a detailed model of the ship in its present condition, to conduct more detailed mapping of the structure, to determine the condition of the hull itself, and survey the wreckage of the *USS Utah*, on the opposite side of Ford Island. It is the only other ship still in the harbor from the attack, and still entombs 55 men.

A two part rendition of the USS Utah *(Illustration by Jerry Livingston - courtesy* USS Arizona *Memorial National Parks Service)*

Considering the expanse of its scope, the entire operation went surprisingly smoothly. In 1986, the biofouling/corrosion study of the *Arizona* was conducted, the survey was completed in more detail, and in 1987, the mapping of the *Utah* was accomplished.

The last phase of the operation spread throughout the harbor to locate any sunken aircraft, and one of the Japanese midget submarines believed to be sunk within the 1000+ foot deep defensive perimeter outside the mouth of Pearl Harbor.

Though diving the wrecks of the *Arizona* and the *Utah* are not possible for the general public, the results of the teams' exhaustive surveys have produced fascinating renditions of the wrecks, published within a comprehensive report on their findings. The 192 page book is a well illustrated, historical documentation of the attack, and subsequent salvage operations, and a scientific study of the wrecks as they lay today. "The Submerged Cultural Resources Study: USS Arizona Memorial and Pearl Harbor National Historic Landmark", by Daniel J. Lenihan, Editor © 1989 is available by writing the Arizona Memorial Museum Association, #1 Arizona Memorial Place, Honolulu, HI 96818. The price for the book is $6.95 plus $3.40 for first class postage and handling.

Regular shuttle boats are run to the shrine from the **Arizona Memorial Visitor Center**. The center's museum has two models of the ship, one above water, and the other in its present condition below. The second most popular tourist destination in the state, you can expect a long wait to get to the memorial, but it is well worth the time. Administered by the U.S Department of Parks and Recreation, the facility has an interesting museum of artifacts, and stories of the event, and regular showings of "Day of Infamy, December 7, 1941." There is a gift shop with periodic literature, and admission is free. Hours are daily from 7:30 a.m. to 5:00 p.m. Children must be at least 45 inches tall, and no bare feet or swimming attire are allowed. Call (808) 422-0561 for information.

Another perspective of the harbor is by way of a cruise around Ford Island. It is a relaxing half-day round-trip excursion from the Kewalo Basin (Fisherman's Wharf) in Honolulu. A very informative narration starts before entering the harbor, and continues throughout the tour timed to point out the highlights as they are being passed, in perspective to the attack. Ford Island is circumnavigated in a clockwise direction, opening up sights otherwise inaccessible to the public, including a close up view of the above water remains and memorial to the *USS Utah*. Paradise Cruise Limited afforded me the opportunity to take their cruise aboard the *Pearl Kai II*. Trips leave twice daily; at 9:15 a.m. to noon, and 1:15 p.m. to 4:00 p.m. Call (808) 536-3641 for information and reservations.

A view of the USS Utah Memorial as seen from one of the tour boats that circumnavigate Ford Island.

From the parking lot of the visitor's center, several signs lead to the adjacent **Bowfin Park**. A fully restored World War II submarine, the *USS Bowfin*, is on display, and open to adults and children over six years of age. The boat is in immaculate condition, and best seen with the help of an audio tour guide. The newest facility is the **Pacific Submarine Museum**, opened in 1988, that houses a superb collection of artifacts, stories, and citations from the war era, and a tribute to the men and evolution of the submarine from its inception, through the modern era. Adults and children of all ages are allowed into the museum which is administered by the non-profit Pacific Fleet Submarine Memorial Association. Hours are daily from 8:00 a.m. to 4:30 p.m. Admission is charged. Contact (808) 423-1341.

The interior of the Pacific Submarine Museum houses a superb collection of artifacts, citations and other memorabilia as a tribute to the men who helped develop, fight in, and die for the "Silent Service". (Photo Dan Murray © 1989. All Rights Reserved. Courtesy Pacific Fleet Submarine Memorial Association)

Chapter 10

The Four Island County of Maui

Moloka'i

Lana'i

Maui

Kaho'olawe

Second largest of the Hawaiian Islands, Maui is actually two islands in one. Two shield volcanoes, connected by converging lava flows, combined to form a fertile, low lying valley between the two. Visitors enroute to the major tourism centers travel between expanses of sugar cane and pineapple, the island's main agricultural products.

Overview: Maui

Nickname .... The "Valley Isle"
Area .... 729 square miles
Coastline .... 120 miles
Highest peak .... Haleakalā - 10,023 feet
Population .... 94,700 in county (12/31/89 estimate)
County seat .... Wailuku
Airports   **Distance to Honolulu:**
 Kahalui .... 101 miles
Kapalua/West Maui .... 81 miles
Agriculture .... cattle
                                  flowers
                                  macadamia nuts
                                  Maui potato chips
                                  Maui onions
                                  pineapple
                                  sugar cane

West Maui

Intricately carved by time and streams, the verdant West Maui Mountains stand as a breathtaking backdrop to the historic village of **Lahaina**. This onetime capital of the islands, whaling port, and fleet anchorage, has not lost touch with its origins, meticulously maintaining the 19th century flavor through building preservation and development.

A survivor of that era is the **Old Indian Banyon Tree** planted on April 24th, 1873. It has grown to two thirds of an acre and a quarter of a mile in circumference. The tree is the congregating place for weary shoppers, struggling artists, boisterous mynah birds and zealous street preachers. It shades the Old Lahaina Courthouse, built in 1859 and is across the street from the Pioneer Inn. The inn has been a fixture on the Lahaina waterfront since 1901 and faces the newly renovated harbor facilities and the *Carthaginian*.

After appearing in the movies, *Hawai'i* and *The Hawaiians*, this 93 foot square rigged bark now serves as a floating whaling museum - a throwback to a lustier, uninhibited era.

The Carthaginian *now serves as floating whaling museum against the backdrop of Front Street in historic Lahaina.*

The *Richmond*

Several years ago, on a vacation to New Bedford, Massachusettes, I happened upon a logbook of the whaling bark *Richmond* in the Melville Room of the city's public library. Log books were kept as a record of the ship's daily position, the weather, ship's damage, the handling of the vessel, behavior of the crew and the results of their hunt. This particular log was intriguing for a number of reasons. It was a first-hand account of the incidents, successes, rigors and tedium of their two and a half year voyage. They made several stops in the Hawaiian Islands during that time, but most of all, it was richly illustrated with simple drawings depicting the day to day operations of the journey.

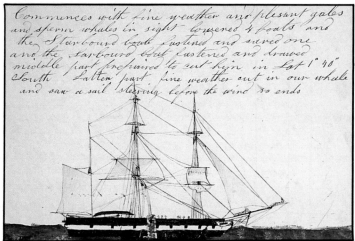

Simple pen and ink drawings in the log of the Richmond *richly illustrate the day to day adventures aboard the 19th century whaling brig. The February 23, 1845 entry reads,* "Commences with fine weather and pleasant gales and sperm whales in sight lowered 4 boats and the Starboard boat fastened and saved one and the Larboard boat fastened and drawed middle part prepared to cut him in Lat. 1° 40" South. Latter part fine weather cut in our whale and saw a sail steering before the wind so ends."

Page after page of the log has simple pen and ink sketches and more elaborate color drawings of ships encountered, islands passed, and the processes of killing and butchering a whale through the eyes of the ship's cooper, Charles F. Morton. With 30 men and officers, they set sail from Provincetown, Rhode Island on October 20th, 1844. It took five months before they first reached the Sandwich Islands (Hawai'i):

"Bark Richmond at Mowee (sic Maui)... Wednesday 25th (March) - Commences with light winds and calms. Lowered our boats and towed in towards the harbour... Came to an anchor about 11 P.M. and the other broke out some casks and carried them ashore for water. . ."

As was true of all vessels visiting Hawai'i, it was hard keeping the men at their posts :

"Monday 31st - Commences with pleasant weather. The watch onshore. Latter part all hands onboard. Six men having left the ship on French liberty (AWOL). Stowed down some water."

To fill the missing manpower needs, locals were often recruited, and wrongdoers swiftly and brutally dealt with:

"Friday 4th (April) - Commences with strong trades lying at Mowee. Latter part got under weigh (sic) and the boat went ashore and returned again about 11 P.M. When we went to sea after obtaining four of our lost men and seeing one of them take one dozen of lashes. We also shipped two natives."

They set sail for the Kamchatka Peninsula off Russia on a dangerous and successful journey:

"Friday 30th (May) - Commences with fine weather and a pleasant breeze… saw two Wright (sic) whales and lowered four boats and the starboard struck one and saved him. The bow boat got capsized and stove. We took along the stoven boat and got out a new one and then took the whale along side, tied him up got supper…Latter part commence cutting."

"Tuesday 10th (June) - Commences with fine weather and a pleasant breeze from the Southeast…Saw whales and lowered but did not fasten at 7 o'clock saw a whale and the starboard boat struck him and he returned the compliment by taking the head of his boat the waist boat picked up the crew and the other two boats fastened to the whale and saved him and took him alongside… Latter part… cut in our whale and saw others and lowered two boats but did not fasten."

Not all of their kills were successful:

"Tuesday 17th - Commences with fine weather and quite clear. Made sail and maned the mastheads and saw whales and the starboard boat struck one and killed him and it shut in thick again (fog) and the ship got to fin to the leeward of him and hauling him with a long line he sunk as usual a sail in sight. Latter part saw whales and the starboard boat fastened to one but his line stranded and fastened with another iron and it drowned and he lost him so ends…"

The Richmond made several returns to the islands during its voyage including stops at Byron's Bay (Hilo), Honolulu, Kaua'i, and Lahaina. It was a commercial success - 110 barrels of sperm oil, 3200 barrels of whale oil, and 36,654 pounds of bone, but not without a toll:

"Thursday 12th (March 1846) - Commences with fine weather… All hands employed mending sails and making spun yarn … Commenced breaking out the blubber room in order to break out some oil to get at a cask that was leaking. After breakfast starboard watch refused to come out on deck until they had a watch below which the Captain (Edward A. Swift) refused to give them until his work was done and after some words on the subject he would allow them five minutes to come on deck and if they did not come within that time then he should bar down the hatches and smoke them out. They not coming within, he closed the forecastle scuttle and locked it. Commenced smoking ship by putting a lot of charcoal and brimstone in the deckpot in the forehold. When he first made the fire he called his 3rd mate, two boat steerers, cooper and one foremast hand to witness that he was going to smoke them because they refused to come on deck or refusedduty. Then put on the hatches and pasted paper over all the joints. Someone remarked that he might suffocate them. When he said they might all go to hell together and after waiting about two hours took off the forehatches and found they had gone through into the forehold and put out the fire by throwing on a barrel of pickels. The captain then ordered four or five muskets to be loaded with shot and one or two of them with a ball and called for an axe to knock down the bulkhead of the forecastle when they agreed to come on deck. He accordingly opened the scuttle one man coming up at a time. Then he put five of them in irons and the others went to their duty. He then took three of the men out of irons and seized them up in the rigging and flogged them on the bare back. Madison (green hand) with ten lashes, he said for being a ringleader and spokesman. Benish Austin (seaman) six lashes for the same alleged crime. John Ballou (seaman) six for the same and six for insolence to his officers and afterwards he read the law to them as given the ship master's assistant. The other two were then let out of irons and they all returned to duty. Stowed off the blubber room. So ends this day."

During their last leg home, the ship hove the tryworks (used to boil down the whale blubber to oil) overboard, signaling the killing was completed and the voyage soon to end. The cooper summarized his feelings in one telltale entry:

"Thursday April 1st (1847) - Commences a real screamer from the S.W. with thunder and lightning, rain and saltwater flying in all shapes. Who would not sell a farm to go to the sea . . ."

Their journey was completed six days later - So Ends.

Lahaina is a registered National Historic Landmark. **Front Street** adds to its scenic waterfront with 19th century structures still in use, only now in an unbroken line of oceanfront art galleries, gift shops, convenience stores, boutiques, restaurants, booking desks, and a number of dive shops.

Traffic congestion and parking problems in and around Lahaina are symptomatic of the growing pains the entire island is going through. The boom of tourism has hit in force with a major airport under construction, two super resort hotels in the works, and a large shopping center - and these are just the high profile projects. Several smaller scaled hotels, condominiums, and housing projects add on to the already overtaxed infrastructure. The inconveniences are real, and alienating, but they are temporary, and well worth dealing with, when considering everything this island has to offer.

Continuing less than a half mile past all of the shops is the **Jodo Mission** with the largest Buddha outside of Asia.

The Jodo Mission adjacent to the Māla Wharf, just north of the commercial center of Lahaina.

The adjacent MālaWharf boasts the remains of a pier where pre-1940 sailors debarked their vessels for liberty…

What Might Have Been

Most people remember December 7th, 1941 as the date the Japanese bombed Pearl Harbor. What many do not know was how close that attack came to being on Lahaina. Prior to 1941, the Lahaina roadstead served as home to the U.S. Pacific Fleet. Māla Wharf was the main dock for sailors coming into town on liberty, and the waters in front of what is now the resort area at Kāʻanapali were anchorage for the Navy's seaplanes.

Battle Fleet at Lahaina Roads (photo credit U. S. National Archives)

The Japanese hoped that the ships would still be at Lahaina when they were to execute their surprise attack. They would have virtually unlimited aerial maneuverability. They would not have to alter the standard torpedo technology for the shallow waters at Pearl Harbor, and once the ships were sunk, they would be too deep to salvage. However, the fleet did move to Pearl in 1940, and the attack was planned accordingly.

Despite the constant flow of intelligence back to Japan, assuring High Command the fleet had not moved back to Lahaina, no chances were taken. The day before the attack, Japanese submarines I-71, 72 and 73 patrolled the waters surrounding Maui, with I-71 sending back the report that no ships were in the area. The evening before the attack, all efforts focused on Pearl Harbor. However, up to the moment of the assault, hoping against hope, a seaplane was launched from the Japanese heavy cruiser *Tone*, to fly a last reconnaissance mission over Lahaina. The report was negative and Pearl Harbor bore the full fury of the attack.

Today, the dilapidated pier at Māla is all that remains of that bygone era. Small fishing, watersport and dive charter boats launch from Māla Wharf to ply the inter-island waters between Maui, Lānaʻi, and Molokaʻi. The demand for **big game fishing** charters is one of the strongest recreational businesses in Hawaiʻi. The allure of catching and battling that "big one" draws the serious, and not so serious from around the world. Boats can be chartered for half or full day bill fishing or bottom fishing trips. Prices vary with the size of the boat, and the rule of thumb is the crew keeps the catch unless other arrangements have been made. Every year the Lahaina Jackpot tournament offers prizes up to $25,000 for the largest fish caught over a four day stretch.

A couple of miles north of Lahaina is the **Kāʻanapali Beach Resort**. An outcropping of high-rise condominiums, resort complexes and hotels, has risen along the wide sandy beaches. The Whaler's Village shopping center is located amid the resort, and is highlighted by the **Whaler's Village Museum**, a small whaling display and gift shop. No admission fees are charged. Further north are the tourist centers at Napili and Kapalua. Both Kapalua and Kāʻanapali are noted for their beautiful, and busy golf courses.

South Maui

Kīhei and Wailea are communities that sit in the rain shadow of the dormant Haleakalā. They are both experiencing rapid development, and Wailea, already the location of some of the nicest hotels in the state, will be home to two new super resorts, now under construction. Touted as the largest marine art exhibition in the world, the **Maui Marine Art Expo** is held at the Maui Inter-Continental Wailea and at the Lahaina Center every February through March. Well known marine artists in all mediums, display and sell their works in the Inter-Continental hotel lobby, with part of the proceeds going to the Cousteau Society. There is quite often a kickoff presentation to meet the artists, with a keynote presentation by local dignitaries, and on occasion, Jean-Michel Cousteau.

Central Valley

Looking back on Maui from a transiting boat can be a breathtaking experience. The shoreline concentration of palm trees, shops, residences, and condominiums is segregated from the mountains by fields of sugar cane. Quite often a billowing plume of white smoke rises lazily in the still air, or lays down with the tradewinds. It signals cane burning time, a necessary step in the process before harvesting the crop. The resultant flakes of ash can coat your car in what is known as "Hawaiian snow". Increased foreign competition has diminished profits from sugar production, so fields are yielding to the more profitable, and succulent pineapple. **Maui Tropical Plantation**, on Highway 30 in Waikapu, is a 60 acre, tourist center designed to present a concentrated example of the different agricultural products of Hawaiʻi.

A short drive from the plantation leads into Wailuku, the center of the island's government. At the intersection of Route 30 (now High Street) and Main, turn left and follow the signs for ' Īao Valley State Park. Its a three mile drive until the road dead ends at the parking lot. A short, but steep walk will lead to a view of the ' **Īao Needle**, a 2,250 foot geological inspiration. A beautiful stream and small waterfalls adds to the tropical setting of exotic foliage.

The 2,250 foot spire ' Īao Needle is the highlight of the pastoral 'Īao Valley State Park.

The heaviest concentration of local population centers around Wailuku, and the harbor city of Kahalui. All of the direct flights from the mainland, and most of the interisland flights land at the island's main airport in Kahalui, where visitors usually fan out to their respective destinations.

Upcountry and East Maui

The eastern half of the island is the 10,023 foot high Haleakalā, a dormant volcano, believed to have last erupted between 1786 and 1793. **Haleakalā National Park**, at the mountain's summit, is the largest tourist draw on the island with 1.3 million visitors annually. Known in legend as "House of the Sun", the crater is an alienesque landscape of cinder cones, multicolored soils, and an unparalleled view of the island.

One of the popular activities here is viewing the sunrise. Catching the first colorful glimpses of the sun's rays requires an early morning drive to the summit, and several layers of warm clothing. There are many trails to hike, but keep in mind the rarefied atmosphere can leave the unprepared exhausted in a hurry. An unusual plant called the silversword, a relative of the sun flower, is named for its silver leaves that reflect sunlight to conserve the moisture. The endangered *nēnē*, or Hawaiian goose, had one time

198

dwindled on the brink of extinction with only 50 of the small geese surviving. Recovery efforts for the state bird have been successful, and domesticated *nēnēs* patrol the grounds around the park ranger's office. If you have ever had the urge to bike down the volcano, here's your chance. Participants are transported to the summit to view the sunrise, or the scenery, then mount their specially modified bicycles for a tightly controlled cruise, 38 miles downhill.

The chilly summit of the 10,023 foot Haleakalā is a transition into an alienesque landscape.

Pāʻia is a roadside town at the beginning of the shoreline drive around the east side of the island. Small speciality shops and decor are a throwback to the 1960's. Hoʻokipa Beach, a short trip from Pāʻia, is to the windsurfing community what the Bonzai Pipeline is to surfers. On any given day, dozens of the board sailors can be seen challenging the elements, and world class tournaments are held here annually.

Continuing along the coast brings travelers to the beginning of a highway featured on T-shirts and bumper stickers with the warning, "I survived the **Road to Hāna**". The drive is only 44 miles one way, but there are 617 curves, and 56 one-lane bridges enroute. Visitors who are still geared for living on the mainland battle tourist buses and other slow traffic, and usually return disappointed by what they've found, or haven't. So, why go through the effort? The secret to enjoying Hāna is first, preparation – fill the gas tank, check the tires, pack plenty of snacks and patience. The entire trek is a combination of coastal vistas, roadside streams and waterfalls, rain forests, bamboo groves, rainbow eucalyptus trees, monkey pod, and the aroma of white ginger as Hana nears. **Waiʻānapanapa State Park** is a great place to stop for a picnic, lounge on a black sand beach, explore large caves, and enjoy the sea and its coastal beauty. There is only one small hotel in Hāna and little else of commercial development, a way of living the residents are fighting to preserve, and a throwback to the natural beauty and lifestyle before the world discovered these natural islands.

The Road to Hāna winds its way to several panoramic opportunities including the feral coastline. (Photo courtesy David Watersun © 1990. All Rights Reserved)

The road does not completely encircle the island as part of it fell into the sea a few years ago. Before retracing your steps, you may wish to stop in **Hasegawa's General Store**, a small country store with a hodgepodge of everything necessary for life in lovely Hāna.

The two questions most visitors ask locals are, "Where is Seven Pools?", and "How do you get to Lindbergh's grave?" Seven miles past the town is the National Park where Palikea stream has cut through 'Ohe'o Gulch to form **Seven Pools**, a misnomer, as there are actually twenty four. About three miles past the park the paved highway ends. The **Palapala Ho'omau Congregational Church** is located on a bluff overlooking the ocean. A simple, rock-covered grave is the final resting place of the "Lone Eagle", Charles A. Lindbergh. His love for the islands was reflected in choosing them as his final resting place, and through his own words,

"Midway across the North Pacific, space, time and life uniquely interlace a chain of islands named "Hawaiian"... These small fragments of land appear offered to the sky by water and pressed to earth by stars."

Overview: Moloka'i

Nickname	The "Friendly Isle"
Area	261 square miles
Coastline	88 miles
Highest peak	Kamahou - 4,970 feet
Population	6,700 (1987 estimates)
County seat	Wailuku, Maui
Airport	Moloka'i Airport
Distance to Honolulu	53 miles
Agriculture	cattle
	pineapple

I live in the Hawaiian islands, and when my wife and I go "on vacation", we like to go to Moloka'i. The greatest appeal of the "Friendly Isle" is its segregation from the mainstream of tourism. We come here to "get away from it all" - literally. The few thoroughfares on the island are well maintained and show little evidence of use. Traffic isn't a problem here, there just isn't any. Some people may find that this fits the definition of "boring", but we find it to be the "perfect escape".

Though small by comparison (measuring 10 miles wide by 38 miles long), Moloka'i nevertheless offers a sprawling oceanside resort, the largest white sand beach in the state, photo safaris through a wildlife preserve, and a panoramic vista that overlooks a reminder of our unenlightened past.

The eastern half of the island is mountainous, rugged and wet. It is best brought into perspective by helicopter tour, which takes passengers through the beautiful Hālawa Valley and to Kahiwa Falls. Cascading in several steps, the 1,750 foot high falls has the longest total elevation drop in the state.

The west side of Moloka'i is primarily rolling hills and a dry climate. Two mile long **Pāpōhaku Beach**, on the island's west coast, is the longest in the state, and within walking distance of the Kaluako'i resort. A very short distance south of the resort, one can step into the wilds of Africa and Asia at the **Moloka'i Ranch Wildlife Park**. Photo safari's are led by Pilipo Solatorio, who can identify all of the 800 residents, and has named those that now feed out of his hand. Tours through the 1,000 acre park are aboard one of their vehicles on spine jarring roads that justify using four wheel drive. The sound of the horn signals snack time to the animals, and visitors can often approach to within a few feet of giraffe, eland, axis deer and black buck. Tours are available seven days a week, weather permitting.

Leprosy is a degenerative nerve disorder that has stirred the fears of people throughout recorded history. Victims suffered the loss of feelings in their extremities leading to opportunistic infections that often resulted in amputations and disfigurement. The bacteria caused disease is mildly contagious, and has spurred the primal fears of society into ostracizing its victims. The Chinese called it *ma'i-Pake*, or the separating sickness.

In 1865, by decree of King Kamehameha V, everyone in the islands that fell prey to the disease were shipped to the remote Kalaupapua peninsula and abandoned. Many were cast into the rough waters surrounding the peninsula and left to make their own way ashore. Several took refuge in caves and the place of exile virtually became a colony of living dead, isolated from the rest of the world.

Father Damien is now honored in part by a statue in front of the State Capitol Building in Honolulu.

Missionaries came the next year to establish the Kalawao settlement, and provide relief and care for the unfortunate. Two years prior to that a priest named Joseph de Veuster arrived in Hawai'i from Belgium. In 1873, he made his first visit to the leper colony at Kalaupapa, and through his compassion spearheaded an era of enlightenment. Known as Father Damien, the next sixteen years of his life were devoted to serving the physical and spiritual needs of the ailing. His work brought dignity to the outcasts, but it eventually consumed him, and on April 15, 1889 at the age of 49, he succumbed to the disease.

In 1946, the discovery of sulfone drugs put a check on the debilitating effects of the illness, now known at Hansen's disease, and by 1969 the quarantine was lifted. The remaining residents stay on a voluntary basis.

Kalaupapua National Historical Park was established to preserve this historic era. Tours are available to anyone over 16, but access to this naturally isolated peninsula is available only by sea or air, or by walking or riding down the 1,600 foot high cliff. The **Moloka'i Mule Ride** follows the Kukuiohapu'u Mule Trail for an hour and a half descent down the cliff, through dozens of switchbacks, and some of the most breathtaking scenery imaginable. Once at the bottom, resident guides greet the incoming groups to conduct tours through the current village and the remnants of the Kalawao settlement. St. Philomena Church was built by Father Damien and stands as a monument to the work of a man that triumphed over the fear and prejudice that spanned thousands of years.

The sound of the horn signals it's feeding time to the residents of the Moloka'i Ranch Wildlife Park.

The southern coast is lined with remnants of ancient fishponds. Belonging to the *ali'i*, or ruling class of the islands, the enclosures were constructed of coral and rocks stacked above the water line. A wooden gate would allow small fish to swim through, grazing in the shallow ponds. When they grew too big to swim out of the gate, they were harvested. **Kaloko'eli Fishpond** is one of the best examples of the surviving ponds. It is located between the Moloka'i Shores condominium and the Hotel Moloka'i just east of the main village of Kaunakakai.

Midway on the northern side of Moloka'i is **Pala'au State Park.** Here, at 1,600 feet, is one of the best vistas in the state overlooking the infamous Kalaupapa Peninsula. The lookout opens to a panoramic view of the land mass, encompassed by the ocean on three sides, and naturally segregated from the main island by sheer cliffs rising over 2,000 feet above sea level.

Overview: Lāna'i

Nickname	The"Pineapple Isle"
Area	139.5 square miles
Coastline	47 miles
Highest peak	Lāna'ihale - 3,370 feet
Population	2,200 (1987 estimates)
County seat	Wailuku, Maui
Airport	Lāna'i Airport
Distance to Honolulu	74 miles
Agriculture	pineapple

At 16,000 acres, Lāna'i is one of the largest pineapple plantations in the world. Over 98% of the island is privately owned by Castle & Cooke Corporation, a subsidiary of Dole Company. Situated in the rainshadow of the West Maui mountains, Lāna'i experiences sparse rainfall which is ideal for its agricultural mainstay.

Throughout the coastal areas of the island are the remnants of civilization gone by. Several *heiaus* and concentrations of petroglyphs are accessible by four wheel drive vehicles and a good pair of hiking boots.

The island is slowly succumbing to the pressures of growth and tourism. The 102 room Lodge at Koʻele is a high ticket resort that opened in 1990 for the well healed traveler. The 250 room Mānele Bay Hotel is planning on opening by late 1990. Both mark Lānaʻi's inevitable first steps to development.

Overview: Kahoʻolawe

Nickname .... The "Target Isle"
Area .... 45 square miles
Coastline .... 29 miles
Highest elevation .... 1,477 feet
Population .... uninhabited
County seat .... Wailuku, Maui

Because Kahoʻolawe borders the southern waters of the Maui County basin, winter home to the heaviest concentration of the endearing cetaceans, it is ironic that the island resembles a large humpback whale resting on the surface. But the island itself is forbidding, and the center of a continuing controversy in the state.

Because it lies in the rain shadow of Haleakalā, eight miles from Maui, the 11 by six mile island is arid (less than 25 inches of rain annually) and desolate. Now under the administration and control of the U. S. Navy, uninhabited Kahoʻolawe serves as an active target range for live bombing and military training missions. RimPac Exercises include ground and troop maneuvers, firing, amphibious assaults, helicopter assaults, and air to ground, and ship to ground shelling.

Archaeological research has unearthed evidence that the island was at one time an ancient Hawaiian settlement. Project Kahoʻolawe ʻOhana is seeking to end the bombing, rid the island of the military, and develop a resource management program. They have succeeded in placing the island on the National Register of Historical Places, and continue to influence countries to drop out of participation in the military exercises.

Chapter 11

The "Big Island" of Hawai'i

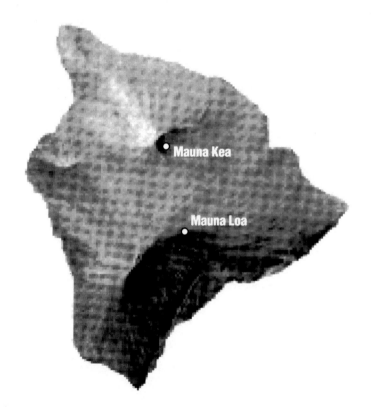

The island of Hawai'i is an paradisal anomaly, with majestic mountains that dominate the backdrop. These rugged formations graphically display their relatively recent volcanic origins. Picturesque valleys have been carved by time and erosion into serene landscapes. The entire island is encased by a feral coastline interrupted by white, green, and black sand beaches.

Overview: Hawai'i

Nickname .... "The Big Isle" - "The Volcanic Isle" - "The Orchid Isle"
Area .... 4,038 square miles
Coastline .... 266 miles
Highest peak .... Mauna Kea - 13,796 feet - dormant shield volcano
Population .... 117,100 (12/31/89 estimate)
County seat .... Hilo
Airports   Distance to Honolulu:
Hilo .... 216 miles
Kailua .... 170 miles
Agriculture .... bananas
                        cattle
                        flowers
                        Kona coffee
                        macadamia nuts
                        papayas
                        sugar cane

The "Big Island" of Hawai'i is the southernmost in the island chain. Located 34 minutes flying time from Honolulu, its land mass is twice as large as all of the other Hawaiian Islands combined, and it is still growing. Hawai'i is often referred to as a continent in miniature. The climate ranges from rain forest wet on the windward side, to desert dry on the leeward. Snow caps the highest peaks during the winter months, and creation's forces can be witnessed first hand, as lava continues to pour from its still active volcano, as it has since 1983.

Hawai'i needs to be experienced over time. A couple of days is not enough time to take in all of the sights, sounds and smells that are by-products of life here. The west side of the island, known as the Kona Coast, is an 85 mile stretch that extends from 'Upolu Point on the north, to Ka Lae Point at the southern extreme. The moderate, sunny, dry conditions along the Kona Coast contribute to its popularity.

The 8271 foot dormant Hualālai volcano towers over **Kailua-Kona**, a small, laid back village, bordered by resort condominiums, and primarily supported by tourism. Kailua Bay gently laps against the breakwall that borders the waterfront of this picturesque village. The main street of Ali'i Drive, lined with restaurants, shops, and history, is easily explored by foot. In the center of Kailua is **Hulihe'e Palace**, the 19th century summer home of King Kalakāua. There is no admission to tour this modest, two story palace of 19th century Hawaiian royalty. Across the street from the palace is **Moku 'aikaua Church**, the oldest missionary church in the state, and still in use today. It was built from coral, rocks, *koa* and *'ohi'a* wood in 1837. On the immediate north side of Kailua Bay is the site where King Kamehameha died. The site, **Kamakahonu**, has been restored and marked by a plaque.

This wooden carving is one of several reproduction artifacts on view throughout the grounds at the Puʻuhonua O Hōnaunau National Historical Park.

The harbor is the kick-off point for the now famous **Ironman Triathalon** competition held every October. The grueling competition (a 2.4 mile swim, 112 mile bike, and 26.2 mile run), attracts world class athletes, and avid spectators line Aliʻi Drive to see who excels and who survives.

The waters off Kailua have gained an international reputation for deep sea fishing action. Hawaiʻi's location next to the abyssal depths brings normally blue water pelagics close in to shore. Pacific blue marlin, black marlin, *ono* (wahoo), *mahimahi* (a type of dorado), and *ʻahi* (yellow-fin tuna), are sought for their sport by the fishermen, and subsequently by the restaurants for their taste. For five days every August fishing teams from around the world congregate here to compete in the invitational **Hawaiʻi International Billfish Tournament**. It is one of the most prestigious marlin fishing tournaments in the world.

South of Kailua is the village of Captain Cook that borders both sides of Route 11 and looms 1,400 feet over the historic **Kealakakua Bay**. In a confrontation with the island's inhabitants, the explorer Captain Cook lost his life on the shore of this bay on February 14th, 1779. A solitary white obelisk stands as a memorial to the islands' discoverer. The bay is accessible only by boat or a very long swim from its opposite shore at Nāpoʻopoʻo Beach Park. The rocky beach is separated from the historic site by a sheer wall. A 4.3 mile, narrow, winding, but scenic road accesses the park and the adjacent Hikiau Heiau.

Petroglyphs

A tangible link with Hawai'i's ancient past is depicted in the simplistic stone carvings found throughout the islands. Human figures, methods of transportation, the supernatural, dots, circles and lettering are found etched on fields of *pāhoehoe* lava, but also on boulders and natural stone walls. They are usually clustered in groups with the most extensive concentration (22,600) on the "Big Island" of Hawai'i.

To record petroglyphs on film, the most vivid contrast can be obtained by filling in the etchings with chalk.

Nondamaging recordings of the petroglyphs can be obtained through rubbings and photographs. Erosion has reduced the contrast between the grooves and their respective mediums necessitating some kind of enhancing highlights. The best methods recommended are outlining with chalk, or wetting the grooves before photographing them.

Although their meaning has eluded archaeologists, L.R. McBride put it into the best perspective in his book, *Petroglyphs of Hawai'i,*

"The complete understanding of Hawaiian rock pictures will probably never occur. Of course, it is unnecessary to fathom their meaning to enjoy them."

His book, as well as *Hawaiian Petroglyphs*, by J. Halley Cox with Edward Stasak, are two of the best on the topic.

Four miles south of Kealakakua Bay is the **City of Refuge**, or Pu'u honua O Hōnaunau National Historical Park. In the times of the ancient Hawaiians, a code of conduct called *kapu* was strictly enforced, usually through capital punishment. One way out for a condemned offender, or a vanquished warrior in battle, was to flee to a *pu'uhonua* or city of refuge, and receive sanctuary. If he could reach the temple, it was considered to be sacred ground, and the priest (*kahuna pale*) would perform the rite of absolution. Subsequently the offender could return home with no threat of recrimination. This city of refuge was reconstructed by the National Parks Service in 1961. They currently administer the facility and charge $1 to walk the grounds of the King Kamehameha dynasty. Bring a camera to record the beauty and mystery of this window into Hawai'i's past.

On the way back to the highway from the park, look for the signs to the **Painted Church**, just off Route 160. St. Benedictines is a tiny church, skirted by a cemetery. Its interior is completely covered with frescoes and murals of religious icons. Standing vigil over the bay, the picture postcard setting is a treat and a challenge to photo buffs.

North of Kailua is another concentration of tourism on the island at **Waikaloa** and Kohala. The $360 million, 1241 room, **Hyatt Regency** at Waikaloa is a resort hotel at its most opulent, and even if you aren't a guest, it's worth a visit. The 3/4 mile long museum walk is lined with a three million dollar Pacific-Oriental art collection and ties together the many towers that comprise the complex. The Dolphin Quest project is located here, and well worth watching even if the waiting list is too long to participate. Near the hotel is a field of ancient **petroglyphs** that has been preserved from the encroaching expansion of civilization.

The Waipi'o Valley cuts into the rugged Hāmākua coastline with a sculptured grace reminiscent of Kaua'i's Nā Pali coast. (Photo courtesy Paul Grulich © 1978. All Rights Reserved)

The "Big Island" is also home to the largest privately owned cattle ranch in the United States. The **Parker Ranch Visitors Center and Museum** offers tours around portions of the 225,000 acres, and a glimpse into Hawai'i's past through the museum. The original house has been preserved, with artifacts and photos of the family, and their ties to 19th century Hawaiian royalty.

A short hike through lush tropical foliage leads to the 442 foot high 'Akaka Falls.

Continuing west to the rugged Hāmākua coastline is **Waipi'o Valley**, known as the "Valley of the Kings". At Honoka'a, turn north onto Route 240, and continue to the end of the road. The overlook faces the northern edge of the valley. A sheer lava wall cut by wind and waves offers a dramatic vista similar to the Nā Pali coast on Kaua'i.

The valley was carved by the Wailoa stream and is framed by 2,000 foot cliffs. It is very lush, relatively undeveloped, and accessible either by foot or 4-wheel drive vehicles only. The road going down from the overlook is very narrow and winding with several switchbacks to navigate. Once there, the road is a rugged step back into a time before pavement or grading existed. Entry signs warn visitors not to go down with less than a 4-wheel drive vehicle, and the police will cite you if you are caught doing so.

Continuing south, **Mauna Kea** is the largest topographical feature on the island. Measured from the ocean floor 18,000 feet below the water's edge, to its summit 13,796 feet above, Mauna Kea is the world's largest mountain. Named the "white mountain" for the snow that intermittently caps its peak during December through April, the dormant volcano is one the world's most important observatory centers. There is snow skiing here, with the best months in December and January. However don't seek this out for a primary skiing destination, as conditions are iffy at best, and undeveloped.

North of Hilo, turn on Route 220 and follow the signs to **'Akaka Falls State Park**. A short looping trail leads from the parking lot through a tropical forest to the 400 foot high Kāhunā Falls, and finally to the park's namesake. At 442 feet, 'Akaka Falls is the longest unbroken waterfalls in the state.

A paved path leads visitors to the most advantageous views of the falls, and on a sunny day, a rainbow can be seen in the cascading mist. The vegetation is as much of a draw as the falls are. Thick, lush and huge by any standards, and the rain forest is an encyclopedia of exotic foliage. The skies can open up without warning, so bring protection if you don't appreciate an unexpected shower. Admission is free.

The city of **Hilo** has the largest concentration of the island's populace and is the center of commerce. Located on the lower third of the windward east coast, Hilo averages 132 inches of rain a year. The rainfall occurs mostly at night though, and serves to water the abundant foliage that has turned this city into a tropical paradise.

The **Hawai'i Tropical Botanical Garden** is located seven miles north of Hilo, just off Route 19 and is accessed from a scenic drive along the northern shoreline of the natural deepwater harbor of Hilo Bay. A donation will enable visitors access to a walking tour through a maze of tropical plants collected worldwide. There are several trails that pass by a waterfall, the ocean front, an ancient Hawaiian burial site, and a collection of five different tropical birds. Guidebooks are available at the walkway to help in identifying 1,048 of the over 1,600 different species of plants.

One event eagerly anticipated throughout the state is the **Merrie Monarch Festival**, staged in Hilo annually. Adults and children (*keikis*), representing the best of Hawai'i's schools, dance both traditional and modern hula for four consecutive nights in April. The competition is intense, and the event is a big drawing card (meaning tickets are hard to come by).

To the south of Hilo is the Puna District. Rich volcanic soil nurtures the exotic flower industry that has spawned here. Drab green and grey tents belie the delicate petals they serve to protect. The Puna District is also home to some of the most scenic **black sand beaches** on the island.

*The geological anomaly of black sand beaches are a source of wonder and feral beauty to a world used to white sand. (Photo courtesy Paul Grulich © 1988. All Rights Reserved) (*__Author's note:__ *The continuing eruption from Kīlauea has covered this picturesque beach since this photograph was taken.)*

Caution

If you plan to use the beaches, be wary about swimming, as currents are unpredictable and treacherous. Find out first, what the prevailing conditions are, and use swim fins. If you find yourself getting swept out to sea by a shift in current or the undertow, it is best to not fight it. Instead ride it out and then swim diagonally back to shore. Your best bet is to enjoy the scenery, have a picnic, catch some rays, and save your swimming for safer areas which abound on the "Big Island".

Plumes of sulfuric smoke emenate from the confluence of the cool Pacific Ocean and the newly exposed lava.

A 1790 eruption permeated a forest of *'ohi'a* trees near Kaniahiku village, coating their outer trunks. When the level of the lava suddenly lowered, a field of surrealistic spires remained to spark the imaginations of countless visitors to **Lava Trees State Park**. Follow Route 130 south from Hilo, turn left at Route 132 and continue south.

Literally, the hottest tourist attraction in the Hawaiian Islands (about 2200°F), is **Hawai'i Volcanoes National Park**, in the Puna district of the "Big Island". On January 3rd, 1983, Kīlauea, one of Hawai'i's two, still active volcanoes, erupted again, and has been providing observers with a view of creation in action. Pumping out about 650,000 cubic yards of lava each day, the eruption has often been spectacular, while at other times being remote and out of sight. Now in its 48th phase from the Kupaianaha vent, plumes of steam mark the site of the most current flow, where fingers of lava enter the ocean announcing the new birth. Over the last six and a half years, 15,000 acres of land have been covered, and the "Big Island" has grown by about 100 acres.

Caution

To access the safely monitored side of the lava flow and not the unprotected east side, it is necessary to use the upper entrance of the park via Route 11 west from Hilo. Park rangers are there to point out safe limits for viewing, while the other side is privately owned, and unmarked hazards can lead to a fatal mistake. Bring a flashlight if you plan to view the action at night for the walk back to your car, and be advised that close viewing can cause problems for people with respiratory ailments.

The day we visited the park, we were able to get within 20 feet of live, flowing lava entering the water, creating a brand new black sand beach, a reconfigured coastline, and virgin underwater topography. The sea and its inhabitants will eventually lay claim to this new territory.

Hawai'i Volcanoes National Park was established in 1916 to preserve the natural beauty of Mauna Loa and Kīlauea, and to provide scientists a safe, active forum to study volcanism. It has become the single biggest tourist attraction to the "Big Island". The park encompasses 344 square miles of the Puna and Ka'ū districts, including portions of the 13,679 foot Mauna Loa, and all of the 4,078 foot Kīlauea, on the larger mountain's back slopes. Both volcanoes are considered active with the most consistent eruptions coming from Kīlauea. Magma is fed to Kīlauea through lateral conduits, that now oozes from vents and lava tubes along the volcano's eastern rift zone.

A Glossary of Volcanic Terms

Knowing the language of volcanoes will help in understanding what to see in Hawai'i Volcanoes National Park. All of Hawai'i's volcanoes are dome shaped **shield volcanoes**, resembling a warrior's shield laying flat on the ground. There are three phases in the lifespan of any volcano. An **active volcano** is one currently erupting, while a **dormant volcano** has erupted during recorded history (deceptive in Hawai'i's case - as there is not an early recorded history of the islands). An **extinct volcano** is one that has not erupted in recorded history. **Magma** is molten material beneath the earth's surface. Once it has erupted, or seeped above ground, it is then known as **lava**. There are two types: **'a'a** (ah-ah) is characterized by a rough, jagged appearance. The black lava has many sharp edges and is high in gaseous content. *pāhoehoe* (pa-hoy-hoy) is smoother lava, often having a billowy appearance, or resembling coiled or bunched rope.

Driving to the park, it is hard to believe while looking at the tranquil, green scenery and landscapes, that you are entering an area where cataclysmic forces are at work. Admission is $5 per car and is good for a week. Just inside the gate is the **Kīlauea Visitor Center** and is open from 7:45 a.m. until 5 p.m. The ten minute introductory video is augmented by a very helpful staff at the information desk, fielding all questions, and providing an explicit map that shows car routes within the park and high points of interest, including location and current status of the eruptions. A small gift shop also sells books and videos as souvenirs of the experience. Recorded information to the volcano's activity can be obtained by calling (808) 967-7977. If you would rather talk to a person who can give you more personalized up-to-the-minute information, call (808) 967-7311, and then have the patience to deal with a number that is often quite busy.

Across the street from the visitor's center is the **Volcano House** hotel. Located at the summit of the crater, the back *lānai* provides a view of the volcano's caldera that measures 2 x 2 miles and drops over 400 feet deep. It is a rustic hotel and a great kick off point if you want to spend more than a day seeking out the park's offerings. The hotel is open all year and reservations are recommended. The **Volcano Art Center** is located nearby and features work of local artisans.

From there you can circle the 11 mile **Crater Rim Drive** or proceed directly to the flow. The Crater Rim Drive will take you through a world of contrasts, from forests of lush tropical foliage to desolate areas devastated by more recent flows.

Chain of Craters Road is the main drag that will take you down the slope of the volcano to the ocean, and to the location of the most recent flow. There are several highlights along the way to stop and experience, and are suggested if you have the time. Before you begin the trek, there are no services along the 65 mile round trip. Travel time without stopping averages two to three hours depending upon the season and the traffic.

The first stop along the way is the **Thurston Lava Tube**. It is a very short walk from the car to an alienesque world of primordial-like vegetation lining the walkway to the tube. The lava tube itself is about 450 feet long and ranges from six to 20 feet high.

Continuing down the mountain, the Chain of Craters Road passes through zones of old lava flow that have put a distinctive mark on the landscape. The older flows are marked by varying degrees of new growth, while more recent flows are as barren as any moonscape imaginable. Beginning at the Pu'u Pua'i Overlook, **Devastation Trail** is a 1.2 mile trail paved by a boardwalk over the thick pumice left by the Kīlauea Iki eruption. Other trails can range from less than 10 minutes hiking time to several miles distance.

Caution

The National Park Service advises that hikers in the park follow a few safety precautions:
- **Stay on the marked trails.** The thick vegetation can conceal deep crevices in the topography.
- Weather can change rapidly, so try to **keep your bearings in mind** in case cloud cover suddenly moves in.
- **Take plenty of water**, as it is very easy to dehydrate in Hawai'i.
- **Leave things undisturbed.** No souvenir hunting please.

The **Pu'u O'o eruption**, which began in 1983, is the current flow at the date of this writing. The unpredictability of the lava's location and its amount is emphasized by the information staff. If it is running, they will advise you to not procrastinate as it can change hourly. At the site of the eruption, the road comes to an abrupt halt where the lava has run over the pavement (in some spots as much as 12 feet thick).

Call before attempting to see the current lava activity. The ever-changing topography may necessitate an unplanned detour.

Cars line the sides of the road to that point, and volcano groupies are directed via rangers and volunteers to the closest safe spot for viewing. The Waha'ula Visitors Center that was built near the site is now but a memory, as the natural forces continue their relentless drive to the sea.

Volcanoes can be both destructive and creative. Trees, homes, roads, power lines, historical artifacts, and a visitor's center have been leveled, covered by mineral rich land. Within three years, moss, followed by ferns, grasp a foothold on the lava. Then seed bearing plants take root in the cracks, and the cycle starts anew. The erosion process has begun, sculpting a weathered face to earth's newest born.

Conclusion

Unusual marine encounters are most commonly written about from remote, exotic locales as an exceptional once-in-a-lifetime experience. In Hawai'i, the unusual has become the commonplace. The people of Hawai'i want you to visit their islands, enjoy their aloha, and experience the underwater world of your 50th state.

"… a framework of tall precipitous mountains close at hand, clad in refreshing green and cleft by deep, cool, chasm-like valleys - and in front the grand sweep of the ocean: brilliant, transparent green near the shore, bound and bordered by a long white line of foamy spray dashing against the reef, and further out the dead blue water of the deep sea, flecked with "white caps," and in the far horizon a single lonely sail - mere accent-mark to emphasize a slumberous calm and a solitude that were without sound or limit. When the sun sunk down… it was tranced luxury to sit in the perfumed air and forget that there was any world but these enchanted islands."

Mark Twain 1872

Photo courtesy David Watersun © 1990. All Rights Reserved.

Appendix A Telephone Numbers

Area Code (808) unless otherwise listed

General

Police, Ambulance, and Fire Emergencies (all islands except Hawai'i)	911
Coast Guard Rescue Center (O'ahu)	.. 536-4336
(Neighbor Islands)	(800) 331-6176
DAN Diver's Accident Network (Emergencies)	(919) 684-8111
DAN Diver's Accident Network (Nonemergencies)	(919) 684-2948
Hyperbaric Center (Recompression Chamber in Honolulu)	523-9155
National Marine Fisheries Service (O'ahu)	
Southwest Enforcement Office	541-2727
State Division of Conservation Resourses Enforcement (O'ahu)	
24 hour hotline	548-5918
Neighbor islands dial "0" ask for	enterprise 5469
U. S. Fish and Wildlife Service (O'ahu)	541-2681

Kaua'i Listings

Civil Defense	245-4001
After hours, Saturdays, Sundays and Holidays	742-1372
Harbor Master's Office	245-6996
Marine Patrol	246-1007
Weather Information	246-4441 ext. 1671
Surf and Marine Report	ext. 1672

O'ahu Listings

Civil Defense	523-4121
Harbor Master's Office (Honolulu)	548-4134
Harbor Agent (Kewalo Basin)	548-4158
Marine Patrol	548-2065
Weather Information	296-1818 ext.1671
Surf and Marine Report	ext. 1672

Maui Listings

Civil Defense	243-7285
After hours, weekends & holidays	244-6400
Harbor Master's Office (Lahaina)	661-3557
Harbor Master's Office (Mā'alaea)	244-7041
Marine Patrol	877-0257
Weather Information	244-8934 ext. 1671
Surf and Marine Report	.ext. 1672

Hawai'i Listings

Ambulance and Fire	961-6022
Police (Hilo)	935-3311
Police (Kailua)	323-2645
Police (Kohala)	889-6225
Police (Volcano)	966-9388
Civil Defense	935-0031
After hours, weekends & holidays.	935-3311
Harbor Master's Office (Hilo)	935-0809
Harbor Master's Office (Kailua)	329-3434
Harbor Master's Office (Honokohau)	329-4215
Harbor Master's Office (Kawaihae)	882-7565
Weather Information	935-1666 ext.1671
Surf and Marine Report	ext. 1672

Appendix B

Getting Around Island to Island

Air transportation between any of the neighboring islands is offered by two primary interisland carriers: Aloha Airlines, Inc., and Hawaiian Airlines. Between the two, over 260 flights are offered daily, meaning that there are plenty of opportunities to fly anywhere within the state, at just about any time, with little delay. The flights are short (see graphic), and have the fastest cocktail service aloft.

Airfares vary depending upon the ticket price wars going on, but in any case, are very reasonable. Be prepared to pay extra baggage fees if you lug around lots of dive equipment. Although airlines are usually pretty good about that (I have only been hit up twice in the last five years), they have the option of changing policy.

The hub of the network is out of Honolulu, Oʻahu to major airports at Līhuʻe on Kauaʻi, Kahalui on Maui, and Hilo and Kailua on the "Big Island" of Hawaiʻi. Smaller airports on Molokaʻi, Lānaʻi, Maui and Hawaiʻi are accessible via smaller trunk lines.

Interisland Distances and Flight Times

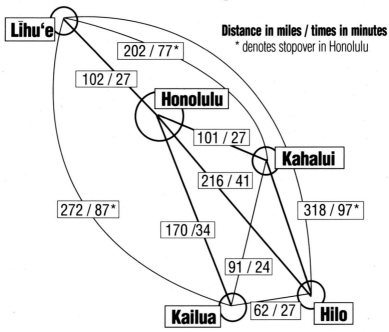

Līhuʻe

202 / 77*

102 / 27

Honolulu

Distance in miles / times in minutes
* denotes stopover in Honolulu

101 / 27

Kahalui

216 / 41

272 / 87*

318 / 97*

170 /34

91 / 24

Kailua   62 / 27   Hilo

Appendix C

First Aid for Marine Encounters

Hawai'i's marine world is a complex ecosystem of predation and survival, relying upon the species' ability to succeed through aggression, speed, camouflage, poison and distastefulness. Interaction between this perfectly balanced realm and the ill-adapted intrusion of man has sometimes resulted in an irritating or painful reminder of an inadvertent contact or an uneducated gamble in mishandling.

A few simple steps can be taken to prevent these kind of encounters:

• Education
The more that is known about the capabilities and behavior of a particular species of marine life, the better the understanding of what the limits are in handling or interacting with them. The best sources for finding this out, are the professionals that dive with the critters daily.

• Buoyancy control
Properly weighted divers that aren't bouncing along the bottom will prevent an untold amount of damage to the corals and their inhabitants, and reduce the chances of an "ow-ee".

• Clothing
A wet suit or a pair of jeans and a long sleeve t-shirt will provide adequate protection from inadvertently brushing up against a marine organism. If you want to wear gloves, by all means do so, but many critters are irritated by or sensitive to the material, and react adversely to it. I personally would rather feel the sea and the marine life that I am handling, but then my fingers and hands have the scars to show for it.

An excellent book to have in your dive bag in case an encounter does occur is *A Medical Guide To Hazardous Marine Life*, by Paul S. Auerbach, M.D. © 1987. Otherwise, the following is a short listing of some potential problems and how to deal with them, in order of what we most commonly see on the boats:

Villains	Results	Treatment
Coral and Lava	abrasion	clean with antiseptic
Long Spiny Sea Urchin	puncture wound spines remain in flesh intense throbing pain	soak in very hot (nonscalding) water (30 to 90 minutes) to deactivate venom seek medical attention prevention is the best
Hydroids	itchy rash burning sensation	make paste of meat tenderizer and alcohol - apply for 10 to 20 minutes
Portuguese Man 'O War (do not handle beached critters - tentacles are still harmful)	prickling, stinging blisters possible allergic reaction	immediately rinse with sea water remove tentacles carefully make paste of meat tenderizer and alcohol - apply for 10 to 20 minutes - do not use sand
Jellyfish	same as man 'o war	same as man 'o war
Crown-of-Thorns Sea Star	puncture severe pain and stiffness inflammation, vomiting	remove loose spines same as sea urchins
Moray Eels	lacerations from bites swelling from reaction to marine bacteria (nonvenomous)	stop bleeding seek medical attention
Fireworms	same as hydroids	same as hydroids
Scorpionfish	puncture wound intense throbing pain	soak in very hot (nonscalding) water - 15 to 90 minutes seek medical attention anti-tetanus shots
Cone shells	puncture wound slight to extreme pain	same as scorpionfish

Appendix D
Marine Life Listings

Within the scientific community, marine life is named in Latin, which necessitates, and results in precise identification, but makes for awkward conversation and difficult memorization. Within the diving community, critters are known by their common names, which can be formal, a nickname or a pet name. There is a lot of room for mistaken identity using this method, as some of the animals are known by more than one moniker. In Hawai'i there are also the local or native names of the critters. Several are much shorter (*ū'ū*) than the common or latin names. Others are longer - much longer (*humuhumu nukunuku ā pua'a*), but are an integral part of daily discussions about marine life in the Hawaiian Islands. In order to avoid bogging down the text with all of the possibilities, the following lists the formal common name in alphabetical order followed in parenthesis by the other known common names, then the Latin listings, and finally the Hawaiian words (when known).

Fish:

Common	Latin	Hawaiian
achilles tang	*Acanthurus achilles*	pā ku'iku'i
amberjack fish	*Seriola dumerili*	kahaka
arc-eye hawkfish	*Paracirrhites arcatus*	pili ko'a
ash-colored (mustache) conger eel	*Conger cinereus*	pūhi ūhā
bandit angelfish	*Holocanthus arcuatus*	
black jack fish	*Caranx lugubris*	ulua
blackside (Forster's) hawkfish	*Paracirrhites forsteri*	hilu pili ko'a
blacktipped reef shark	*Carcharhinus melanopterus*	manō
bluestripe pipefish	*Doryrhampus excisus*	
bluestripe snapper	*Lutjanus kasmira*	ta'ape
boar fish	*Histiopterus typus*	
brown sting ray	*Dasyatis latus*	hī hī manu
canine-toothed (viper) moray eel	*Enchelynassa canina*	puhi kauila
Commerson's frogfish	*Antennarius commersonii*	
common (undulated) moray eel	*Gymnothorax undulatus*	puhi lau milo
convict tang	*Acanthurus triostegus*	manini
cornet fish	*Fistularia petimba*	nunu peke
devil scorpionfish	*Scorpaenopsis diabolus*	nohu 'omakaha
dorado	*Coryphaena hippurus*	mahi mahi
eastern flying gurnard	*Dactyloptena orientalis*	loloa'u
fantail filefish	*Pervagor spilosoma*	'ō'ili 'uwī'uwī
fire goby	*Nemateleotris magnifica*	
Fisher's angelfish	*Centropyge fisheri*	
flame angelfish	*Centropyge loriculus*	
garden eel		
(giant) manta ray	*Manta alfredi*	hāhālua
grand-eyed porgy fish (bigeye emporer)	*Monotaxis grandoculis*	mū
gray reef shark	*Carcharhinus amblyrhynchos*	
great barracuda	*Sphyraena barracuda*	kākū
Hawaiian dascyllus (shadow damsel)	*Dascyllus albisella*	'alo 'ilo'i
Hawaiian morwong	*Cheilodactylus vittatus*	kīkākapu
Hawaiian sergeant (major)	*Abudefduf adbominalis*	mamo

Common	Latin	Hawaiian
Hawaiian turkey (lion) fish	*Pterois sphex*	
Henshaw's snake eel	*Brachysomophis henshawi*	
leaf scorpionfish	*Taenianotus triacanthus*	
leopard (dragon) moray eel	*Muraena pardalis*	puhi ao
lined butterflyfish	*Chaetodon lineolatus*	kī kākapu
longnose butterflyfish	*Forcipiger flavissimus*	lau wiliwili nukunuku 'oi'oi
longnose (black) butterflyfish	*Forcipiger longirostris*	
longnose hawkfish	*Oxycirrhites typus*	
lowfin chub	*Kyphosus vaigiensis*	nenue
mackerel scad fish	*Decapterus pinnulatus*	'ōpelu
milk fish	*Chanos chanos*	awa
milletseed (lemon) butterflyfish	*Chaetodon miliaris*	lau wiliwili
moorish idol	*Zanclus cornutus*	kihikihi
oceanic white-tipped shark	*Pterolamiops longimanus*	
orangemouth lizardfish	*Saurida flamma*	'ulae
peacock (razorhead) wrasse	*Hemipteronotus pavoninus*	lae nihi
pennantfish	*Heniochus diphreutes*	
Picasso's (reef or painted) trigger	*Rhinecanthus aculeatus*	humuhumu nukunuku āpua 'a
pinktail durgon	*Melichthys vidua*	humuhumu hi'u kole
porcupinefish	*Diodon hystrix*	kōkala
pyramid butterflyfish	*Hemitaurichthys polylepis*	
raccoon butterflyfish	*Chaetodon lunula*	kī kākapu
razor wrasse fish	*Hemipteronotus mubrilatus*	lae nihi
rockmover (clown wrasse)	*Hemipteronotus taeniourus*	
saddleback butterflyfish	*Chaetodon ephippium*	kī kākapu
saddle wrasse	*Thalassoma duperrey*	hīnālea lau wili
scalloped hammer-head shark	*Sphyrna zygaena*	manō kihi'kihi
scrawled filefish	*Aluterus scriptus*	'O'ili lepa
short bodied blenny	*Exallias brevis*	pāo'o kauila
shoulderbar soldierfish (menpachi)	*Myripristis kuntee*	'ū'ū'
snowflake moray eel	*Echidna nebulosa*	pūhi kāpā
spotted eagle ray	*Aetobatus narinari*	hī hī manu
spotted (peacock) flounder	*Bothus pantherinus*	pāki'i
spotted puffer (white spotted balloon)	*Arothron meleagris*	'o'opu hue
spotted trunkfish	*Ostracion meleagris*	moa
striped mullet	*Mugil cephalus*	'ama 'ama
threadfin butterflyfish	*Chaetodon auriga*	kī kākapu
thread-fin jack fish (thread-fin ulua)	*Alectis ciliaris*	ulua kihi kihi
tiger shark	*Galeocerdo cuvieri*	māno pā'ele
Tinker's butterflyfish	*Chaetodon tinkeri*	
titan scorpionfish	*Scorpaenopsis cacopsis*	nohu
trumpetfish	*Aulostomus chinensis*	nūnū
unicorn surgeon fish	*Naso brevirostris*	ka la
whale shark	*Rhincodon typus*	
whitemouth moray eel	*Gymnothorax meleagris*	pūhī 'oni'o
whitespotted surgeonfish	*Acanthurus guttatus*	'api
white-tipped reef shark	*Triaenodon obesus*	
yellowfin goatfish	*Mulloides vanicolensis*	weke 'ula
yellowfin tuna	*Gnathanodon speciosus*	'ahi
yellow-headed moray eel	*Gymnothorax petelli*	
yellowmargin moray eel	*Gymnothorax flavimarginatus*	pūhi-paka
yellow-spotted snake eel	*Callechelys luteus*	
yellowtail coris	*Coris gaimard*	hīnālea-'aki-lolo
yellow tang	*Zebrasoma flavescens*	lua'ī-pala
zebra moray eel	*Gynomuraena zebra*	pūhi

Invertebrates:

Common	Latin	Hawaiian
aeolid nudibranch	Pteraeolidial ianthina	
anemone crab	Lybia edmondsoni	kūmimī pua
antler coral	Pocillopora eydouxi	
banded coral shrimp	Stenopus hispidus	'ō pae hund
banded mantis shrimp	Lysiosquilla maculata	'alo 'alo
black coral	Antipatharia dichotoma	'ēkaha kū moana
blue spotted sea urchin	Astropyga radiata	
box crabs	Calappa hepatica	poki poki
brittle star (fish)	Ophiocoma pica	
cauliflower coral	Pocillopora meandrina	ko'a
checker cowry	Cypraea tessellata	
Christmas tree worm	Spirobranchus giganteus	
Chinaman's hat	Cellana exarata	'opihi
collector urchin	Tripneustes gratilla	
commensal shrimp	Stegopontonia commensalis	
crown-of-thorns sea star	Acanthaster planci	hōkū ka'i
day octopus	Octopus cyanea	he'e mauli
emporer shrimp	Periclimenes soror	
finger coral	Porites compressa	
ghost shrimp (fountain shrimp)	Stenopus Pyrsonotus	
gold lace nudibranch	Halgerda terramtuentis	
groove tooth cowry	Cypraea sulcidentata	
(hairy) hermit crab	Aniculus maximus	pāpa 'i iwi pūpū
harlequin shrimp	Hymenocera elegans	
Hawaiian lobster	Enoplometopus occidentalis	
helmet shell (conch)	Cassis cornuta	'olē
hydroids		limu
leviathan cowry	Cypraea leviathan	
lobe coral	Porites lobata	
long-handed spiny lobster	Justitia longimana	ula
long spiny sea urchin	Echinothrix diadema	wana
marlin spike auger shell	Terebridae maculata	
mole lobster	Palinurella wieneckii	
night octopus	Octopus ornatus	he'e pūloa
octocoral	Sinularia	
orange tube (cup) coral	Tubastraea coccinea	
pebble collector urchin	Pseudoboletia indiana	
pincushion star (shark's pillow)	Culcita novaeguineae	
plate coral	Porites rus	
Portuguese-man-o'-war	Physalia physalis	pā malau
reticulated cowry	Cypraea maculifera	
rock boring sea urchin	Echinometra mathaei	'ina uli
rough spined urchin	Choneroidaris gigantia	
scrambled egg nudibranch	Phyllidia varicosa	
sea cucumber	Holothuria atra	
sea mouse (heart urchin)	Brissus carinatus	
7-11 crab	Carpilius maculatus	'ala kuma
slate pencil sea urchin	Heterocentrotus mammillatus	hā'uke'uke 'ula'ula
sleepy sponge crab	Dromidiopsis dormia	makua o ka līpao
slipper lobster	Scyllarides haanii	ula pāpapa
snakehead cowry	Cypraea caputserpentis	
spaghetti worm	Loimia medusa	

224

Common	Latin	Hawaiian
Spanish dancer nudibranch	*Haxabranchus sanguineus*	
spiny lobster	*Panulirus marginatus*	ula
sunburst starfish	*Luidia*	
swimming crab	*Charybdis hawaiiensis*	
textile (common) sea star	*Linckia multifora*	
textile cone snail	*Conus textile*	pūpū
tiger cowry	*Cypraea tigris*	leho kiko
triton's trumpet	*Charonia tritonis*	pū puhi
violet shell	*Janthina fragilis*	
wire coral	*Cirrhipathes anguina*	
xanthid crab	*Lybia edmondsoni*	

Mammals:

Common	Latin	Hawaiian
false killer whale	*Pseudorca crassidens*	
humpback whale	*Megaptera novaeangliae*	koholā
melon-headed whale	*Peponocephala electra*	
monk seal	*Monachus schauinslandi*	ʻīlio holo i ka uaua
Pacific bottlenose dolphin	*Tursiops gilli*	
Pacific spotted dolphin	*Stenella attenuata*	nai'a
pigmy killer whale	*Feresa attenuata*	
short-finned pilot whale	*Globicephala macrorhynchus*	nu'ao
sperm whale	*Physeter macrocephalus*	
spinner dolphin	*Stennella coeruleoalba*	nai'a

Reptiles:

Common	Latin	Hawaiian
green sea turtle	*Chelonia mydas*	honu
hawksbill turtle	*Eretmochllys imbricata*	ʻea
leatherback turtle	*Dermochelys coriacea*	

Bibliography

Auerbach, Paul S. M.D. *A Medical Guide To Hazardous Marine Life*. Jacksonville; Progressive Printing Co., Inc., 1987

Balcomb III, Kenneth C. *The Whales of Hawaii*. San Francisco; The Marine Mammal Fund, 1987.

Blanding, Don, [et.al.]. *Hawaii, Island Paradise*. San Carlos; World Wide Publishing, Tetra, 1987.

Bryan, William Alanson. *Natural History of Hawaii*. Honolulu; Hawaiian Gazette Co., Ltd., 1915.

Cox, J. Halley with Edward Stasak. *Hawaiian Petroglyphs*. Honolulu; Bishop Museum Press, 1970.

Daws, Gavan. *Shoal of Time*. Honolulu; University of Hawaii Press, 1974.

Decker, Robert and Barbara. *Volcano Watching*. Honolulu; Hawaii Natural History Association, 1987.

Fielding, Ann. *Hawaiian Reefs and Tidepools*. Taipei; Color Printing Company, 1982.

Fielding, Ann and Ed Robinson. *An Underwater Guide to Hawai'i*. Honolulu; University of Hawaii Press, 1987.

Gardner, Robert. *The Whale Watcher's Guide*. New York; Julian Messner, 1984.

Gay, Lawrence Kainoahou. T*ales Of The Forbidden Island of Ni'ihau*. Honolulu; Topgallant Publishing Co., Ltd. 1981.

Graves, William. *Hawaii*. Washington D.C.; National Geographics Society, 1970.

Gurnani-Smith, Ruth. *The Essential Guide to Kaua'i*. Honolulu; Island Heritage, 1988.

Gurnani-Smith, Ruth. *The Essential Guide to O'ahu*. Honolulu; Island Heritage, 1988.

Hargreaves, Dorothy and Bob. *Hawaii Blossoms*. Kailua;Hargreaves Company, Inc., 1958.

Hopper, Dr. Carol. *Waikiki Aquarium, A Guide to the Galleries*. Honolulu; Waikliki Aquarium, 1987.

Ingmanson, Dale E. and William J. Wallace. *Oceanology: An Introduction*. Belmont; Wadsworth Publishing Company, Inc., 1973.

Johnson, Scott. *Living Seashells*. Honolulu; Oriental Publishing Company, 1982.

Kaufman, Gregory Dean and Paul Henry Forestell. *Hawaii's Humpback Whales*. Kihei; Pacific Whale Foundation Press, 1986.

Kay, E. Alison. *Reef and Shore Fauna of Hawaii, [Vol. 4] Hawaiian Marine Shells*. Honolulu; Bishop Museum Press,1977.

Lenihan, Daniel J. [et. al.]. *Submerged Cultural Resources Study, USS Arizona Memorial and Pearl Harbor National Historic Landmark*. Santa Fe; National Parks Service, 1989

Lott, Arnold S., LCDR, USN (Ret) and Robert F. Sumrall, HTC, USNR. *Pearl Harbor Attack*. Honolulu; Fleet Reserve Association, 1977.

McBride, Leslie R. *Petroglyphs of Hawai'i*. Hilo; The Petroglyph Press, Ltd. 1969.

Michener, James A. *Hawaii*. New York; Fawcett Crest, 1959.

Morgan, Joseph R. *Hawaii, a geography*. Boulder; Westview Press, 1983

Mrantz, Maxine. *Hawaii's Whaling Days*. Honolulu; Aloha Publishing Company, 1976.

1990 Commercial Atlas & Marketing Guide. Chicago; Rand, McNally & Co., 1990.

Prange, Gordon W. *At Dawn We Slept, The Untold Story of Pearl Harbor*. New York; Mc Graw-Hill, 1981.

Puku'i, Mary Kawena and Caroline Curtis. *Tales of the Menehune*. Honolulu; Kamehameha Schools, 1985.

Puku'i, Mary Kawena. Hawaiian Dictionary: *Hawaiian – English, English – Hawaiian*. Honolulu; University of Hawaii Press, 1986

Randall, John E. *Underwater guide to Hawaiian Reef Fishes*. Newtown Square; Harrowood Books, 1981.

Rice, Captain William T., USNR (Ret). *Pearl Harbor Story*. Honolulu; Tongg Publishing Co., Ltd., 1965.

Runge, Jonathan. *Hot On Hawaii*. New York; St. Martin's Press, 1989.

Scott, Susan. *Oceanwatcher*. Honolulu; Green Turtle Press, 1988.

Shallenberger, Robert J. *Hawaii's Birds*. Honolulu; Hawaii Audubon Society, 1984

Simpson, MacKinnon and Robert B. Goodman, *Whale Song, A Pictorial History of Whaling and Hawai'i*. Honolulu; Beyond Words Publishing Company, 1986.

Slackman, Michael. *Remembering Pearl Harbor, The Story of the U.S.S. Arizona Memorial*. Honolulu; Arizona Memorial Museum Association, 1984.

Sherman, Stuart. *The Voice of the Whaleman*. Providence; Providence Public Library, 1965.

State of Hawaii Data Book, The, 1988, A Statistical Abstract. Honolulu; Hawaii Department of Business and Economic Development, 1988.

Stone, Scott C.S. *The Essential Guide to Hawai'i, The Big Island*. *Honolulu;* Island Heritage, 1988.

Stone, Scott C.S. *The Essential Guide to Maui*. Honolulu; Island Heritage, 1988.

Suiso, Ken and Rell Sunn. *A Guide to Beach Survival*. Honolulu; Water Safety Consultants, 1986.

Sunset, Editors of. *Beautiful Hawaii*. Menlo Park; Lane Magazine & Book Company, 1972.

Taylor, Leighton R., LJV Compagno, and Paul Struhsaker, "Megamouth, a New Species, Genus and Family of Lamnoid Shark (Megachasma pelagios, family Megachasmidae) From the Hawaiian Islands". In *Proceedings of the California Academy of Sciences*, Vol. 43 #8, pp. 87-110, 1983.

Thrum, Thomas G. "Hawaiian Temple Structures", *Special Publications of Bernice P. Bishop Museum*, Vol. 7, pp. 86-90, Honolulu, 1921.

Tinker, Spencer Wilkie. *Fishes of Hawaii*. Honolulu; Hawaiian Service, Inc., 1982.

Tinker, Spencer Wilkie. *Pacific Crustacea*. Rutland; Charles E. Tuttle Company, 1965.

Tinker, Spencer Wilkie. *Pacific Seashells*. Rutland; Charles E. Tuttle Company, 1958.

Titcomb, Margaret. *Native Use of Marine Invertebrates in Old Hawaii*. Honolulu; The University Press of Hawaii, 1979.

University of Hawaii. *Atlas of Hawaii*. Honolulu; University of Hawaii Press, 1983.

Watts, A.J. and B.G. Gordon. *The Imperial Japanese Navy*. London; Macdonald & Co. Ltd., 1971.

Wisniewski, Richard A. *Hawaii: The Territorial Years, 1900-1959 (A Pictorial History)*. Honolulu; Pacific Basin Enterprises, 1984.

Index of Dive Sites and Points of Interest

Site names listed in **bold**

Index of Sidebars and Photo Tips